The American Art Museum

Contemporary Issues in Museum Culture
Series Editors: Susan M. Pearce and Elaine Heumann Gurian

Other volumes in the series:

The Authorship of Art Institutions: The Social Construction of British Art Institutions 1750–1950
Gordon Fyfe

Cultural Diversity: Developing Museum Audiences in Britain
Eilean Hooper-Greenhill

Experiencing Material Culture in the Western World
Edited by Susan M. Pearce

Material Obsessions: Postmodernity and the New Collecting
Steve Chibnall

Museums and Popular Culture
Kevin Moore

The American Art Museum

Elitism and Democracy

NANCY EINREINHOFER

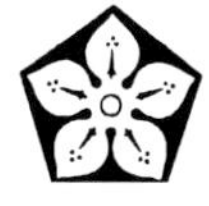

Leicester University Press
London and Washington

Leicester University Press
A Cassell Imprint
Wellington House, 125 Strand, London WC2R 0BB
PO Box 605, Herndon VA 20172

First published 1997

British Library Cataloguing in Publication Data
A catalogue record for this book is available from the British Library.

ISBN 0 7185 0042 3

Library of Congress Cataloging-in-Publication Data
Einreinhofer, Nancy.
The American art museum : elitism and democracy / Nancy Einreinhofer.
p. cm.
Includes bibliographical references and index.
ISBN 0-7185-0042-3
1. Art museums—United States. 2. Art and society—United States. 3. Art patronage—United States. I. Title.

N510.E45 1997
708.13—dc21 96-48135
CIP

Typeset by BookEns Ltd., Royston, Herts.
Printed and bound in Great Britain by Biddles Ltd,
Guildford and King's Lynn

Contents

"The trouble is," said Si, speaking straight in a way that had become rather rare with him, "that in literature, just as in anything else that's serious, nothing's really any good at all that isn't based on the recognition of the very best that's ever been possible. If you begin recommending the second-rate—let alone the third-rate and the fourth-rate, as the Readers' Circle sometimes does—you're not gradually educating people, as Warren claims he is, so that they'll be able to appreciate something better: you're simply letting down the standards and leaving people completely at sea. The most immoral and disgraceful and dangerous thing that anybody can do in the arts is knowingly to feed back to the public its own ignorance and cheap tastes."

Edmund Wilson
Memoirs of Hecate County

Plates

Figures

Tables

Preface

The American art museum was born in the nineteenth century, the child of wealthy industrialists who viewed the collecting of art as a symbol of prosperity, wealth, and power for themselves and for the new nation. From its beginnings, the art museum was understood to define the American nation as an advancing culture, one rich, not only in the art collected, but also in the methods and means of sharing those treasures with all the people. The American art museum proclaimed a new society based on industry, commerce, democracy, and capitalism.

The democratic and capitalistic underpinnings of the museum created an institution sometimes at odds with itself since the holdings of the institution were of a rarefied nature, precious, even spiritual, and required a certain level of knowledge for full appreciation. The contradictions and conflicts arising from these democratic and elitist impulses are the subject of this book. The book is intended to provide a view of the American art museum as a distinctly American institution. It means to present an observation, not finely drawn, but sketched with broad strokes, of the origins of some of our policies and procedures and the motivating factors which shape our present circumstances.

The study is divided into three main parts. It begins (Chapters 1–4) with an examination of the motives and systems of art patronage in the American society of the nineteenth century, and a consideration of how these shaped the American art museum (Chapter 1). The art museum stood as a symbol of the triumph of democracy and capitalism on the North American continent (Chapter 2), first made concrete in the architecture and collections of the Metropolitan and Boston Museums (Chapter 3). The democratic/elitist legacy of the Metropolitan, as America's first great museum, continues today in the American art museum as powerful boards manage the acquisition of rare and valuable objects for institutions pursuing democratic missions. In the public sector, democratic concerns sometimes prove intrusive in the institutions funded by federal tax dollars. A review of the programs of the National Gallery and the National Endowment for the Arts sheds light on areas of concern (Chapter 4).

The second section (Chapters 5–7) examines three major influences on the American art museum: modernism, democracy, and capitalism.

Modernism, first introduced to America in the Armory Show of 1913, influenced not only American art, but museum architecture and design. The art propagated by modernism required a specific museum context in which to be displayed and, because of the difficulty of the new art forms, that museum context included a logical, instructional focus for the public. Education, a pillar of democracy, was a central mission of the American art museum. Perhaps more than any other internal force in museum administration, the growth of educational programming reflected both democratic and economic concerns. Educational programming attracted large numbers of visitors who in turn supported the museum through admission fees, membership dues, and bookstore and restaurant spending. The popular appeal of the art museum also attracted corporate sponsors who greatly influenced museum administration.

The final section (Chapters 8 and 9) is a case study of the Museum of Modern Art in New York City, America's first museum devoted exclusively to modernism.

I would like to thank the museums whose collections and libraries are offered for the advancement of knowledge, in particular the Metropolitan Museum of Art and the Museum of Modern Art, New York. Special thanks to the museums that participated in the survey and supplied additional information: Herbert Johnson Museum at Cornell University, the Philadelphia Museum of Art, the Whitney Museum of American Art, and the Worcester Museum of Art. Thanks go also to the Boston Museum, the Cleveland Museum, the Guggenheim Museum, and the National Gallery.

The advice of Susan Pearce, Head of the Department of Museum Studies at the University of Leicester, England has been invaluable. The artists Vito Acconci and Hans Haacke were most generous in sharing their time and their ideas. I wish to acknowledge also the support of William Paterson College in allowing me the opportunity and resources to complete this project.

Sincere appreciation goes to Judi Stevens for typing this manuscript, for her patience and attention to detail. Gratitude goes also to the Niland family, especially Pauline, who made her home my home.

Finally, my thanks go to my husband and my son whose support and love made this happen.

1

The motives of art patronage during the American Renaissance and how they influenced the American art museum

We may do as France has done: go and sit at the feet of the masters and learn to achieve that wider art which embellishes not only our individual houses but our city. For France has sat at the feet of Italy. She has sent her architects, painters, sculptors to Rome ... As it is in Paris, so, let us hope, it shall one day be in America when we shall have put our best art where it belongs, at the top, in public building.

Edwin Blashfield, *Mural Painting in America*

Introduction

America's art museums were built, for the most part, by wealthy individuals whose fortunes resulted from capitalist enterprises. The founders and developers of the first museums, the likes of J. P. Morgan and Henry Clay Frick, saw themselves as the kings of industry and looked to art collecting and art patronage as another way of establishing their place in history while gaining status and pleasure in the present. They organized these institutions based on a corporate structure to be governed by a private board of trustees and funded with private dollars (see Chapter 3). This uniquely American situation and the amassing of great works of art that resulted was viewed with pride by the still young nation as the activity of an advanced culture (Veysey, 1979: 81). The major influence to be cited during this period is the Italian Renaissance, which impacted both on the society and on individual patrons. The Havemeyers, Corcorans, and Morgans looked to the early capitalists and found a model for art patronage in the Medici family. To understand what motivated the Americans, we must look to their models.

The Italian Renaissance was viewed by nineteenth-century Americans as the epitome of high culture, and so would serve as a model for the new civilization in the new world (Wilson, 1979: 39). The leaders of the Renaissance, in particular the great Florentine banking family, the Medici, would serve as models for the new American leaders, establishing the concept of princely donorship and strengthening the link between collecting and social status. (The role of the late-twentieth-century Medici, the corporation, is discussed in Chapter 7.) This social motivation for collecting, conspicuous accumulation, served to spark the imaginations of America's industrial giants who considered themselves the royalty of the new empire. Both the motives and the systems of art patronage during this period determined the shape of the American art museum.

We will first note how the Italian Renaissance served as model for the American Renaissance and then briefly review the patronage of the Medici family as a general model for American art collecting. We will also review the Renaissance systems of patronage, the role of the Vasarian Canon and their influence on American thinking. The motives of art patronage and collecting during the fifteenth century (piety, prestige, and pleasure) will then be compared to those of nineteenth-century America (patriotism, prestige, and pleasure through moral elevation).

The Italian Renaissance as model

Nineteenth-century America looked to European culture to locate a model for the new nation. The Italian Renaissance, as it was viewed in nineteenth-century America, was a period in which the arts flourished, an interest in and then an imitation of the classical period began, and an interest in the secular and the individual emerged. To the nineteenth-century mind these events or trends were indications that the Middle Ages were over and the modern world had begun (Murray, 1979: 9). While historians generally agree that the Renaissance man did not perceive his time as a distinct period, our concern here is with the perceptions of nineteenth-century Americans.

The use of the term "Renaissance" to denote a definite epoch in the history of art was well established in France by about 1855 (Murray, 1979: 9). From there it spread, without being translated, to Germany and was adopted in England by about 1860. From recognizing the Renaissance as a period in the history of art, it was a short step to the application of the term in other areas of culture.

One important contribution to the nineteenth-century idea of the Renaissance is the fact that the period was full of "firsts." It was the time of the first oil painting and the development of linear perspective. Other methods used to create the illusion of depth, such as color theory, foreshortening, proportion, and relative positioning, were also employed. This age also witnessed the first copperplate, the first printed book and the first woodcut. The concept of "firsts," of new discoveries resulting in an advancement of culture, held great appeal as a model for a

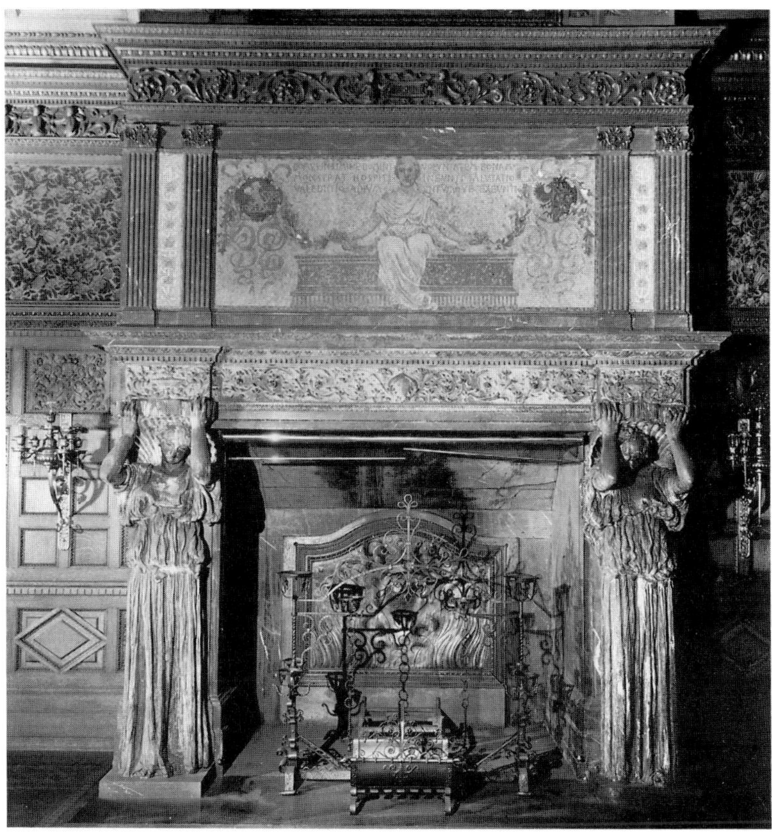

Mantelpiece by Augustus Saint-Gaudens (1848–1907) as reinstalled in the Billiard Room, Cornelius Vanderbilt II house, in 1894. Mosaic by John LaFarge (1935–1910). Installation designed by Francis Augustus Lathrop. Marble, mosaic, wood.
The Metropolitan Museum of Art, Gift of Mrs. Cornelius Vanderbilt, Sr., 1925 (25.234).

young nation evolving its own identity. It imbued the new with a potential for greatness, a notion that seems to be still in play today.

The neoclassical enthusiasm of the nineteenth-century was another important stimulus to interest in the Renaissance as was the revival of the humanist tradition. Nationalistic pride and a sense of America's place in history also exerted an influence on attitudes toward the Renaissance, and the neoclassical art and architecture could express this pride. The ideal form established by the ancient Greeks and rediscovered in the Renaissance was considered valid for all people, for all time (Alsop, 1982: 111). America would be no exception. The neoclassicists in America supported and preserved the Vasari tradition which held the art of Greece and Rome as the model to be emulated. At the same time, the emphasis on moral earnestness and Christian piety found models in Renaissance art and expression in national sentiments.

The Renaissance was depicted as an age characterized by individualism and typified by powerful personalities: scholars, artists, poets, princes, popes. Their biographies became inspiration to those Americans who sought a place in history and believed in the importance of intellect and of personal as well as national wealth as the economic foundation of an advanced culture. They understood that during the Renaissance, the foundations of economics had shifted from the medieval land to the urban center and perceived Florence as the ideal city. They noted how community was replaced by society, and religiously sanctioned political power was replaced by intellectually supported economic power. All this seemed rational and realistic, and as emphasized earlier, individualistic. In short, the Renaissance became the prototype for the new American society as Americans identified with the ways in which early capitalism caused changes in the social structure and created entrepreneurs whose dominance depended on wealth and intellect. The nineteenth-century historians' emphasis on the role of capitalism is understandable since capitalism was key to the social and cultural genesis of the Renaissance.

So nineteenth-century historians looked at the despair of the Civil War period in America and drew a parallel to the Middle Ages. They looked at the postwar American civilization, its industry, commerce, democracy and art, and declared it the legitimate heir to the concept of the Renaissance. This identification by many Americans, including artists, scholars, politicians, and industrialists, with the Italian Renaissance resulted in the introduction of the term "American Renaissance" to describe that period in American history dating from approximately 1876 to 1917 (Wilson, 1979: 12).

In almost every area there were made analogies with the Renaissance. Artists attempted to assume the humanist example: painting murals and designing buildings, sculpting as well as etching. There was also great collaboration among the artists, architects, designers, and decorators as public art projects took as a model the various architectural styles of Europe.

Three churches in New Jersey of three distinct architectural styles, when compared and contrasted, provide an example of this. St. Paul's Episcopal Church in Paterson (1895) was modeled after Durham Cathedral in northeast England and is Romanesque in style with heavy walls and piers to support the vaulted ceilings. It was designed by William Wood of Newark and submitted through the prominent architectural firm of the period, McKim, Mead, and White. In a typical collaborative trend of the day, the windows were designed by Louis Comfort Tiffany and are considered to be among his most successful ecclesiastical commissions (Duncan, 1980: 218). It is a significant footnote that the Tiffany Workshop was similar to the Renaissance workshop in that he acted as the master instructing the apprentices and overseeing his productions from inception to completion. Tiffany also designed the woodwork in St. Paul's.

The Cathedral of the Sacred Heart (1899) in Newark was planned in the soaring Gothic style in order to inspire awe by "drawing mankind to a closer awareness of the Divine Presence" (O'Hara, n.d: 15). A huge edifice, its dimensions are: length, 365 feet; nave width, 50 feet; transept width, 165 feet. It contains eight chapels, the largest of which is the Lady Chapel with windows by Zettler and the altar of Carrara marble by Raggi. The Cathedral contains four rose windows by Zettler and "an organ of nine divisions and one hundred forty ranks" (Bishop McNulty Dedicatory Homily, October 19, 1954, quoted in O'Hara, p. 30). Its size and effects are an interesting contrast to the single, direct design of the Central Presbyterian Church of Montclair.

This unpretentious example of nineteenth-century classical inspired American architecture was designed by the New York architectural firm of Carrera and Hastings, both of whom were educated at the École des Beaux Arts in Paris and worked for the firm of McKim, Mead, and White. Both men preferred the classical architectural styles of ancient Greece and Rome to be integrated with the spirit of the new world to create a new architecture. The Central Presbyterian Church has a classical portico with a pediment supported by six Doric columns. But in keeping with American provincial church architecture, a spired tower reaches one hundred and eighty-five feet above the ground ending in the New England tradition, with a weather vane (Einreinhofer, 1990: 66). Carrera and Hastings also designed the New York Public Library and the Senate and House Office Buildings in Washington, D.C., great monuments to the neoclassical.

There was also of course the analogy of the American robber baron to the Italian merchant prince. In this way the Medici became models for the Whitneys, Morgans and Fricks. We will now look to the history of the Medici family and their influence on art patronage in nineteenth-century America.

The Medici as model patrons

From about 1300 the feudal society of the Middle Ages with its agricultural economy and church-dominated intellectual life was transformed into a centrally controlled society with a commercial economy dominated by lay patronage of the arts and education. The Italian Renaissance was an urban phenomenon occurring in cities such as Florence, Milan, and Venice. The wealth concentrated in these cities allowed the arts to flourish. The arts, along with humanistic studies, were encouraged through the financial support of the leaders in commerce and politics such as the Sforza of Milan and the Doges of Venice (Murray, 1979).

The Medici, the wealthy banking and political family that long ruled Florence, were among the greatest collectors and patrons of the Renaissance. Cosimo de Medici, the founder of Medici power and rule in Florence, was the first of a long line of rich and influential Italians to become ardent collectors of art. A look at Cosimo, his son Piero, and his grandson Lorenzo, will provide some insight into an example that exercised influence on Western art right through to America in the nineteenth-century.

In the middle of the fifteenth century the city of Florence had much of which to be proud. Intellectual life had never been more vital, and art and architecture had begun the move away from medieval models. The Medici family was established as one of the great dynasties of European history and already had a reputation as dutiful servants to the community and bankers to the Pope. The Medici bank was the most successful commercial enterprise in Italy due to the efforts of Giovanni de Medici but also to his son Cosimo (Hibbert, 1987: 37).

Giovanni left his fortune to his son Cosimo, who was known early on as a patron of scholarship and would initiate the Medici role as patrons of art. Cosimo began his role as a patron of the arts in 1429, at the age of forty, upon the inheritance of the family fortune. From this point on, but especially after his return from his brief banishment in 1434, Cosimo supported both church projects and personal artistic commissions.

The first great act of patronage undertaken by Cosimo was the comprehensive enlargement of the church and convent of San Marco. One outstanding component of the complex was the library. Cosimo acquired the book collection of Niccolo Niccoli upon his death in 1437 and transferred it to San Marco. This was an extraordinarily vast collection and was made accessible not only to the residents of San Marco but to all citizens with scholarly interests (Hibbert, 1987: 69), a gesture to be emulated by the "princes" of nineteenth-century America. The industrialist, Andrew Carnegie, for example, is credited with establishing America's public library system (Carnegie, 1986: 45). Cosimo saw also to the acquisition of other works and to the production of copies for the library.

Another major project of this same period was the expansion of San Lorenzo which had been begun by Giovanni and which would now occupy Cosimo. This monumental project placed Cosimo in a position of princely donorship rather than the donorship of a private citizen. It was by assuming the sole responsibility for a whole great church and establishing San Lorenzo as the church of the Medici that Cosimo moved beyond the concept of private patronage (Wackernagel, 1981: 232). This model of public patronage would also be noted in nineteenth-century America, especially in the establishment of art museums (Veysey, 1979: 82).

> In San Lorenzo only the secondary chapels were erected and patronized by individual families in the customary manner. All main parts, however, including the whole stock of furnishings, were the result of donations solely from the house of Medici. In the context of other private patronage of the

> time this represented a completely unique accomplishment that can be explained only through the no less unique development of Cosimo's position in the commercial and political life of the city republic and that may stand as the most evident monumental demonstration of this. (Wackernagel, 1981: 233)

Upon the death of Cosimo in 1464, his son Piero inherited the family fortune, the palace, the villas, and the role as benefactor to the arts. His role in Florentine art and life was a brief one because Piero died just five years after his father. But in that short period of time he strove to be recognized as a friend and patron of artists (Hibbert, 1987: 107, 108). His personal involvement with the artists, and the types of projects he commissioned, represent a transition from the more public oriented patronage of Cosimo to what can be seen as the more personal involvement of Lorenzo. There is also with Piero a trend toward more conspicuous acquisitions, an important influence on nineteenth-century patrons who, for the most part, wished to demonstrate their good taste. Piero's son, Lorenzo, noted when reviewing the family's fortune upon his father's death in 1469:

> I find that from 1434 till now we have spent large sums of money. .. They amount to 663,755 florins for alms, buildings, and taxes, let alone other expenses. But I do not regret this, for though many would consider it better to have a part of that sum in their purse, I consider that it gave great honor to our State, and I think the money was well expended, and am well pleased. (Brucker, 1971: 27)

Shift in style: Lorenzo as collector

Lorenzo would surpass his father in personal aggrandizement. He would be known to all men as Lorenzo the Magnificent and, moving beyond his father and grandfather, would become the most famous art collector and patron Europe had seen since the decline of the Roman Empire (Hook, 1984: 119).

Lorenzo was barely twenty-one years old when his father Piero died leaving him to the business of governing the city state. Lorenzo would also assume a role as patron of the arts though, unlike his father and grandfather, his commissions proceeded mainly from personal motives rather than the magnanimous donor's intentions (Hook, 1984: 120).

Lorenzo came to be known as the "laurel who sheltered the birds that sang in the Tuscan spring" (Hibbert, 1987: 122). His personal connections to artists and artistic support systems would serve as a model in nineteenth-century America. His relationship with Michelangelo, for example, would be particularly inspirational.

Giorgio Vasari recorded the stories of the relationship between Lorenzo and Michelangelo and in the following recounted how the friendship was sealed. Michelangelo was engaged in copying in marble the head of an old faun.

> Michelangelo succeeded in copying the faun so well that Lorenzo was amazed. Then, when he saw that Michelangelo had departed a little from the model and followed his own fancy in hollowing out a mouth for the faun and giving it a tongue and all its teeth, Lorenzo laughed in his usual charming way and said, "But don't you know old people never have all their teeth; there are always some missing."
>
> As soon as Lorenzo had gone away, Michelangelo broke off one of the faun's teeth and dug into the gum so that it looked as if the tooth had fallen out; and he waited anxiously for Lorenzo to come back. And after he had seen the result of Michelangelo's simplicity and skill, Lorenzo laughed at the incident more than once and used to tell it for a marvel to his friends. He resolved that he would help and favour the young Michelangelo; and first he sent for his father, Lodovico, and asked whether he could have the boy, adding that he wanted to keep him as one of his own sons. Lodovico agreed, and then Lorenzo arranged to have Michelangelo given a room of his own at the Palazzo Medici and looked after him as one of the Medici household. Michelangelo always ate at Lorenzo's table with the sons of the family and other distinguished and noble persons, and Lorenzo always treated him with great respect ... (Vasari, 1568: 330–31)

Systems of patronage

This system of patronage exemplified by Lorenzo and his relationship with Michelangelo was the most common during the Renaissance period. Known as the household system, it entailed the providing of room and board and often supplies and presents to the artist by a rich man in return for artistic production. A similar system, also very popular and very personal, was an arrangement of short duration ending upon the completion of the commission. Such agreements with artists, architects, and craftsmen would be imitated in nineteenth-century America. Biltmore House, discussed later in this chapter, is a good example of this.

There was also at this time the beginning of a market system. In this case the artist produced objects in his studio and then sold them directly to a client or sometimes enlisted the assistance of a dealer. This last system would eventually allow for a broader patronage since works would become more affordable and more easily transferable. It would no longer be necessary to commission a mural when one could purchase a painting from the artist's studio and bring it home. This painting could, at some future point, be transferred to another household thus broadening the concept of collecting. The market system would also encourage more individualized expression since decisions of content were left more and more to the artist.

One can see how the household systems were tied to princely patronage while the market system would lead to a pattern of collecting related to that of modern times. The market system would also fit well with nineteenth-century capitalism and ideas about individualism. Before examining the Renaissance motives for patronage and/or art collecting, let us see how certain trends developed during this period.

There is some evidence that art collecting existed in ancient Greece, perhaps as early as the later fourth century B.C., and in Rome until about the fourth century A.D. But with the twilight of the classical art tradition came an end to art collecting until the beginning of the fourteenth century. With the Renaissance there came a new tradition of collecting which developed into what we are familiar with today.

During this period in Italy, art collecting again established itself for the first time in over eight hundred years. Italian collectors of this period were keenly interested in classical works of art. This interest grew in the following century and very important classical collections were formed. The influence of classical art was imposed on the artists of the day and they were encouraged to imitate the ancient forms. The art lovers and art makers of the Renaissance bestowed the highest status on antique art thus establishing that form as the standard against which all art should be measured (Alsop, 1982: 111).

The artists who would become the old masters of Western culture began to paint secular subjects on the walls and ceilings of private domestic interiors. These included all the favorite kinds of ornamental, vegetable, heraldic, and even narrative figural subjects, all with a nod toward the ancient ideal. A series of frescoes, for example, was executed in the Medici villa of Spedaletto by the great Florentine painters Botticelli, Ghirlandaio, Perugino, and Filippino Lippi (Hook, 1984: 132). Commissioned by Lorenzo Magnifico, the four masters produced images from Greek mythology. This type of commission and collaboration would be imitated by nineteenth-century patrons and artists. For example, in 1893 Augustus Saint-Gaudens referred to the Chicago Exposition as "the greatest meeting of artists since the fifteenth century" (Wilson, 1979: 12).

Murals commissioned by the Medici or other wealthy patrons are far outnumbered by paintings on wood and canvas which were more easily collected. These also took as their subjects classical mythology or classical forms. Paolo Uccello, for example, painted a series of three equestrian battles, while Pollaiuolo and Botticelli painted enthroned figures representing seven virtues. Botticelli's famous Venus scenes represent yet another reference to antique mythology. Classic subjects and forms would be incorporated into the paintings and sculpture produced in the American Renaissance, and would very often represent virtues or abstract ideals.

According to the historian Joseph Alsop, the circulation in the mid-sixteenth century of Giorgio Vasari's *Lives of the Artists* established the "ancients" as the models for all art. Alsop labels this influence the "Vasarian canon." This canon dominated artistic thinking in nineteenth-century America and influenced collecting and the structure of the American art museum (see Chapter 3).

The Vasarian canon ended the random approach to art collecting.

> The canon first of all ruthlessly excluded all works of art produced in Europe throughout the Dark and Middle Ages, with an extremely minor exception for Italian Romanesque architecture. This exception was made, in turn, because Vasari devoutly believed that the "ancients" were the necessary models for all art; and buildings like the Cathedral of Pisa passed muster because they were regarded by Vasari as near enough to the works of the "ancients". It can be seen, then, that Vasari's viewpoint strongly confirmed the canonical status of the great artists of antiquity.
> (Alsop, 1982: 111)

Alsop goes on to state that Vasari's other contribution to the new canon was his analysis of the development of art in Italy.

> Vasari conceived the story of Italian art in the fourteenth and fifteenth centuries as a majestic but difficult progression, consisting of a long series of triumphant solutions of technical problems mainly concerning the accurate, but also the graceful and harmonious representation of the thing seen. Within this majestic progression, the masters of the late thirteenth and early fourteenth centuries were warmly praised for their roles in art's "rebirth", but in Vasari's eyes, they were sadly imperfect artists. The great Renaissance masters of most of the fifteenth century were then applauded for coming much nearer to perfection ... Vasari held, however, that true "perfection" was only reached when Leonardo da Vinci showed how Perugino could be much improved upon; and Western art's first canonical masters were therefore Leonardo, Raphael, Michelangelo, Titian, and the other giants of the High Renaissance. (Alsop, 1982: 112)

So Vasari established a canon comprised of the great artists of antiquity and the masters of the High Renaissance who he believed had surpassed the ancients for the first time in history. This canon would determine art collecting in the whole of Europe until the eighteenth century, fostering a narrow definition of what was acceptable to imitate and what was worth acquiring. We will see this canon dominate again in the nineteenth-century as the young American nation takes the Renaissance as its model.

Motives for art patronage

The motives for art patronage and art collecting during the period of the Italian Renaissance have been identified by Renaissance scholar Peter Burke as piety, prestige, and pleasure (Burke, 1986: 97). Similar motivating factors will be found in nineteenth-century America. We will first review the Renaissance motives outlined by Burke and then compare them to the patronage of the American Renaissance.

Piety is easily demonstrated as a widespread, socially acceptable motive through the predominance of religious themes in paintings and sculpture and the number of commissions issued for the love of God. Prestige as a motive for patronage is evidenced by the inscriptions in commissions celebrating the honor and glory of the patron, or the depictions of patrons dressed in luxurious clothing in the company of saints and popes.

The *Adoration of the Magi* (collection of the Uffizi Gallery) commissioned by Piero de Medici is an excellent example of how prestige can be derived from a work of art. In this case the painting serves to document the greatness of the Medici family, but prestige can come in other ways as well. Other outstanding demonstrations of prestige as a motivating factor are the previously described projects by Cosimo de Medici of the enlargement of the church and convent of San Marco and the marvelous expansion of San Lorenzo. Here, the huge expenditures of money become a key factor in gaining prestige. The tabernacle commissioned by Piero de Medici for the Church of the Annunziata was inscribed with the words: "Costo fior. 4 mila el marmo solo" ("The marble alone cost 4,000 florins") (Wackernagel, 1981: 239).

Looking to the third motive identified by Burke, that is the motive of pleasure, we observe it defined by him as "a more or less discriminating delight in paintings, statues and so on, whether as objects in their own right or as a form of interior decoration" (Burke, 1986: 98). It is noted that the pleasure taken from objects of art reached a level of importance and self-consciousness in Renaissance Italy unprecedented anywhere in Europe for a thousand years. The desire to acquire art for its own sake is generally found in people who have received a humanist education, according to Burke. As has already been demonstrated, the study of the humanities was an important part of Cosimo de Medici's life and gained in importance in the lives of his son Piero and grandson Lorenzo. Lorenzo surrounded himself with artists, writers, and scholars and became the most famous patron of the arts in all of Europe.

Renaissance patronage motives revived

Looking at the motives for art patronage during the Italian Renaissance as they have been identified by Peter Burke, that is piety, prestige, and pleasure, let us see how they continued as forces in the American Renaissance.

Piety, demonstrated by the number of religious commissions in the Italian Renaissance, may find a parallel in patriotism during the American Renaissance. The American Renaissance was, by both definition and action, intensely nationalistic. While it appropriated the styles and symbols of the Italian Renaissance, it used them to create the image of a new American civilization.

Americans, from the beginning, were proud and outspoken about their capabilities and achievements. Following the Civil War, however, a great surge of nationalism found form in every aspect of the culture including art (Cashman, 1984: 4). This new awareness of a national identity was defined in word and image and, with the celebration of the centennial and the focus on American history, the images became monumental. Nationalism inspired art and architecture and they, in turn, inspired nationalism.

The Boston Public Library (McKim, Mead, and White, 1887–95) is a fine example of what the American Renaissance built for patriotic and democratic purposes (Cashman, 1984: 44). The very concept of a public library, a place holding the potential for every citizen to gain knowledge, a place that is both free and open, is at the heart of American democracy. However, the library, though financed with public funds, was in fact the result of the movement of Boston's elite. The design is based on a Renaissance palazzo, and on either side of the triple arched entrance are classically inspired personifications of Art and Science. Across the frieze are carved the words: "The Public Library of the City of Boston Built by the People and Dedicated to the Advancement of Learning." Inside the library rooms of rich marble are memorials of heroes and patriots by Louis Saint-Gaudens and Frederick MacMonnies. There are Venetian-style ceiling paintings and great bronze doors designed by Daniel Chester French (Wilson, 1983: 135–9).

The Boston Public Library is but one example of a movement that crossed the continent and in every American city brought together the businessmen, architects and artists for the purpose of civic beautification.

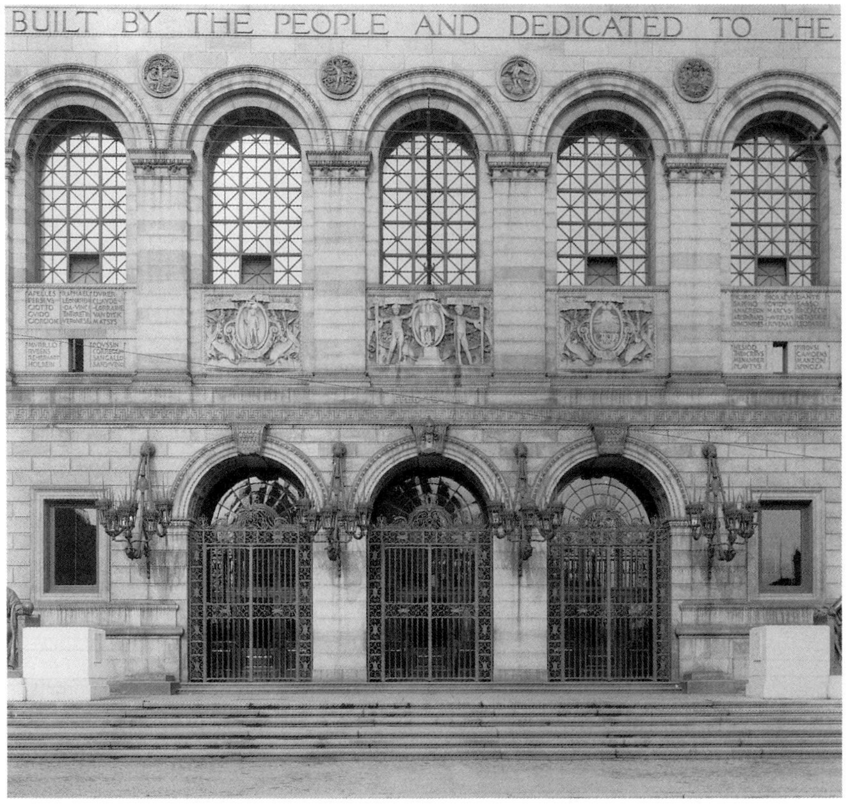

Boston Public Library (entrance), McKim, Mead and White, architects.
Reproduced from the Collections of the Library of Congress.

The movement was portrayed as American and democratic. The muralist Edwin Blashfield echoed the three motives when he wrote:

> The names of public buildings are the century-marks of the ages ... wherever the footprints of the spirit of civilization have rested most firmly some milestone of human progress has risen to be called Parthenon or Notre Dame, Giotto's Tower or Louvre, and to teach from within and without, by proportion and scale, by picture and statue, the history of the people who build it; to celebrate patriotism, inculcate morals, and to stand as the visible concrete symbol of high endeavor the effort of man in his own handiwork to prove himself worthy of the creator whose handiwork he is.
> (Blashfield, 1913: 18)

Prestige as a motive for patronage is tied to the expenditure of money, and the Vanderbilt family were among the Medicis of the late nineteenth-century. Between 1876 and 1917, the Vanderbilts constructed at least seventeen mansions including the Biltmore in Asheville, North Carolina, which was constructed on a 125,000-acre estate at a cost in excess of $5,000,000. The Biltmore (1895) is a massive structure of Indiana limestone designed by the architect Richard Morris Hunt, who referred to the project as "the most permanently important public work" and "the most distinguished private place, not only of America, but of the world" (Baker, 1986: 417–21).

Biltmore House is reminiscent of early French Renaissance architecture in its mass of chimneys and gables and pinnacles. The library, the most richly decorated room in the house, is paneled with Circassian walnut with a muraled ceiling originally attributed to the Venetian master Tiepolo. George Washington Vanderbilt filled this luxurious room with over twenty thousand beautifully bound volumes on art, architecture, history, and forestry. Over the mantel is a late-seventeenth-century tapestry flanked by modern wood carvings done in a baroque manner (Baker, 1986: 428; Lynes 1980: 122).

The banquet hall, which measures 42 by 72 feet and has a ceiling 75 feet above, was designed to be the grandest room in the house. This room, dominated by a triple fireplace at one end, is medieval in style and decorated with five large sixteenth-century Flemish tapestries and numerous modern carvings depicting period themes and executed in period fashion (Baker, 1986: 424; Lynes 1980: 122).

The 90-foot-long tapestry gallery contains a series of early sixteenth-century Brussels tapestries (Baker, 1986: 428), and the print room holds a collection of Dürer engravings and a chess set once owned by Napoleon I (Lynes, 1980: 122). "There were forty masters' bedrooms in the house and the steep roof that covered it was the largest, whether for a public or private building, anywhere in the country" (Lynes, 1980: 22). This clearly illustrates the hold the Italian Renaissance had on the American imagination and demonstrates the link between collecting and social status.

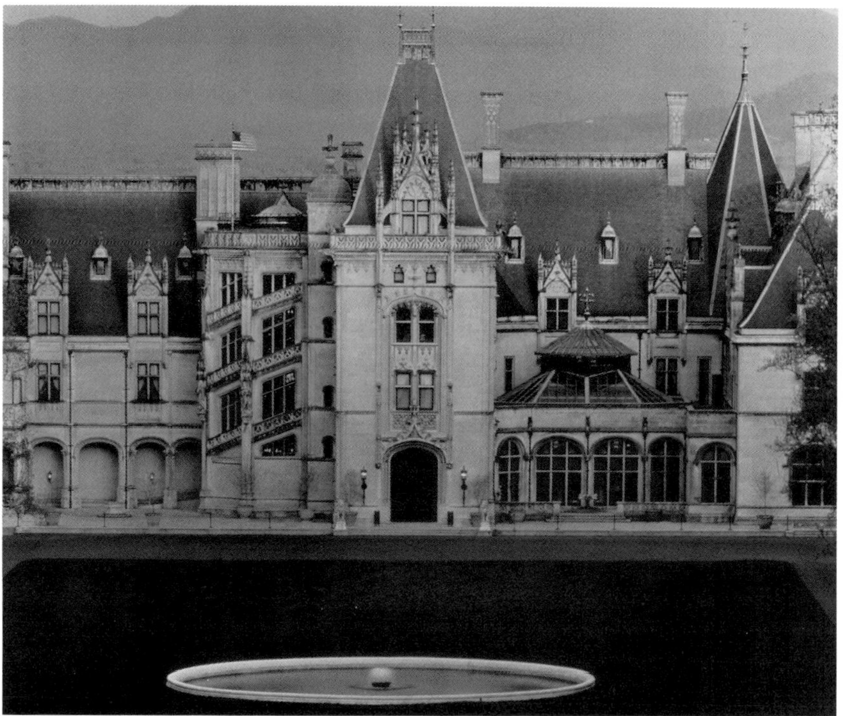

The Biltmore House, Asheville, NC, 1895, Richard Morris Hunt, architect. *Biltmore Company.*

The American Renaissance art and architecture, whether private or public, was inextricably tied to capitalism. The artists of this period designed the Italian palazzos in which the new Medici would spend their time. They designed the great public buildings and cultural institutions that were generally funded by wealthy patrons or philanthropic organizations. This period did witness the founding of America's libraries, orchestras, operas, universities, and of course, America's museums. "The large European Old Master holdings of many art museums were tied directly to both a vision of America equaling the Old World in artistic property and to the pillaging activities of Bernard Berenson, Stanford White, and others" (Wilson, 1979: 21).

Appropriately, the artists also designed the currency of capitalism. Saint-Gaudens designed both the ten- and the twenty-dollar gold piece; Adolph Weinman designed the Liberty dime; James Frazer, the Buffalo nickel; Victor Brenner, the Lincoln penny.

As we look to Burke's third motive for collecting, we find that Americans take great delight in the fine arts and the decorative arts as well. The new rich sought exotic and beautiful furnishings from all parts of the world and were quick to commission American artists to paint, sculpt, and otherwise enhance their surroundings. The pleasure motive taken with things beautiful was also tied to the prestige derived from the wealth and knowledge required to choose and purchase art. It was somewhat nationalistic too in that art was seen as an index of civilization.

There was also for American patrons the notion of art giving pleasure by uplifting the spirit. This was the didactic notion that elevated aesthetics would produce elevated morals (Adam, 1929: 53). It was connected to the motive of patriotism in that the superiority of the morals of the American nation were at stake. Better art would make better citizens.

The similar motivating factors in the collection of art speak to the way in which Americans adopted the symbolism of art collecting as established in the Italian Renaissance. For the American people, art collecting symbolized the establishment of, on the North American continent, an advanced culture enlightened and ready to assume a leadership role among world powers. It meant they were a nation rich in treasures, money, culture, and learning. For the individuals who amassed large numbers of paintings and sculptures—millionaires like the Astors, Whitneys, and Fricks—the art collection stood as a symbol of wealth, power, and prestige. They viewed themselves as the new Medici and took great pride in the role of patron. These patrons represented the sense of confidence and intellectual prowess that characterized America's coming of age.

Conclusion

Bernard Berenson, art scholar and advisor on art collecting, wrote in 1894

> We ourselves because of our faith in science and the power of work ... are instinctively in sympathy with the Renaissance. Our tasks are more difficult because our vision is wider, but the spirit which animates us was anticipated by the spirit of the Renaissance, and more than anticipated. That spirit seems like the small rough model after which ours is being fashioned. (Berenson, 1894: n.p.)

And later:

> We, too, are possessed of boundless curiosity. We, too, have an almost intoxicating sense of human capacity. We, too, believe in a great future for humanity, and nothing has yet happened to check our delight in discovery or our faith in life. (Berenson, 1894: 57)

The European model as defined here was first classical and second individual. The classical art and architecture of Greece and Rome furnished the basic styles that were adapted to American needs. It became the custom of the day for artists to study in Europe where the standards of Classic and Renaissance art would be taught. Berenson defines the consequences of this interest in the classical as a growing worship of human greatness, which led to the celebration of the individual and a love of glory of the individual. Art patronage would follow and a means to insure that glory (Berenson, 1894: 6).

In architecture, a variety of buildings with reference to the past were designed. Temple fronts were a common theme as were great domes and triumphal arches, and the classical orders were found everywhere. Sculpture was used to enhance the buildings, and the human figure idealized was the most frequent form. Usually, these figures were abstract allegories representing Wisdom, Justice, Truth, or Beauty, Knowledge, Mercy, Courage.

The generation of American artists that returned home from various European academies in the 1870s and 1880s returned with a new knowledge, a keen sense of European history, and the ability to design in a number of different styles. They had learned about the Renaissance through art schools in Munich and Paris as well as in Rome. They had learned that architecture is a means by which a group could communicate its ideas and ideals, could define in stone its public identity; and America, having only a recent architectural past, would connect its identity to European history. "We want to belong somewhere and to something, not to be entirely cut off by ourselves as stray atoms" (Dow, 1979: 45). Thus the concrete symbols of American civilization, the art and architecture, were modeled after the Old World.

Note that a study of John La Farge's mural in the Church of the Ascension in New York reveals an unmistakable reference to Raphael's Vatican mural entitled "Transfiguration." According to Richard Guy Wilson, however, it draws upon several other works as well: "the figures of the apostles are derived from Palma Vecchio's 'Assumption of the Virgin' (Venice, Accademia), the background is indebted to Japanese landscape, and the painting style comes from Titian and Delacroix" (Wilson, 1979: 61). Wilson goes on to point out that the mural is located in a Gothic Revival church (Upjohn) with decoration by Stanford White after Bramante, flying angels by Saint-Gaudens after Donatello, and kneeling angels by Armstrong after Giotto. The entire composition expresses the contrary attitude of individualism inherited from the Renaissance while honoring the Renaissance as the primary stylist inspiration. John La Farge himself expressed the feelings of the period when he wrote regarding his European contemporaries: "We are not as they are ... fixed in some tradition; and we can go where we choose ... to the greatest influences, if we wish, and still be free for our future" (quoted in Wilson, 1979: 61).

In conclusion, it was the collection of art, the commissioning of art, both privately and publicly, that elevated the sights of nineteenth-century America. It said that America was no longer only a frontier society of great natural resources but also rich in cultural things. America's art collecting proclaimed a new society based on the success of industry, commerce, democracy, and capitalism, a society in which the new Medici could flaunt that success by the accumulation of art. An understanding of the motives behind the patronage of art in nineteenth-century America, (patriotism, prestige, and pleasure through moral elevation) provides an understanding of the nation's need to establish the art museum. Patriotism could be demonstrated in the art and in the architecture of the public building. The triumphal arches outfitted with statues representing civic virtues would in turn inspire patriotism. The pleasure the work of art provided, it was believed, was morally uplifting for the masses and therefore would create better citizens. The prestige provided by the art would touch both the individual and the nation and would solidify the vision of America as a great civilization, the new bearer of the torch of Western culture. The American Renaissance, therefore, was the perfect climate and soil for the establishment of America's first art museums.

2

The American art museum, a symbol of democracy

Introduction

The origins of the symbolic meaning of the American art museum can be found in eighteenth-century Paris, in the evolution of the Louvre Museum and its connections to the French Revolution. Nineteenth-century Americans viewed the Louvre as a symbol of the triumph of democracy and adopted it as a model for the development of an American art museum (Tomkins, 1989: 31). Just as the collection of art was seen as a symbol of prosperity, power, and prestige by both the American people and their leaders (see Chapter 1), the collection of art within the museum context would confer that status on the American nation and establish it as an advanced culture whose system of democracy had succeeded. The seeds of the democratic/elitist paradox of the American art museum can be found in the choice of the Louvre as a model.

The idea of the museum as a symbol will be explored first, followed by an overview of the museum as an educational system, education being at the core of the democratic purpose. The Louvre as a model for the American museum includes its architectural image, its collections, and its place as a symbol in French culture. These will be reviewed and connected to America's counterpart, the Metropolitan.

The museum as symbol

There are images that reside in the mind's eye of the American people that, because of their persistence and universality, come to stand for and express feelings and beliefs about the American nation. These images range from the majestic Statue of Liberty and the American eagle to the pop icons of cowboy hats and Chevrolets. What they have in common is the desire of their creators to be the people and live in the society the symbols represent.

Generally speaking, symbols may be defined as "things which stand for or express something else." Symbols are substituted for all known real and imaginary actions and objects and the relations among them. For our purposes, a sociologically-based definition will serve the discussion.

> The essential components of a symbol are the sign and its meaning, the former usually being the outward perceptible form which is culturally identifiable and recognizable, the latter being the interpretation of the sign, usually composed of concepts of what is being interpreted and the positive and negative values and feelings which "cluster about" the sign. The sign's meaning may refer to other objects or express and evoke feelings. The values and feelings may relate to the inner world of the person or be projected outward on the social and natural worlds beyond.
>
> (Warner, 1965: 4)

The American flag with its stars and stripes is a prime American symbol. Like all symbols it is comprised of a sign and its meaning. The sign is the red, white, and blue stars and stripes in that specific configuration that is known across the land and around the world. The meaning or interpretation of the sign, as stated earlier, can be either referential or evocative or both. In the case of the American flag, the thirteen stripes refer to the nation's beginnings in the thirteen original colonies, and the 50 stars symbolize the unity and equality of the 50 states. The flag also symbolizes the sacrifices of our forefathers through the color red; the purity of their intentions through the color white; and their bravery through the color blue. These are specifically designated meanings, but the flag also refers generally to more abstract concepts that the American people associate with their nation, such as liberty, equality, and justice. The flag, or any symbol, might also inspire feelings such as love of country and loyalty, or negative feelings such as anger and fear.

The creation of a symbol involves the attribution of meaning as a result of experiences that are visible, perceptible, and available to the group. The meaning of the American flag within the American culture is generally unanimous because that culture, though large and diverse, maintains a common core of understanding. The flag states symbolically what the nation collectively believes, how it perceives its history, and what it wants to be.

The American art museum is a national symbol as well because, not only does it represent the wealth of a great nation and that nation's belief in the preservation of culture, but it also symbolizes the triumph of American democracy, for it stands with its doors open, its treasures gathered for the benefit of all the people (Adam, 1939: 49, 51). In other words, it projects an image of what Americans want to believe and what they want to be. The concept of the American art museum along with most of what it symbolizes can be traced to France and to the Louvre Museum.

The originating concept and call for an American art museum was sounded not in Washington, New York, or Boston, but in Paris. This may be viewed as prophetic when one considers the connections and competitions between American and French art and museums that have continued through the twentieth-century.

John Jay, an American lawyer and grandson of the first chief justice, addressed, at a Fourth of July, 1866 dinner party, a group of wealthy Americans vacationing in Paris. Jay stated that it was "time for the American people to lay the foundations of a National Institution and Gallery of Art" (quoted in Lerman, 1969: 12). The desire to establish a cultural institution in America similar to the wonders observed in Paris and London caused these men to pledge to support the goal. The vehicle for support would be New York's Union League Club of which these men were members, and the object of their support would be the Metropolitan Museum of Art.

It would take about four years for the Union League's art committee to present a full report and recommendations and to organize the solicitation of sponsors. At the end of 1869, a meeting attended by the city's business and cultural leaders confirmed that America would have a great encyclopedic art museum in New York City.

A key speaker at this meeting was Princeton's George Fiske Comfort, who laid out the various educational aspects of the art museum. According to Calvin Tomkins, Metropolitan Museum historian,

> Comfort's ideas were really rooted in the revolutionary origins of Europe's museums. Art museums as we know them today are recent developments in Western society. They appeared at the same historical moment as the first encyclopedias, toward the end of the eighteenth century, and like the encyclopedias they were strongly influenced by the radical currents of French thought that helped to bring on the French Revolution. The first public museum was born in 1793, when the Louvre Palace, with all its treasures, confiscated by the republican regime, was declared open to the people. (Tomkins, 1989: 31)

So from its inception, the American art museum in the form of the Metropolitan had as its model the European museum born of revolution. In order to understand the originating concept of the American museum one must understand the originating concept of the Louvre and its place in French culture and in Western culture in general. We will look first at the Enlightenment and its impact on eighteenth- and nineteenth-century thought.

The museum as educational system

The period preceding the French Revolution was one in which great emphasis was placed on rational thought and education. It was no coincidence that the concept of the public museum of art would arise during this period, considering the values of the day (Veysey, 1979: 81). New discoveries in science led people to believe that a strict use of reason would result in progress and that this progress would change the world as people were educated in it. Humanity was perceived as capable of progress in science, progress in the arts, progress even in moral values. The belief in both the possibility and the necessity of progress was pervasive, as was the belief that humanity could be improved intellectually and morally through proper education (Gay, 1984: 14–17; Ozouf, 1988: 198–203).

Proper education meant education through observation and through experience, both guided by reason. According to the seventeenth-century philosopher John Locke, whose influence was still strongly felt at this time, knowledge was not innate but was gained through education. He regarded the mind of a person at birth as a *tabula rasa*, a blank slate upon which knowledge would be imprinted by experience. Locke also held that all persons are born good, independent, and equal. His *Essay Concerning Human Understanding* (1690) was very important to the period that gave birth to the French Revolution and American democracy, and in fact his philosophy was incorporated into the United States Constitution.

Locke's concept of education through observation matches perfectly with the museum format where objects are set out and one may study and compare several or focus on one specifically. For Americans, the educational opportunities presented by the museum enhanced it as a symbol of democracy. (For a discussion of the museum as an educational institution, see Chapter 6.) In addition, the desire at this time for the display of rational thought processes was well satisfied with the museum's systematic presentations of art (Alexander, 1982: 10). (For an analysis of the impact of modernism on exhibition design, see Chapter 5.)

What had previously governed the arrangement of paintings in private galleries was the desire to achieve a harmonious, decorative effect. Paintings were arranged according to their size and shape and, no doubt, how well they fitted the available wall space. But now a new didactic approach was taken. With the public's access to the art gallery there developed an educational approach to the display of paintings (Alexander, 1982: 195–6).

When the Ancien Régime opened the galleries in the Luxembourg Palace to the public at mid-century, the paintings were installed in a way that encouraged contrast and comparison of style and subject. In its desire to create a public museum, the Ancien Régime installed about one hundred paintings in the east wing of the Luxembourg Palace in what Andrew McClellan refers to as a system "with a pedagogic and theoretical coherence grounded in mainstream art theory of the late seventeenth and early eighteenth centuries" (McClellan, 1994: 30). This was a system that juxtaposed works by different artists and of different genres. The gallery provided artist and amateur alike with an "eclectic mix of artists. . . who embodied a competitive historical field in which French artists took on their Italian and Northern rivals" (McClellan, 1994: 44).

This system probably derived from a theory developed by Roger de Piles in 1708 which held that a painting contained the four elements of color, design, composition, and expression and that one could best study painting by comparing each individual element. This would best be achieved by the juxtaposition of artists, styles, and subjects, thus allowing the viewer continuous contrast (Piles, 1706: 29–38).

This system was later abandoned in favor of a more progressive order. Paintings were hung chronologically and according to school. Works at the Imperial Gallery in Vienna were classified by region and then arranged to illustrate art historical developments within each school. The plans for the Grand Gallery of the Louvre, set in motion in 1779, probably included the installation of art in the new progressive order, the arrangement by school and chronology (McClellan, 1994: 77–8). The Louvre in the late 1790s displayed the French school at the Salon end of the Grand Gallery, followed by the Northern and Italian schools. Within the schools, artists were grouped in chronological order. This system of display was in keeping with the Vasarian, or Renaissance canon, which was enthusiastically embraced by nineteenth-century Americans (see Chapter 1). Therefore, the galleries of both the Louvre and the Metropolitan Museum would welcome art exhibited in a progressive historical order.

The Louvre and its architectural influence

The Louvre Palace was to be the first great museum, an encyclopedic collection housed in a palace and opened to the public for the purpose of enlightenment and inspiration. It's beginnings can be traced as far back as the reign of Charles V, who employed an army of architects and artists to enlarge and "modernize" the then 150-year-old buildings which had functioned mainly as arsenal and prison. In about 1400 Charles V established the Louvre as his palace and, in addition to the royal treasures housed there, established also a library rich in illuminated manuscripts, the nucleus of the present-day Bibliothèque Nationale. (Bazin, 1979: 9; Huyghe, 1967: 11).

During the reign of Charles VI, the English conquered the French and occupied Paris. For more than a century the Louvre was neglected, becoming again a prison and arsenal. But with the rise of Francis I, the Louvre once again became a royal court and the symbol of the wealth and culture of the French nation.

Francis I began a collection of contemporary Renaissance paintings and also began the additions to the palace which would eventually lead to a complex of unprecedented magnificence and monumental size. Every sovereign that followed Francis, and each administration since the Revolution, left a mark on the evolution of the Louvre, making it a palace, a seat of government, and a repository of the nation's treasures (Laclotte, 1989: 25).

The entire architectural tradition of this great palace was an inspiration to America, whose first museums, the Metropolitan and the Boston Museum of Fine Arts, would be designed to look like palaces. When the Metropolitan's Fifth Avenue facade was completed, New York City's *Evening Post* of December 23, 1902 praised it as "the only public building in recent years which approaches in dignity and grandeur the museum of the old world."

The Louvre continued to grow with the erecting of the Petite Galerie and part of the Palace of the Tuileries by Catherine de Medicis. Henry IV completed the work begun by the queen mother, and spanned the distance from the Petite Galerie to the Palace of the Tuileries with the Grande Galerie (Laclotte, 1989: v). On the lower floors of this structure, which is more than a quarter of a mile long, hundreds of artists lived and worked as guests of the King. (This tradition continued until Napoleon I.)

Succeeding Henry, Louis XIII planned the present court to be four times the size of Henry's. Louis XIV, sparing no expense, took both architecture and art as the symbols of a great and glorious reign. New wings were built for the Palace of the Tuileries, which became home to Louis XIV. Other additions included the north, east, and south buildings of the old Louvre quadrangle, the Gallery of Apollo to replace the Gallery of the Kings, and the enlargement of the Petite Galerie (Bazin, 1979a: 39–41).

The Academy of Painting was founded in Paris in 1648 and held biannual exhibitions which were installed in the Louvre beginning in 1673. Beginning in 1681, many of Louis' paintings were exhibited to a semipublic audience in the Louvre. Thus there was established early on a tradition of both the creation of art and the exhibition of art in the Louvre.

However, when Louis XIV built Versailles he moved his court to this luxurious estate outside Paris. During the eighteenth century, as Versailles continued as the seat of power, the Louvre fell into disrepair. The artists continued living and working there and were joined by shop owners and private tenants. There were also still some government offices, but the building deteriorated, due to the absence of real power.

The Ancien Régime talked of renovation and the creation of a great public museum, but plans continued slowly. With the fall of the Bastille in 1789, the monarchy came into jeopardy. The concept of a public museum may have originated with the Crown, but it was realized in the end through the efforts of the Revolution (Bazin, 1979: 54–9). It is said with a smile that one of the reasons the Revolution was so popular was because it got things done.

The day the Bourbon monarchy finally collapsed (August 10, 1792) and the king's art collection was declared national property was the true beginning of the Louvre Museum. Louis XVI was taken prisoner, and the National Assembly declared its interest in the museum and assigned responsibility for its completion to the Girondin Jean-Marie Roland, Minister of the Interior. Roland appointed a committee of six men headed by the artist Jacques-Louis David. Their assignment was to refurbish the Grand Gallery for exhibition and to select the various paintings and decorative arts to be exhibited. By February, 1793, arrangements for the first display in the Louvre were complete. When the Republic celebrated its first birthday on August 10, 1793, it celebrated also the inauguration of the museum.

A palace in New York City

When the Metropolitan Museum of Art opened almost one hundred years later (see Chapter 3), its home in Central Park was a newly built Gothic palace. This first building, designed by Calvert Vaux and Jacob Wrey Mould, was part of a larger architectural plan to be executed over the years. The final Fifth Avenue facade would be designed by the first American to study at the École des Beaux Arts in Paris (Baker, 1986: 443; Howe, 1974: 276). Richard Morris Hunt was famous for his facility with historical styles and created for America's art museum a monumental, neoclassical, Indiana limestone building with a look of elegance and greatness emulating a European museum. The subsequent wings on either side of the Hunt facade would be designed by McKim, Mead, and White.

The new building was strictly symmetrical and clearly articulated in its advancing and receding planes. The coupled columns are a common feature of Beaux-Arts Classicism, as are the arched and linteled openings between the columns and the sculptural elements that enliven the skyline. The monumental flight of steps (which was further expanded in 1970) was also characteristic. (For the influence of modern architecture on the museum, see Chapter 5.)

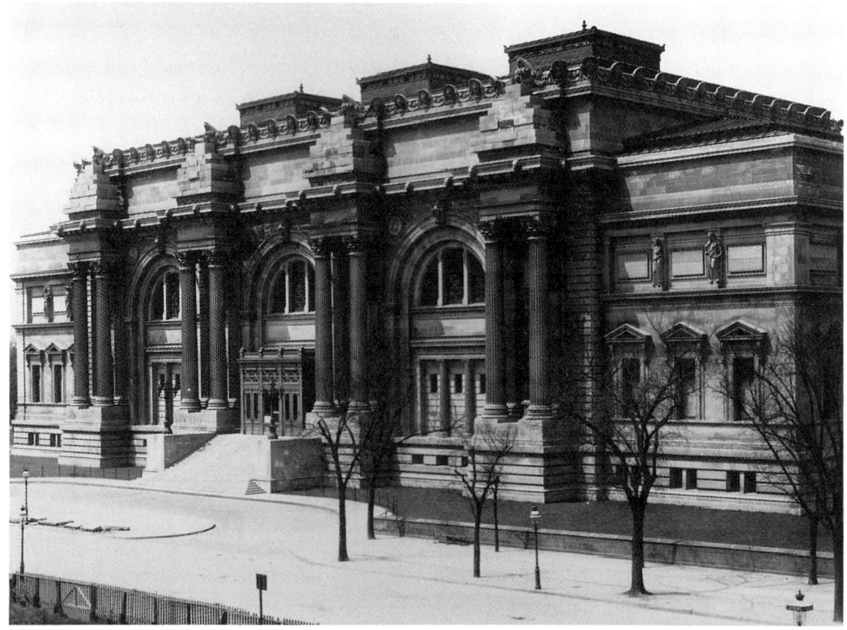

The Metropolitan Museum of Art, 1910, Richard Morris Hunt, architect.
The Metropolitan Museum of Art.

The interior of the Metropolitan was just as grand, with the great hall and its mighty staircase designed to awe the visitor. The enormous scale was intended to impress the public and let them know the importance of the museum in the American culture.

The museum developed its collections and its facility and approved the expansion plans presented by the prestigious New York architectural firm of McKim, Mead, and White. The Fifth Avenue wing would be extended north (funds approved 1904), a new library would be built, and by 1910 a wing for the decorative arts would be added (Lerman, 1969: 124; Howe, 1974: 309–10).

McKim, Mead, and White, like Richard Morris Hunt before them, had been trained in Europe, McKim at the Ecole des Beaux-Arts, Mead at the Accademia delle Belle Arte in Florence, and White, informally, through a year of travel on the continent. They were therefore knowledgeable of contemporary styles as well as European historical styles (Wilson, 1983: 10–12). This firm spearheaded the revival of Georgian and Federalist architecture and completed 215 significant commissions between 1879 and 1887, when the Boston Public Library marked the emergence of their mature work (Roth, 1978: xxiv).

They set the pace for Neoclassical Revival, according to Richard Guy Wilson (1983), and designed the largest and one of the finest Neo-classical Revival buildings: Pennsylvania Station in New York City. They were experienced and highly respected in the practice of adapting historical styles to modern purposes, and the wings they designed for the Metropolitan Museum served the art they held and also served the public.

Having established the primary symbol of the palace for the people, the Metropolitan Museum could begin to collect artifacts of historical and aesthetic significance. A country with no aristocracy and only a very recent history looked again to the European model for inspiration. Just as the American museum had transplanted the Old World palace onto the isle of Manhattan, so would it also appropriate treasures similar to those held in Europe's great houses.

The Louvre collection

The collection of fine art and decorative art held in the Louvre grew with each new sovereign, sometimes fed by the collections of disposed nobles from around Europe. With the rise to power of Napoleon Bonaparte, and the establishment of the Louvre as a museum, the treasures held there would mount rapidly.

General Napoleon Bonaparte, in his various military campaigns and conquests, set about to systematically confiscate the best paintings, sculptures, and other cultural treasures from invaded lands and store them in the Louvre Museum. Belgium was the first victim in 1794 giving up many paintings by Rubens and Van Dyke. Italy's confiscated treasures included paintings by Correggio and Titian. Napoleon employed official art experts who, upon entering the invaded territories, would examine, catalog, pack and ship everything worthwhile back to Paris (Alexander, 1983: 89; Bazin, 1979a: 56).

Following his conquest of Italy (1797), Bonaparte, with the help of his art experts, returned to Paris with one hundred paintings, five hundred manuscripts, and seventy-three sculptures including the Apollo Belvedere, the Laocoon, and the Lion of St. Mark.

> The arrival in Paris of the largest convoy of the confiscated art works from Italy in July, 1798 led to a great two-day-long "fete de la liberte". The triumphal parade worked its way from the Jardin des Plantes to the Champ de Mars, where it formed a triple circle around the Altar to Liberty. Enormous wagons pulled the four bronze horses from St. Mark's Basilica in Venice, the carefully packed statues, huge crates labeled in large letters, "Transfiguration by Raphael" or "Christ by Titian", and cages of bears and lions followed by plodding camels. There was a band, there were marching artists, scholars, and prominent statesmen, speeches, patriotic songs, and wild applause resounded from a huge crowd.
>
> (Alexander, 1983: 89)

Most of these masterpieces would be returned to their rightful owners following Napoleon's defeat, but the reputation of the Louvre as the great encyclopedic museum was firmly established during this period. Napoleon understood the symbolic significance of the possession of these works of art and the far-reaching impact of the parade through the streets. The Louvre became the depository for the spoils of war, but was also established, both by the Revolutionary government and later by Napoleon as emperor, as an educational institution for the common people. This, according to Germain Bazin, was another democratic twist: "Previously, the education of the artist had been in the hands of a master." But now the galleries were open and full of copyists and so... "henceforth, from Delacroix to Matisse, by way of Courbet and Renoir, it was the great masters in the Museum who supervised artistic education" (Bazin, 1979a: 62).

Napoleon had little, if any, aesthetic appreciation for art, but he clearly understood its function as a symbol of glory and, as his power increased, saw how the museum could bring attention and splendor to his reign (Dowd, 1969: 133–4). The man who helped guide Napoleon in this direction was Dominique Vivant Denon (1747–1825), an aristocrat from Burgundy. Denon came to Napoleon with a thorough knowledge of Europe and its art, a knowledge of art history, and an ambitious, hard-working personality. In 1798 Vivant Denon joined Napoleon's army of 38,000 men and 328 vessels to sail for Alexandria. The expedition resulted in many notes and drawings that went into his monumental book on Egypt, *Voyage dons la Haute et al Basse Egypte*, which he dedicated to Napoleon (Denon, 1973: n.p.). This publication no doubt influenced Napoleon's decision to appoint Denon chief administrator of the Louvre Museum.

Denon and Bonaparte agreed that the Louvre must be the most beautiful, most important museum in the world. Denon began renovation plans immediately and, to guarantee Napoleon's continued support, suggested a change in the name of the museum, calling it Musée Napoleon (Alexander, 1983: 90; Bazin, 1979a: 58).

Denon accompanied Napoleon on his campaigns in order to secure the conquered land's best art for his beloved Musée Napoleon. Denon was by nature an avid collector of art, so in his position as museum director and chief collector for the empire he truly excelled.

The Grande Galerie of the Louvre was 1,200 feet long and contained nine bays which, by 1811, held almost 1,200 paintings. Denon had arranged the bays according to schools. Four bays were devoted to Italian schools and showed 25 paintings by Raphael, 24 by Titian, fifteen by Veronese, ten by Tintoretto and seven by Leonardo da Vinci to name a few. The Northern school was given four bays to show the 600 Dutch, Flemish, and German paintings including 54 by Rubens, 33 by Rembrandt, fifteen by Holbein, and fourteen by Van Dyck. It was assumed that providing the opportunity for comparison within each school made it possible for visitors to perceive the historic course of art. The clustering of works by a single artist within the school allowed for comparison and an understanding of that artist's concerns and development.

The Louvre continued to grow in size and importance under the directorship of Denon and the illustrious reign of Napoleon. Following the unsuccessful Russian campaign of 1812, however, Napoleon was defeated in a series of battles and abdicated in 1814. Louis XVIII was restored to the throne and, not wishing to disturb the French people, the allies postponed the restitution of art works to former owners. But when Napoleon escaped from Elba in 1815 and was finally defeated at Waterloo, the allies changed their policy. Deciding that the French people needed to be punished, and understanding the symbolic meaning of the museum and its treasures, the allies began restitution procedures (Bazin, 1979: 67–9). The despoiling of the Louvre took only six months but was a bitter and humiliating experience for the French people, who were deeply angered and openly displayed their feelings. The removal of treasures from the Louvre symbolized the loss of the nation's greatness.

The Louvre had become such a precious symbol, however, that it could not be abandoned. Louis XVIII and those who followed him attempted to imitate Napoleon's cultural policies while the French people allowed for their tax monies to support the museum. Today, the Louvre is no doubt a greater museum in many ways than it was in 1814, and its life as a symbol is still vital. The symbol of the Louvre, of the palace filled with world treasures and opened to the public for the purpose of education and gratification, was adopted by the American art museum.

From the Louvre to the Metropolitan

The influence of the Louvre was felt across Europe and across the Atlantic Ocean to the shores of America. It was seen as a symbol of the triumph of democracy, equality, and freedom: the world's first great public museum, a palace filled with the world's art treasures, open to all the people. The architecture and the encyclopedic contents were powerful symbols of intellectual, moral, and democratic progress and inspired the patrons of the Metropolitan Museum to strive to build a collection of similar status.

The main exhibition hall of the Metropolitan, when the museum first opened, was filled with large stone sculptures from Golgoi and smaller objects from Cyprus, all part of the Cesnola Collection. The "Old Masters" were located in the painting galleries on the floor above. These were mainly seventeenth-century Dutch and Flemish paintings and sixteenth- to nineteenth-century Italian, French, Spanish, and English works from the collections obtained for the museum by William T. Blodgett. Two galleries were set aside for temporary exhibitions, opening with nineteenth-century canvases borrowed from the William H. Vanderbilt collection (Lerman, 1969: 66).

It soon became very fashionable to give works of art to the Metropolitan, and in short order the museum's collections reached world status. One early gift of paintings that pushed the museum forward was from the collection of Henry Gurdon Marquand and included works by Rembrandt, Vermeer, Van Dyck, Franz Hals, Turner, and Gainsborough. The European masters were now in New York. (Chapter 3 provides a more in-depth look at the development of the Metropolitan's collection.)

The fascination with the European masters obscured for some time the idea of collecting American art. To Americans of the late nineteenth and early twentieth centuries, only European art was real art and carried the proper symbolism needed for the great and prosperous American nation. (This attitude influenced exhibits at the Museum of Modern Art well past 1950. See Chapter 8.) This love affair with European art, and especially the art held by the Louvre Museum, continued well into the twentieth-century and was demonstrated by the stir surrounding the arrival at the Metropolitan in 1969 of the famed *Mona Lisa*.

As referred to earlier, Francis I began a collection of contemporary Renaissance paintings during his reign. This included the work of Raphael and Leonardo da Vinci and four works by da Vinci remain in the Louvre to this day. The *Mona Lisa* was in the royal collections and was shown at Versailles. It hung in Napoleon's bedroom at the Tuileries and later, when the state collections opened to the public, it was given a place of honor in the Louvre. It had become the most famous portrait of all time, a point of pilgrimage at the Louvre Museum. The *Mona Lisa* was placed on loan by the Louvre (the French government) to the Metropolitan Museum (officially to President Kennedy) in 1963. Surrounded by elaborate security measures, including twenty-four-hour surveillance by secret

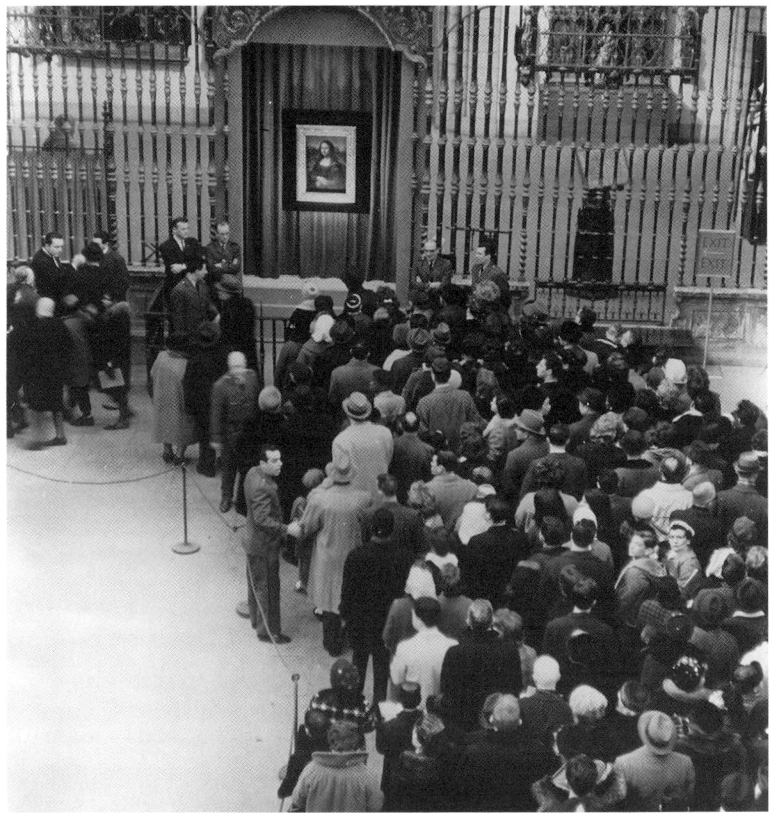

Visitors view the *Mona Lisa* in the Medieval Sculpture Hall at The Metropolitan Museum of Art, February 10 through March 4, 1963.
The Metropolitan Museum of Art.

service agents, and bullet-proof glass, the *Mona Lisa* was viewed by more than a million people during its one-month stay in New York (Metropolitan Museum of Art, *Bulletin*, February, 1963; *Annual Report*, 1962–63). This is an example of how the American people and the American art museum hoped to assume symbolic meanings by way of association.

The painting of the *Mona Lisa* represents many things, including wealth, history, and high culture. The possession of such a treasure suggests power, and its presence at the Metropolitan worked to transfer all of these attributes to that institution and, by further association, to the people viewing it. Day after day, in spite of the severe winter weather, lines formed before the museum opened. Once in motion, they stretched from the medieval hall where the painting was displayed, through the early Christian gallery, across the great hall, out the front doors and down Fifth Avenue for several blocks. The lines demonstrated the American admiration for the masterpiece and demonstrated also the American desire to achieve a museum of status similar to that of the Louvre.

The *Mona Lisa* was exhibited also at the National Gallery in Washington, D.C. and there too attracted large numbers of visitors. It is said that a general agreement on signs and symbols results in legitimacy. The American people recognized and agreed on the meaning of the *Mona Lisa* and turned out in record numbers to demonstrate that. The fact that this important and valuable painting was made available to the masses confirmed in the American culture the strength of democracy and the importance of art and the art museum as a symbol of democracy.

Conclusion

It was in eighteenth-century France, perhaps more than any other country at the time, that social currents found accurate reflection in the visual arts. The changes brought about by the Revolution were clearly articulated in the shift from the Rococo to the Neoclassical. The exuberant and decorative gave way to the austere; straight lines and simple forms replaced the undulating, curling shapes; the subjects of flirtatious and frivolous ladies of the court found in the paintings of Jean-Honoré Fragonard (1732–1806), were replaced by stoic characters of tough moral fiber exemplified in paintings by Jacques-Louis David (1748–1825). The new art had as its desire the objective analysis of history, art, human nature, and the forces of destiny. The Neoclassical gave contemporary themes classical dignity and thus gave the people a needed sense of history and the historic. The paintings by David gave artistic expression to the ideals and ambitions of the Revolutionaries and idealized patriotic virtue. The *Death of Socrates* (Collection of the Metropolitan Museum) for example, demonstrated both the educational and the propagandistic potential of art. The Americans, as well as the French, identified with the heroic and moral tone of the lesson.

David was also largely responsible for the creation of the Louvre Museum as a symbol of the triumph of democracy. The rich historical associations of the Louvre as palace, and its position, not only in the history of Paris, but also its physical position in the city, made it a powerful symbol of the triumph of the people. There stood the most conspicuous royal building, overflowing with treasures representing wealth and knowledge, now flung open to the public, welcoming the "rightful" owners.

The Museum Commission, according to Andrew McClellan, had deliberately planned the museum to dazzle the public with the spectacle of the nation's great treasures. "It would be appropriate to bring together ... everything that will enhance our precious collection of treasures to impress upon those who are coming to Paris ... that our present political problems have in no way diminished the cultivation of the arts among us" (McClellan, 1994: 99).

But while the museum would stand for stability and the greatness of the nation, it would also stand for education. David, who had nothing of the pedantic scholar about him (Ozouf, 1988: 76), wrote: "The Museum is not supposed to be a vain assemblage of frivolous luxury objects that serve

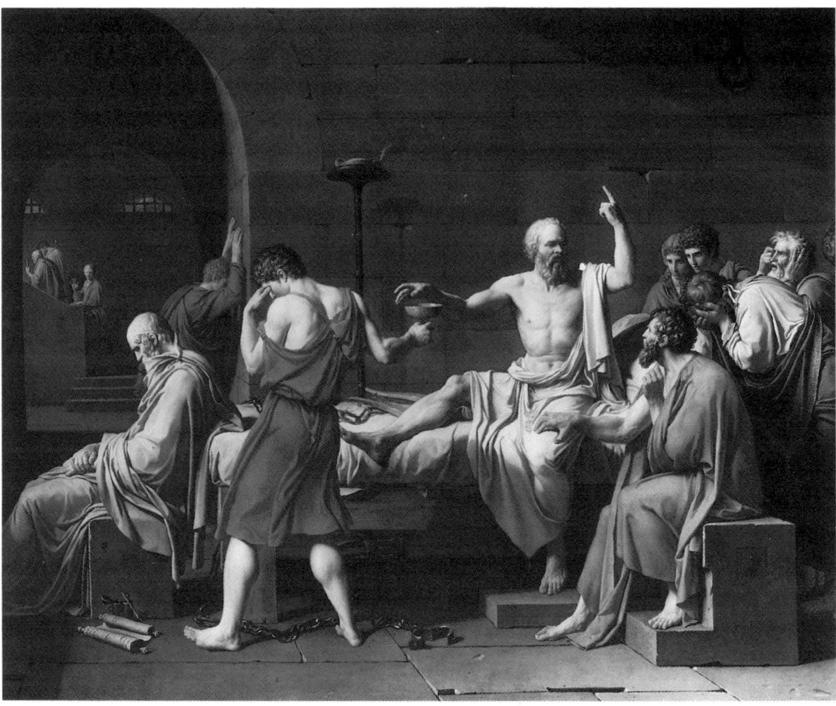

The Death of Socrates by Jacques Louis David (1748–1825), oil on canvas, 51 × 77½ in. (129.5 × 196.2 cm).
The Metropolitan Museum of Art, Catherine Lorillard Wolfe Collection, Wolfe Fund, 1931 (31.45).

only to satisfy idle curiosity. What it must be is an imposing school" (McClellan, 1994: 106). This dual symbolic role was adopted by the founders of the Metropolitan, thereby establishing the objectives for all American art museums and setting the paradoxical stage. The palace was meant to serve the people, its treasures offered for educational purposes.

So it was that the symbolic meanings of art and the art museum, described and defined in Paris during the period of the French Revolution, were appropriated by the American nation and made concrete first in the form of the Metropolitan Museum. The American palace on Central Park, filled with the world's treasures, continues to flourish and serve ever-increasing numbers of visitors. The Metropolitan, along with America's other art museums, stands, in part, because of the desire of the American people to live in a great society, a powerful society that can gather together world treasures; a good society that believes in the preservation of history, knowledge, and culture; a democratic society that provides educational opportunities to all its citizens. The American art museum stands because Americans want to be the people and live in the society represented by this symbol.

3

America's first museums: The Metropolitan Museum of Art and The Boston Museum of Fine Arts

We Americans have collected a little differently from other people. We were denied the historic opportunities afforded to proconsuls and viceroys ... Our interests as collectors grew out of our interests as manufacturers and merchants, as promoters and organizers, and followed them into every corner of the world and every epoch and activity of man ... Our art collections, like our industrial organization, are our heritage from the heroic age of American private enterprise.

A. Hyatt Mayer, "The Gifts that Made the Museum"

Introduction

Art, by its nature, is not democratic. The whole of what we call Western art was created by superior craftsmen of high intelligence and astute sensibilities. This art was often created for the wealthy rulers, well-educated leaders, the merchants, industrialists, and bankers of refined taste. To complicate this matter further, modern Western art has been based primarily on the artist's personal vision and the personal expression of that vision. The modern artist has been highly educated and highly trained, and his intention has largely been to communicate on his level, not necessarily to enlighten the masses.

The art museum in America has come to stand for, among other things, the triumph of American democracy. Museums supported by private funds and by money from the United States government have flourished in a fashion unprecedented in history. Their growth in this strange shadow of the paradox of elitism and democracy is a tribute to the fertility of the democratic, capitalistic, American soil. A soil so vast and with such variety of life would prohibit the homogeneity of the American art museum. However, the establishment of the first art museums did set the standards for all that followed. They formed, in a sense, the skeletal structure on which could be fashioned a variety of museums which would satisfy the complex American culture.

The first museums, the Metropolitan Museum in New York and the Boston Museum of Fine Arts, shared much in common at their beginnings. They were incorporated in the same year—1870—and were founded by private citizens with private funds as educational institutions. (Chapter 4 will address the art museums funded by the government.) Their constitutions and bylaws dictated the course of the American art museum for the next century, and for this reason their foundations deserve examination.

There were three main objectives perceived by the founders of these first museums: the museum would be an educational institution, it would have a moral mission, and it would foster national pride and prestige. (The origins of these three objectives are the subject of Chapter 1.) Education was the most important objective because it could merge with democratic principles and provide possibilities for the masses. But art could also be used toward moral betterment since, the founders reasoned, art had a moral dimension. The third objective of fostering patriotism and increasing the nation's prestige could be accomplished both through the public perception of the museum institution and its holdings as symbols of greatness and also through the eventual acquisition and exhibition of American works of art.

We will look at the beginnings of these two museums, scan their developments and the paths they took toward the fulfillment of their objectives, and then make note of the legacy which impacts on the American art museum today.

The Metropolitan Museum

The first public meeting where the idea of an institution for New York City was presented was held at New York's Union League Club on November 23, 1869. The Union League Club was primarily a political organization established in 1863 to provide support for Lincoln and the Union during the Civil War. Its members were prominent businessmen, bankers, and lawyers, as well as cultural and educational leaders. The November 23 meeting was attended by more than three hundred people, including members of the National Academy of Design, the Institute of Architects, and the New York Historical Society. The event was presided over by New York's cultural mavin, William Cullen Bryant.

Bryant, poet and journalist, delivered a speech full of national pride and pride in America's great city, New York.

> Our city is the third greatest city of the civilized world, our republic has already taken its place among the great powers of the earth; it is great in extent, great in population, great in the activity and enterprise of its people. It is the richest nation in the world

but a nation without a museum of art. Convincing arguments presented by Bryant included a comparison to European countries and their museums of art and the sad fact that should treasures be bequeathed to the public by private collectors there would be no place to exhibit them or store them. Also, American artists, though growing in number and respectability, still had to study in Europe and exhibit there, so poor was our cultural provision.

> It is like a bird in a cage which can only take short flights from one perch to another and longs to stretch its wings in an ample atmosphere.
>
> (Howe, 1974: 107–10)

At this meeting the speakers established not only the need for the Metropolitan Museum, but also some basic principles of purpose including the education of the general population. George Fiske Comfort of Princeton University described in his speech a museum offering educational outings for school children and gallery lectures for adult visitors. It was clear from the beginning that the museum would be an instrument for educating the proletariat. One could also sense the museum's role in satisfying the social needs of New York's moneyed class.

Approximately two months after this meeting, in January 1870, the first board of trustees was elected and the 27-man committee (21 elective and six ex-officio members including the mayor and the governor) was a good mix of money and art expertise and included the painters Frederick Church, Eastman Johnson, and John F. Kensett. Princeton's George Comfort and the publisher George P. Putnum were also on board for the selection of John Taylor Johnston as the Metropolitan's first president (Lerman, 1969: 15; Howe, 1974: 123).

By April of that year the New York Legislature voted the incorporation of the Metropolitan Museum of Art for the purpose of "encouraging and developing the study of the fine arts, and the application of the arts to manufacture, of advancing the general knowledge of kindred subjects, and, to that end, of furnishing popular instruction and recreation."

Johnston and the board then launched a public membership campaign, devising different classes and rates, in the hope of raising $250,000 toward the purchase of the paintings that would be the nucleus of the collection. At the same time they began negotiations with the City of New York to acquire municipal funding for property and construction of a museum building.

At this point two very different men became extremely important in the development of the museum. The first was William T. Blodgett, a prominent New Yorker with a keen interest in art and a passion for collecting. Blodgett was a member of the 1869 committee which initiated the organization of the Metropolitan, was one of the museum's incorporators, and was the first Chairman of its Executive Committee. Blodgett spent long periods of time in Europe, but his absences did not reduce his zeal for the museum and its collections. He was responsible for the acquisition of the first important collection to be owned by the Metropolitan. One hundred and seventy-four Flemish and Dutch paintings were purchased by Mr. Blodgett with his own resources (totaling $116,180.27) and then offered to the museum trustees at cost and with the generous agreement that the museum could reject any picture the authenticity of which was not fully established, and deduct that cost from the purchase price (Metropolitan Museum of Art (MMA), *Bulletin* February, 1906). John Taylor Johnston wrote to Blodgett on the receipt of the first shipment: "The quality of the collection as a whole is superior to anything I had dared to hope while the number of masterpieces is very great ... the Metropolitan Museum will make a splendid start in life" (Howe, 1974: 137).

During this same period options for a museum building were being explored. The man most responsible for the Metropolitan being located in Central Park was Andrew Haswell Green, the president of the Central Park Commission. Green was influential in the passage of a bill by the city legislature authorizing the Park Commission to "erect, establish, conduct and maintain in Central Park ... a Museum and Gallery of Art, and the buildings therefore, and to provide the necessary instruments, furniture, and equipments for the same" (Howe, 1974: 138). The next step was a legal petition asking for $500,000 to erect a building which would be owned by the city but whose contents, the art collections, would be owned and controlled by the museum trustees.

In 1874, three years after the financial foundations for a building and the nucleus of a collection had been established, ground was broken in Central Park for a red brick Gothic structure designed by Calvert Vaux and Jacob Wrey Mould. This first building, completed in 1880, was part of a larger architectural plan that allowed for further expansion (MMA, *Bulletin*, Summer, 1965).

These were lean years for the Metropolitan due to several factors, not least among them the Wall Street Panic of 1873 which was followed by a depression that lasted until 1878. The temporary quarters for the museum required $9,000 per year for rent and the entire budget from the city government was only $15,000 a year. The Annual Report ending May, 1878 shows cash on hand as $615.16, but immediately celebrates the museum's brief history as "abundant reason for congratulation." There was very little support from the citizens of New York, so according to museum records, the trustees and members who were still solvent following the Panic paid the deficits out of their own pockets. John Taylor Johnston noted that year:

> In times of such unexampled business depression as has characterized the last year, such an attempt seemed almost hopeless; but the Trustees congratulate the members on the visible fact that the Museum has such a strong hold on its friends that they have responded most liberally and cheerfully to its call for assistance ... The Trustees entertain the hope that ... the Museum will be relieved from all embarrassment and be in condition hereafter to devote such funds as it may have over its expenses to the purchase of objects of art. (MMA, *Annual Report*, 1876)

The annual reports from those years reveal a refreshing optimism and clarity of principles. The reports continually voice the conviction that the Metropolitan Museum was first among its kind and steadfast in its goal of "the education of the public and the cultivation in our country of a high standard of artistic taste." It was noted that the Museum had succeeded "in directing the tastes of the community to a higher standard ... our citizens are beginning to gather around them objects of artistic beauty ... and thus children are surrounded by the refining and elevating influences of art" (1876). "The Museum today is not surpassed as an educational power among the people by any university, college, or seminary of learning in the metropolis" (MMA, *Annual Report*, 1876: 78). Yet there was also expressed the frustration resulting from lack of support from the private sector.

By the end of the Depression in 1878, and with the return of confidence in New York's financial center, there came a renewed interest in the support for the Metropolitan. The museum hired, in 1879, General Cesnola as its first paid director and shortly thereafter moved its small collection of treasures into its new home in Central Park. These events marked the beginning of the Metropolitan Museum of Art.

The Metropolitan Museum is today counted among the world's greatest, while the Boston Museum of Fine Arts reached and maintained the status of a great city museum, never moving into world class. There is evidence that it was the elitist and puritanical attitudes of the Boston Museum's founders that ultimately stunted the growth of the BMFA. We will now review the founding of the Boston Museum and explore those issues which may have restricted the museum's growth.

The Boston Museum of Fine Arts

At the opening ceremony of the Museum of Fine Arts, Boston's mayor described the city's museum as "The crown of our educational system." There is some question, however, as to who this educational system was designed to serve, since the city of Boston had no role, financial or philosophical, in either the establishment or maintenance of the museum. Unlike the founders of the Metropolitan, who arranged some involvement of the New York City government, the founders of the Museum of Fine Arts were independent of municipal authorities and proud that no public money was received, perhaps in the conviction that their standards would never be compromised by any city involvement. So with the exception of the city land on which the museum was erected, the funding for the Museum of Fine Arts, its collections, building, and operations, was raised by private subscription. These subscriptions came mainly from those associated with the Boston Athenaeum, the Social Science Association, Harvard College, and the Massachusetts Institute of Technology. The $260,000 raised for the construction of the Museum's first building was donated by one thousand private citizens (Gilman, 1907: 42).

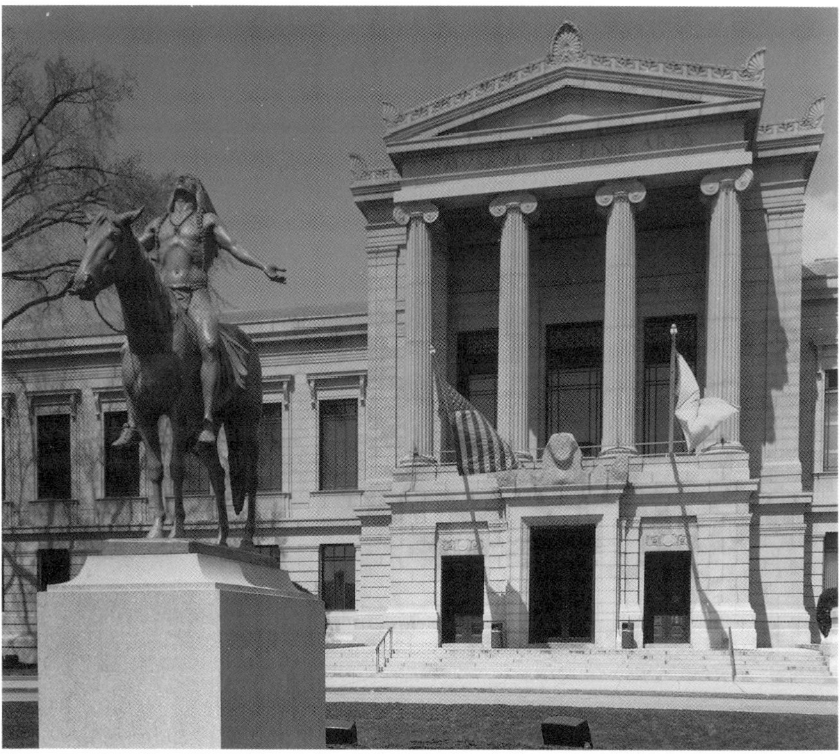

Museum of Fine Arts, Boston, Huntingdon Avenue facade with Cyrus Dallin's *Appeal to the Great Spirit*.
Museum of Fine Arts, Boston.

Nathaniel Burt in his social history of the American art museum, *Palaces for the People* (1977), discusses the backgrounds of the creators of the Boston Museum of Fine Arts. While the Metropolitan's founders were self-made men, the men in Boston were men of family.

> The Boston Museum of Fine Arts inherited a collection, prestige, the backing of Boston's Best and its best institutions, everything but public assistance and cash ... Boston from the beginning was scholarly, intense, serious but poor. Neither surprises nor disasters were characteristic.
> (Burt, 1977: 106)

The Museum of Fine Arts had healthy subscriptions but, unlike the Metropolitan, no major benefactors in the early years. The strength of the Boston Museum of Fine Arts was its close ties to Harvard University, which provided expert curators and trustees with a keen knowledge of and interest in the fine arts. Both Harvard and the Massachusetts Institute of Technology had representatives on the museum board including Harvard President Eliot (Gilman, 1907: 43). In spite of the limited budget, the Museum of Fine Arts managed to purchase remarkable artifacts due, in large part, to the Harvard people. The Egyptian collection and the collection of classical art were built by Harvard men and are the major strengths of the Boston Museum.

The Egyptian collection was launched with an important gift from C. Granville Way in 1872 and rapidly increased under the direction of Albert Lythgoe (Gilman, 1907: 44). Lythgoe, the first curator of the Egyptian collection, was responsible for its growth and its unmatched quality. Lythgoe had the proper connections in Egypt and built the Boston Museum's Department of Egyptian Art to be the finest in America and then deserted Boston for New York and the Metropolitan where, beginning in 1907, he would repeat his performance as superb acquisitor.

The collection of Greek art held by the Boston Museum of Fine Arts was praised as a museum marvel. It was said to be superior in quality to the Metropolitan or any other American Museum, and sections were compared to the holdings of the great museums of Europe by experts in the field (Furtwangler, 1904: 22). Its excellence was due to another Harvard man, Edward Robinson, and to a Bostonian in exile, Edward Perry Warren.

Edward Robinson graduated from Harvard University in 1879 and studied classical archaeology abroad for several years, excavating in Greece. He also worked in German museums, where he acquired a knowledge of and respect for German methods of organization. Robinson served first as curator of Classical Antiquities at the Boston Museum of Fine Arts beginning in 1885 and in 1902 assumed the directorship (MMA, *Bulletin*, January, 1906).

Edward Warren was educated in England and upon graduation from Oxford University decided to dedicate his time and fortune to the collecting of Greek art. Acting on his own behalf and also on behalf of the Boston Museum he launched a large-scale purchasing operation. At this time many of the classical collections that had been acquired in Europe during the nineteenth-century were appearing on the market. Warren kept in touch with dealers and collectors, attended all the classical sales and consistently outbid his competitors. His activity in the field on behalf of the Museum of Fine Arts was triggered, according to Nathanial Burt, by the puritanical attitude prevalent in Boston. Because Edward Warren was a homosexual, he felt at odds with Boston society (Burt, 1977: 121). He chose to live in Europe to escape the puritanism which was also the thrust of the philosophy of the Boston Museum of Fine Arts. That philosophy held that art was not for the purpose of pleasure but rather for moral enrichment. In his acquisitions for the museum, Edward Warren set out to challenge that concept of art. "I have always said and believed that it was hate of Boston that made me work for Boston. The collection was my plea against that in Boston which contradicted my pagan love" (quoted in Burt, 1977: 121).

It is an ironic historical note that the Boston Museum's crowning glory, its classical collection, was achieved because of these opposing views. The trustees thought they were nourishing the moral character of the citizenry with these perfect Grecian forms, while Edward Warren supposed he was spurring the society to question its set definition of morality.

In any case, and with whatever motivation, it was the dedication of Robinson and Warren that built the Boston Museum of Fine Art's collection of classical antiquities. Later a series of peculiar circumstances would take these men along with Lythgoe, to the Metropolitan Museum in New York.

In August of 1905 Edward Robinson resigned as director of the Boston Museum of Fine Arts, a resignation which was accepted as of December 9 (*MMA Bulletin*, 1906). Robinson felt strongly that the Boston Museum's plan to move from Copley Square in downtown Boston to a new building in the Fenway was a mistake (Burt, 1977: 123). Robinson's main interest was, of course, classical antiquities, and the move to Fenway would deplete the funds for acquisition. Robinson also believed in the educational value of casts, which had fallen from favor with the board, and in fact, the design of the new building did not allow for the display of casts (Museum of Fine Arts, *Bulletin*, June, 1907: 31). He felt his authority had been undermined and his time at Boston had come to an end. Reviewing museum records, the Trustees seem to have been caught by surprise by the resignation and formed immediately a committee to consider the reasons leading to the resignation. They determined, after extensive interviews and investigations, not only that the authority of the Director was ill defined but that the situation had caused "strained relations among the officers and confusion in the minds of subordinates." They did not succeed in convincing Robinson to withdraw his resignation but set the museum on a course of reform with plans to rewrite the bylaws and recast the museum administration (Museum of Fine Arts, *Bulletin*, February, 1906: 2–3). In the April 1906 *Bulletin*, the Trustees issued a disclaimer regarding the casts: "No proposition to banish casts from the new Museum building is or ever has been approved by the Trustees."

Hearing of his resignation, the Metropolitan trustees rather quickly offered Robinson the newly created position of assistant director under Sir Purdon Clarke. Robinson instituted his professional museum methods at the Metropolitan, reorganizing various departments and assuming the classical curatorship in addition to his administrative duties of building a competent staff (MMA, *Bulletin* January, 1906).

At the same time Edward Warren transferred his allegiance from Boston to New York and began purchasing Greek and Roman art for the Metropolitan. His reasons for leaving the Boston Museum were similar to Robinson's. Warren was interested mainly in the classical collection and knew the move to Fenway would dry up those funds. It was generally believed that the opportunity to purchase classical art would be shortlived and therefore should take precedence over the new building.

It is interesting to note that the allegiance of both Robinson and Warren was not so much to the Boston Museum as it was to classical art. The Boston Museum's righteous philosophy did not inspire loyalty in these men, and so the conflicts caused by Boston's "moral mission" were in part responsible for the rift. Responsible also was the attitude of the board of trustees toward the museum's educational policies in general and the use of casts in particular. Matthew Prichard, Assistant Director, is quoted in Burt as representing the prevailing view: "The aim of a museum of art is to establish and maintain in the community a high standard of aesthetic taste." It's function is "to collect objects important for their quality" (Burt, 1977: 123). Casts were not included in this definition. Prichard also noted, however, that the public was not interested in looking at "Greek vases, Japanese pottery, or any series of small objects." This was part of his recommendation to divide the Museum of Fine Arts into exhibition collections and study collections in order to cut expenses and allow more space for fewer objects (Whitehill, 1970: 183–5).

At this time Edward Warren's brother Samuel was the president of the Boston Museum and was a strong backer of the Fenway move. His position no doubt added to the alienation felt by Edward Warren and Edward Robinson since he had previously been supportive of their endeavors. In the 1904 President's report, Samuel Warren stated bluntly that "The purchases of classical antiquities, begun in the year 1895, have come to an end" (Burt, 1977: 123).

The end at Boston, however, meant a bright beginning in New York. Metropolitan director Sir Purdon Clark confided proudly in a letter "I have been able to transfer to the Metropolitan Museum the men and the methods by which the collection of Greek and Roman antiquities in the Boston Museum of Fine Arts have been so successfully built up since 1895" (quoted in Tomkins, 1989: 123). Robinson and Warren began promptly to build the collection of Greek and Roman art with full support from the board of trustees.

Building the Met's collections

The men who made up the board of trustees of the Metropolitan Museum at this time were men who possessed a love of art, and a vision of the art museum as a force for good in a democratic society. They were not all men of great wealth. Though some were privileged and willing to lend financial support to the dream, others gave of their time and talents. One such man was Louis Palma di Cesnola, the Metropolitan's first director.

Louis Palma di Cesnola (1832–1904) was an Italian military man who also served in the Eleventh New York Calvary Regiment and received from President Lincoln the rank of brigadier general following his valiant efforts in the Civil War. Following the war, Cesnola was assigned the post of United States Consul at Cyprus, where for the next eleven years he would engage his passion for archaeology. During this time he amassed a huge collection of artifacts, his major discovery coming in 1870 at a site near the ancient town of Golgoi, where several monumental stone sculptures and assorted smaller objects were discovered. These findings

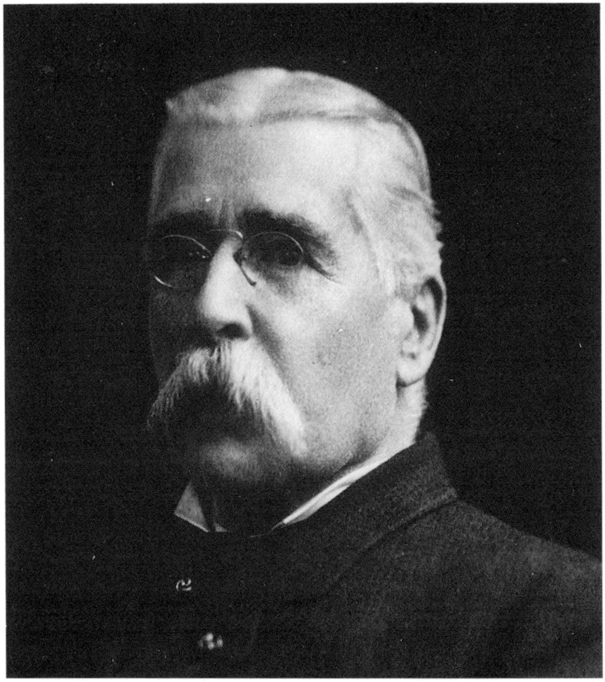

Louis Palma di Cesnola, first Director of the Metropolitan Museum of Art (1879–1904). *The Metropolitan Museum of Art.*

and others, a total of six thousand objects, were sold as a collection to the Metropolitan Museum for the sum of $60,000 in 1872 (MMA, *Bulletin*, 1873).

Four years later, in 1876, the second major Cesnola Collection known as the "Treasure of Curium" was sold to the Metropolitan Museum for $60,000 (MMA, *Annual Report*, 1876).

Cesnola returned to New York with the collection in 1877 and was invited to become a member of the board of the Metropolitan Museum. The Museum had no staff, so members of the Board of Trustees, under Cesnola's direction, began the task of unpacking between 30,000 and 50,000 objects contained in the Cesnola collection. Each object had to be examined and cataloged with a complete description. "The magnitude of the work," wrote John Taylor Johnston, "becomes more manifest as case after case is opened and the importance as well as the number of the objects become visible." To this undertaking the Trustees gave all their spare hours just short of abandoning their own businesses. All this labor was toward the "great purpose of educating their fellow citizens" (MMA, *Annual Report*, 1878). Cesnola was rewarded in 1879 for his energy and dedication with the directorship of the Museum. It was at this time that the new museum building in Central Park was completed and Cesnola began to ready the collections for the move.

Once settled in the new quarters, Cesnola launched a membership drive as a means of gathering popular support for the museum as well as a steady cash flow. By the time the museum marked the tenth anniversary of its first exhibit (1881) the *Annual Report* showed a cash balance with all debts paid and property in excess of $600,000. The museum considered its condition "prosperous" and reminded patrons and members of the mission to build a museum for the "generations to come after us." Over the next ten years the museum memberships reached one thousand annual members at $10.00 a year plus the members in categories of Fellow and Patron for a cash income of $18,300 (MMA, *Annual Report*, 1890). The members' dues helped maintain the institution's dept-free status and the security of its holdings, thus providing the right atmosphere for the donation of art treasures.

These years would set certain very important gift trends, including endowed collections, that would move the Metropolitan Museum to a position of affluence. Three bequests during this period are of special interest, the first being the collection of Catherine Lorillard Wolfe, which was donated to the Metropolitan with an endowment of $200,000. The endowment was to be used for the maintenance and expansion of the collection, a very welcome innovation because, after all, "This Museum is not like the museums of Europe, the property of the people with a national purse for its support. Every gift to it entails expenses in the conservation of that gift" (MMA, *Annual Report*, 1887). This was the first donation of both paintings and funds, thus the first donation to be self-sufficient.

The second bequest was made by Henry Gurdon Marquand, trustee and later president of the Metropolitan Museum board. Marquand set the painting department on track when he donated 37 truly excellent European paintings including Rembrandt's *Portrait of a Man*, and Vermeer's *Young Woman With Water Jug*, the first Vermeer to be held by an American museum (MMA, *Annual Report*, 1890).

By far the strangest and in some ways most important story is of Jacob Rogers, the reportedly obnoxious and surely eccentric manufacturer of locomotives, from Paterson, New Jersey. Rogers never married, had few friends and consistently refused to donate any money to charitable causes. He had little interest in art, and no collection of his own, but was, since 1883, a ten-dollar-a-year member of the Metropolitan Museum. When Jacob Rogers died the summer of 1901, he left to the museum his fortune of more than $5,000,000 "for the purchase of rare and desirable art objects, and for the purchase of books for the Library of said Museum, and for such purposes exclusively" (MMA, *Annual Report*, 1902). The settlement yielded at that time an annual income of about $200,000 (MMA, *Annual Report*, 1905). When one considers that the museum's annual operating budget was about $180,000, the importance of Rogers' bequest in catapulting the museum to a place of power in the art world becomes exceedingly clear. It was the Rogers Fund that Robinson and

Warren used to build the Metropolitan's collection of classical antiquities and that allowed the Museum to support the excavations in Egypt from 1906 through 1936.

The Metropolitan Museum would have many generous benefactors, Jacob Rogers being among the first and J. P. Morgan being among the greatest. When Joseph H. Choate, lawyer and member of the Metropolitan Museum Board, gave his speech at the inauguration of the Metropolitan's building, he rallied the new millionaires with talk of the glory they could share with the museum if they would

> convert pork to porcelain, grain and produce into priceless pottery, the rude ores of commerce into sculptured marble, and railroad shares and mining stocks—things which perish without the using—and which in the next financial panic shall surely shrivel like parched scrolls into the glorified canvases of the world's masters, that shall adorn these walls for centuries.
> (Howe, 1974: 200)

Very important to the "conversion of pork to porcelain and produce to priceless pottery" is the American tax law known as the charitable deduction. The Congress of the United States, beginning with the Federal Revenue Act of 1917, has allowed a tax deduction for all contributions to non-profit organizations. The giving of paintings and other works of art to American museums is therefore made a more profitable deal for the donor than passing works on to descendants or putting works on the auction block.

The 1995 Tax Guide for Individuals published by the Internal Revenue Service states that the taxpayer "can deduct the fair market value of the property at the time of the contribution," irrespective of how much the donor may have paid for the property. Furthermore, the donor is not taxed on any increase in value. For example, a gift to a museum of a painting or drawing bought some time ago for $5,000 but presently worth $20,000, would net the taxpayer a deduction of $20,000. By comparison, should the collector sell the painting or drawing for $20,000, he would be obliged to pay a capital gains tax on the appreciation. State income taxes will also take their toll, thus making the charitable gift still more attractive.

Under these circumstances, it can be more beneficial to the taxpayer to donate works of art than to sell them. In responding to his sense of altruism, the astute collector may be able to benefit not only his soul but his bank account.

The other important fiscal measure was the Payne–Aldrich Tariff of 1909, which allowed for the duty-free importation of works of art more than twenty years old. This was altered in 1913 to include all works of art, even those less than twenty years old. The United States Congress was actively encouraging American collectors in their foreign purchases and as shown above in their donations to American museums. This legislation is clearly and directly related to the growth of art museums in the United

States. The Metropolitan benefited immensely from these acts of Congress, and it is safe to say that the Metropolitan's ascent to a position of world prominence would not have occurred without them.

The Payne–Aldrich Tariff was the solution to the import tax problem of the Metropolitan's president and kind donor John Pierpont Morgan (Canfield, 1974: 158; Saarinen, 1958: 82). J. P. Morgan held a mansion in Hyde Park, London, which he had inherited from his father, and in which he accumulated most of his art collections. The stiff duty on imported art prior to 1909 prohibited the transfer of these works to the American shore and the Metropolitan Museum. Legend has it that Senator Nelson Aldrich dined with J. P. Morgan in the Hyde Park estate, and while being escorted through the collection he was assured that if the tariff law were altered, the paintings would go to the Metropolitan.

With the new Payne–Aldrich law in effect, Morgan began the giant year-long chore of packing for shipment the Hyde Park collections. The cases of art, which numbered 350, were taken upon arrival in the United States to the storerooms of the Metropolitan Museum (Saarinen, 1958: 83–4). However, upon the death of J. P. Morgan the following year, circumstances would reduce the number of objects accessioned by the Metropolitan to less than half. What the trustees and staff of the Metropolitan Museum did not know was that J. P. Morgan spent everything he earned and spent half of it on art. After inheritance taxes and the other obligations of his estate had been satisfied, the remaining works of art were given, as he had requested, "for the instruction and pleasure of the American people" (Canfield, 1974: 161).

J. P. Morgan: the formative influence

John Pierpont Morgan's involvement with the Metropolitan began in earnest in 1901, and he directed great energy and attention to the museum until his death in 1913. Morgan was a founding patron of the Metropolitan in 1871, and joined the board of trustees in 1888, serving for 25 years. He was elected to the Executive Committee and Finance Committee in 1892 but served only two years in that capacity due to other obligations. He joined the Executive Committee again in 1901 and was elected First Vice-President and then President in 1904. (MMA, *Bulletin*, May, 1918).

Morgan became notorious for purchasing art in huge quantities, and was easily considered the greatest collector of his time. He had great confidence in his own eye for quality and saw no reason why he should not possess an entire collection if he so desired (Canfield, 1974: 122). The stories of his acquisitions are legendary as was his generosity to the Metropolitan Museum.

The first major gift from J. P. Morgan to the Metropolitan occurred in 1902 (MMA, *Annual Report*, 1902) and was also his first purchase of an entire art collection. The collection, which belonged to the banker, James

A. Garland, consisted of about two thousand Chinese porcelains which were on loan to the Metropolitan. The curators hoped Garland would leave the collection to the Museum but learned that, upon his death, it had been purchased by an art dealer for half a million dollars. J. P. Morgan went immediately to the art dealer, purchased the two thousand porcelains, changed the name to the Morgan Collection and presented it to the Metropolitan (Tomkins, 1989: 99).

When Edward Steichen photographed Morgan in 1906, he captured the giant financier as most Americans imagined him: large, fierce, arrogant, and intense—with eyes (as Steichen described them) like the headlights of a freight train bearing down on you. Steichen captured the light on the arm of the chair in such a way so as to confuse the image with that of a dagger and confuse, or perhaps confirm, the viewer's response. The public generally was suspicious of Morgan and the means by which he acquired his wealth. His achievements in the world of finance, (such as the formation of United States Steel Corporation, the world's largest business enterprise, or the consolidation of most of America's railroads) were generally held in suspicion outside that world, while his importance and power were clearly communicated.

Morgan was the son of a successful Boston banker who was headquartered in London. For this reason Morgan received much of his

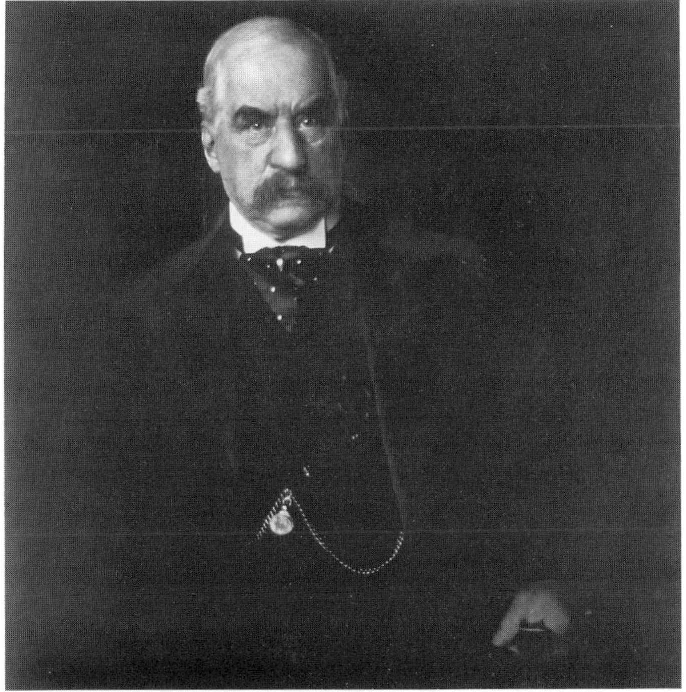

J. P. Morgan by Edward Steichen (1879–1973).
The Metropolitan Museum of Art, The Alfred Stieglitz Collection, 1949 (49.55.167).

education in Europe. Early on he showed an ability for mathematics and an interest in collecting, although he did not begin seriously to acquire art until about 1902 (Canfield, 1974: 15–18). The first collections Morgan compiled were collections of books and manuscripts. He moved on to collect tapestries, armor, bronzes, and carved ivory as well as paintings and, perhaps most importantly, furniture and other decorative arts.

The Metropolitan's Department of Decorative Arts was formed in 1907 when J. P. Morgan presented, as a gift to the museum, the Hoentschel Collection (MMA, *Bulletin*, June, 1907). George Hoentschel was a French architect and designer who had built two major collections of French decorative art. One was a collection of Gothic sculpture, tapestries, and architectural elements such as columns, mantels, and chair stalls. The other was a collection of French eighteenth-century decorative arts which Morgan intended "should be made the nucleus of a great collection of decorative art" (MMA, *Bulletin*, June, 1907).

The organization of the Metropolitan at this point was threefold. There was the Department of Greek and Roman Art, the Department of Egyptian Antiquities and the Department of Paintings. With the formation of a Department of Decorative Arts, there was a place to put everything in the museum that did not fall under the three existing departments. For this reason, the Department of Decorative Arts would give birth to new divisions throughout the coming years. According to Museum Reports, in 1915 the Department of Far Eastern Art was born (MMA, *Bulletin*, July, 1915); Near Eastern Art came into existence in 1932 (MMA, *Bulletin*, January, 1932), 1933 witnessed the birth of three new departments: Renaissance and Modern Art, Medieval Art, of which the Cloisters collection formed an important part, and the American Wing (MMA, *Bulletin*, November, 1933).

J. P. Morgan determined that the Department of Decorative Arts should have its own wing and commissioned the architectural firm of McKim, Mead, and White to submit the design. The wing was completed in 1909 and William R. Valentiner became its first curator (MMA, *Bulletin*, February 1910).

Morgan was responsible, directly and indirectly, for the rapid growth of the Metropolitan Museum, for gifts and legacies were strengthened by his presence. When Morgan assumed the presidency in 1904, the museum's annual operating budget was just over $200,000, of which $150,000 was supplied by the City of New York (MMA, *Annual Report*, 1904). When Morgan died in 1913, the annual budget was $363,000, with the city contributing $200,000. The museum's earned income had more than tripled during the nine years of his presidency (MMA, *Bulletin*, April, 1914). The museum operated with a huge deficit. Morgan's solution was to fill the slots on the board of trustees with millionaires such as Henry Clay Frick and George Baker in order to insure the needed funds. "His usual procedure was to announce the figure at a meeting of the board, and then go around the table, his express-train eyes interrogating each trustee in turn, until the deficit had been erased. Morgan's own check was invariably the largest" (Tomkins, 1989: 100).

It was under Morgan's presidency that the Metropolitan gained the Robinson–Warren team for the building of the Department of Greek and Roman Art. Morgan also made great contributions to the Painting Department and, as we have seen, was fully responsible for the founding of the Department of Decorative Arts. Morgan was also the instigator for the founding of the Egyptian Department.

The year was 1905 and the Egyptians were still allowing foreign archaeologists to excavate under an agreement that 50 percent of the artifacts discovered would go to the Egyptian government. The Metropolitan had been participating in a subscription plan with England's Egyptian Exploration Fund and therefore received some antiquities for its collection every year. J. P. Morgan decided it was time for the Metropolitan to begin its own archaeological expeditions in Egypt so as to supply an Egyptian Department that would "rank permanently as the best in America" (MMA, *Bulletin*, November, 1906).

The Harvard University–Boston Museum of Fine Arts expedition had made the Egyptian collection at the Boston Museum of Fine Arts the best on the North American continent. Knowing this, Morgan visited the site of the Harvard–Boston dig and offered Albert Lythgoe, founder of the Boston Museum of Fine Arts' Egyptian Department, the curatorship of Egyptian Art at the Metropolitan (Tomkins, 1989: 136). The offer must have been a very attractive one because Lythgoe resigned from the Boston Museum and from Harvard, where he taught a course in Egyptology, and became the Metropolitan's first curator of Egyptian Art.

Lythgoe would go on to fulfill J. P. Morgan's dream by building a brilliant staff and establishing the expedition's base at the site of the ancient city of Thebes. Thebes had been the seat of the XI Dynasty which reunited upper and lower Egypt. This period was one of peace and prosperity and saw the production of much beautiful and delicate art. The Metropolitan's collection became rich in works from this period.

J. P. Morgan saw to the building of a large, comfortable base headquarters for the expedition. Known as Metropolitan House, the base overlooked the fertile plain on one side and the desert hills on the other. It was spacious and civilized and welcomed many trustees (Tomkins, 1989: 138). In this way, Morgan guaranteed not only the health and morale of the staff, but also the continued support of the board.

The Painting Department of the Metropolitan also grew under Morgan's presidency. Bryson Burroughs, curator of the Painting Department from 1906 until 1934, had been trained as an artist. Perhaps it was his artist's eye that allowed the acceptance of art forms of an advanced nature, many of which had been rejected by his contemporaries. Burroughs ignored fads and fashion and purchased well for the Metropolitan. Burroughs was responsible for the acquisition of the first Cézanne painting to enter a public American collection (MMA, *Bulletin*,

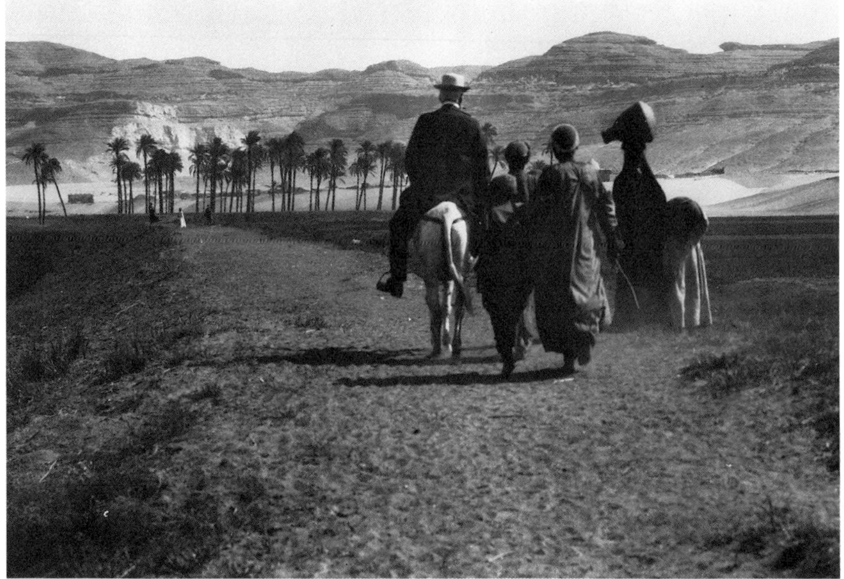

J. P. Morgan in Egypt: The Prince of Wall Street in the Saddle. The Metropolitan Museum of Art, Photograph by the Egyptian Expedition.

May, 1913) as well as several paintings by the French Impressionists (MMA, *Bulletin*, April, 1910; July, 1910).

Two collections would be acquired by the Painting Department that would move its status to the ranks of the world's greatest museums: The Altman Collection in 1913 and the Havemeyer Collection in 1929 (MMA, *Bulletin*, November, 1913; February, 1929).

Benjamin Altman, the New York department store owner, was the son of Jewish immigrants from Germany. Altman never married and devoted his energy and intelligence to building his business and his art collection. He studied the art he collected, reading books and traveling, and developed a keen aesthetic sense. Altman's painting collection included Botticelli, Titian, Holbein, Vermeer, Dürer and Velasquez among others. All were of the highest quality (MMA, *Bulletin*, November, 1913).

Altman was planning to establish the "Altman Museum of Art" as a way to keep his collections together and available to the public. It was through the complex negotiations initiated by President J. P. Morgan that the Metropolitan reached an agreement with Altman. The bequest, which totaled nearly one thousand objects and included a collection of Chinese porcelains and snuff bottles, also included thirteen paintings attributed to Rembrandt. It was said to put the Metropolitan Museum in the forefront of the world's treasure houses (MMA, *Bulletin*, November, 1913).

If any major gaps remained in the museum's collection of paintings, they would certainly be filled by the second, truly significant bequest, the Havemeyer Collection. Henry Osborne Havemeyer made his fortune with the American Sugar Refining Company. He was said to be a difficult personality, overbearing and aggressive, a born competitor, which, no doubt, contributed to the development of his collection (Saarinen, 1958: 147). He pursued his paintings like prey and, stimulated by competition, was willing to pay any price to acquire them.

Havemeyer had an intelligent and knowledgeable wife, Louisine, who contributed many valuable paintings to the Metropolitan, anonymously. Among her gifts was the ceiling, painted by Giovanni Battista Tiepolo, for the Palazzo Barbaro, Venice, given anonymously in 1923. Louisine Havemeyer's dear childhood friend and later art consultant was the painter Mary Cassatt (Saarinen, 1958: 144). Under the guidance of Cassatt, the Havemeyers purchased the works of Courbet, Manet, Degas and Cézanne. Advised again by Mary Cassatt, they bought Spanish paintings including works by El Greco and Goya.

After H. O. Havemeyer's death in 1907, Louisine Havemeyer continued to add to the collection. When she died in 1929, she left 197 items to the Metropolitan and instructions for her children to add to this gift as they pleased (MMA, *Bulletin*, March, 1930). The children consulted with the Metropolitan's curators to insure that the works given were wanted and would be on permanent display. The children then added an additional 1,972 works of art to the Havemeyer bequest.

Under the presidency of J. P. Morgan, therefore, the Metropolitan Museum moved forward, leaving the Boston Museum of Fine Arts to its provincialism, and emerged as first among American museums and on a par with the great museums of the world. As recorded in the Metropolitan's *Bulletin* of May, 1918, the museum's course was set by "his sure knowledge of the field, the largeness of his instinctive methods, his dauntless courage, his vision, and his faith ..."

When J. P. Morgan died on March 31, 1913, he left a legacy not only to the Metropolitan but to the entire museum world. His influence would be a dynamic force for years to come and would be most strongly felt in two areas: the profile of the board of trustees and the attitude toward the acquisition of master works.

Conclusion

As we have seen, both the Metropolitan Museum and the Museum of Fine Arts in Boston had early boards composed of a mix of old families, the landed gentry, and professional men. These were not necessarily people of great wealth but were men with a strong interest in art who were willing to contribute their time and talents to the museum. The Metropolitan was blessed early on with an abundance of artists and men of culture such as William Cullen Bryant. The Boston Museum had the intellectual backing of Harvard and M.I.T. When J. P. Morgan assumed the presidency of the Metropolitan he began to fill the slots on the board with millionaires and those seats have continued to be filled with wealthy patrons. The

Morgans, the Rockefellers, the Whitneys, and the Sulzbergers have held positions on the Met's board, often from one generation to another.

Wealthy board members generally dominate today in the major American art museums, having replaced the nineteenth-century model which included artists and intellectuals whose careers did not generate large incomes. There are no artists or art historians or professional art scholars on the board of the Metropolitan Museum today. "Increasingly" comments William Rubin, director emeritus of the painting and sculpture department at the Museum of Modern Art, "people are being put on museum boards because of their financial clout" (Rubin, 1984: 129).

One reason why the American art museum has continued to move toward the wealthy board membership is the always growing need for financial support from the private sector. A comparative look at the income sources of arts institutions in Europe, for example, reveals that while museums in Italy and France are totally supported by the government, and while museums in Great Britain obtain 90 percent of their income from the government, museums in the United States are likely to rely on government support for only 15 percent of their budgets and on earned and private income for 85 percent. Wealthy board members can assist with that 85 percent.

A 1994 survey conducted by The National Center for Nonprofit Boards revealed that board members of arts and culture organizations were "most likely" to have made a personal financial contribution to their organization (80 percent) and further, that the organization was most likely to require a contribution (59 percent). The survey also reported that 73 percent of the boards of arts and cultural organizations with annual revenue at $10 million or more were male and that 75 percent of the board members were selected by current board members (Slesinger and Moyers, 1995: 9–12), a condition actually recommended by the American Association of Museums.

The museum is no longer a quaint and quiet repository. It is a complex business operation with a board likely to be composed of businessmen who are accustomed to large administrations and who are likely to establish organizational tables like those of corporations. So we have the situation being perpetuated by the board members in power, and necessitated by the museum's financial needs, and perhaps further guaranteed by the development of a bureaucratic structure.

In general, American art museums tend to follow the Morgan board member profile. The American Association of Museums' publication *Museum Trusteeship* by Alan D. Ullberg recommends that the primary criteria for trusteeship be "an individual's sense of social responsibility and his desire and ability to render service to the museum" (Ullberg, 1981: 36). The trustee's "ability" these days may be directly related to his bank account. When, in February, 1996, the Museum of Modern Art announced the purchase of a hotel and two "brownstones" adjacent to the Museum on 53rd Street, in a $50 million transaction, Glenn D. Lowry, the Modern's director, said the money came from a small group of trustees who wished to remain anonymous (Vogel, 1996: 1).

While there have been recorded in recent years, board appointments that, "yielding to both public criticism and the need for government aid, have elected to membership a handful of blacks, 'ethnics', and community leaders" (Meyer, 1979: 225), this attempt at democratization rarely carries any impact in the major art museums.

The second legacy of J. P. Morgan concerns the acquisition of masterpieces for the museum. Calvin Tomkins, in his book *Merchants and Masterpieces*, contends that when J. P. Morgan assumed the presidency of the Metropolitan, the concept of the museum underwent a fundamental change.

> No longer would the Metropolitan defer to European institutions, or limit itself to the utilitarian and educational ... casts, reproductions, and second rate works of art might still retain some usefulness for artisans and students, but the emphasis had shifted unmistakably to the great and original masterpieces, the treasures that old Europe proved only too willing, after all, to relinquish. (Tomkins, 1989: 99)

With J. P. Morgan the purchase of art took on an excitement that is still conveyed. When the fierce and influential Morgan turned his energy to art, the concept of collecting changed from something persnickety to something powerful, and the collector from someone dainty and refined to someone influential and fascinating.

The American art museum has become a superlative collecting machine. There is not at this moment any historical parallel for what has been achieved. One person who has understood and articulated this passion for acquisition is former Metropolitan Museum director, Thomas Hoving (see also "Thomas Hoving and the corporate–museum partnership", Chapter 7).

Hoving, who served as director of the Metropolitan Museum from 1967 until 1977, was known for his ability to capture not only masterpieces, but also the public's imagination. "The chase and the capture of a great work of art is one of the most exciting endeavors in life," he wrote, "as dramatic, emotional, and fulfilling as a love affair" (Hoving, 1975: 1). Hoving also demonstrated an aggressiveness that may very well be part of the Morgan legacy in that it seems to express the ambitious temperament of the Morgan-type trustee and the kind of director he might seek to head the museum.

Relating the events leading to the Metropolitan's acquisition in 1970 of the Velazquez painting *Juan de Pareja*, Hoving describes the special session of the Acquisitions Committee where approval of funds was to take place. Coming up at auction, it was estimated that the painting would fetch $5.2 million, a sum Hoving found "beyond comprehension." "It took us a day to get used to the idea. Where, in God's name, would all that money come from? Even borrowing from both restricted purchase funds would be insufficient." According to Hoving, part of the solution would be found in the Acquisitions Committee: Charles Wrightsman pledged $200,000 of his own funds; Arthur Houghton pledged $100,000; Andre Meyer pledged $100,000; Joan Payson pledged $200,000; Brooke Astor —"I am a poor little girl, so forgive me if I pledge only fifty thousand dollars," and Douglas Dillon pledged $100,000 for a total of $750,000 in gifts collected at that meeting in just a matter of minutes (Hoving, 1993: 264–6).

This business of elite boards and the acquisition of masterworks may be quite undemocratic. The Morgans who served on boards and set this course for America's art museums did not necessarily give consideration to the role of democracy in the art museum; rather, they made autocratic decisions which resulted in procedures still followed today. These procedures became in time traditions which were adopted throughout the country, throughout the century, simply, because they worked. One person might call this American pragmatism; another might attribute it to capitalist know-how. The motivations and continuations of these "traditions" will be explored in Chapter 7 when we examine more closely the impact of capitalism on the American art museum.

The original mission of the Metropolitan and the Boston Museum of fostering pride and prestige in American society, of moral betterment and education for all, that mission, as defined in 1870, continues to be pursued in diversified ways as is fitting to the ever-changing American democratic culture. It is a pursuit full of contradictions, for although America's first museums were based on the Louvre, they were founded and administered by private citizens with private dollars. American artists debated the European aristocratic ideals of connoisseurship even while American patrons poured millions of dollars into acquisitions. Those same patrons hired the great architects of the day to fashion palaces to house those treasures. And while curators celebrated the rare, the enigmatic, the profound object, educators dreamed of making the American art museum truly accessible to the general public. America's first museums set the paradoxical stage for all to follow.

4

The role of the federal government: The National Gallery, Washington, D.C., and The National Endowment for the Arts

Introduction

In examining the impact of democracy on America's art museums, that is, looking at the conflicts which naturally arise when an elitist activity is set down in the people's park, one area that can be revealing is that of federally funded art museums. One can be sure that where there is money awarded, there is influence exercised. If the money belongs to the taxpayers of the United States of America, the influence may very well reflect democratic concerns.

The national museums are gathered under the umbrella of the Smithsonian Institution, which is funded by federal dollars. The federal government, by an act of Congress in 1965, created a federal agency for the dispersal of federal funds to independent art museums and other nonprofit art institutions, that is the National Endowment for the Arts. We will consider these two government institutions, their policies, practices, and influences, beginning with an overview of the Smithsonian, and focusing on the National Gallery as the major art museum within that structure. The National Gallery's record of acquisitions and exhibitions will be analyzed. The record of the National Endowment, established to "foster the arts and to broaden their availability," and the influence of the Congress on the Endowment will then be examined.

The Smithsonian umbrella

The Smithsonian Institution administers thirteen museums and galleries, the National Zoological Park, and a number of research facilities around the United Sates and in Panama. Ten of the thirteen museums are concerned with art. The Cooper-Hewitt Museum in New York exhibits architecture, design, and the decorative arts. The other nine institutions are located in Washington, D.C.: the Arthur M. Sackler Gallery and the Freer Gallery specialize in Asian and Near-Eastern art; the Anacostia Museum and the National Museum of African Art specialize in black culture and African art; the American museums include the National Portrait Gallery, the National Museum of American Art and the Renwick Gallery (American crafts); the Hirshhorn Museum and Sculpture Garden exhibits nineteenth- and twentieth-century sculpture and painting; and finally, the National Gallery of Art, a collection of American and European paintings, sculpture, and the graphic arts, which will be the focus of this study.

The Smithsonian Institution is the world's largest museum complex and is primarily funded by the federal government. The Smithsonian was founded by an act of Congress in 1846 with a bill officially designating a National Cabinet of Curiosities and the Smithsonian Museum, a marriage which would result in the National Museum of the United States. This situation resulted following years of debate over the proper use of the generous gift designated to be used for "the increase and diffusion of knowledge," a vague directive to be sure (Goode, 1901: 93).

In 1835, it became known that the Englishman James Smithson, who had died six years earlier in Genoa, had bequeathed his whole estate to the United States of America "to found at Washington, under the name of the Smithsonian Institution, an establishment for the increase and diffusion of knowledge among men."

This information was given to the Congress of the United States by the then President Van Buren in December and the gift was accepted through an act of Congress in July, 1836. In 1842, following numerous proposals and long debates, Congress approved an act to incorporate the National Institution to "promote science and the useful arts" and to entrust the entire management of the Smithsonian fund to the National Institution (Senate Bill, No. 245, Twenty-sixth Congress, 1839–41, Section No.4). The two institutions would occupy buildings erected at the cost of the Smithson bequest, and all collections of art and natural history owned by the United States would be deposited in these buildings. In this act is the germ of the National Museum idea including a proposition for an appropriation from the National Treasury to pay for those things not covered by the Smithson fund (Goode, 1901: 98).

Then, by 1846, it was resolved by the Smithsonian Regents that

> it is the intention of the act of Congress and in accordance with the design of Mr. Smithson, as expressed in his will, that one of the principal modes of executing the act and the trust is the accumulation of collections of specimens and objects of natural history and of elegant art, and the gradual formation of a library of valuable works pertaining to all departments of human knowledge, to the end that a copious storehouse of materials of science, literature, and art, may be provided, which shall excite and diffuse

> the love of learning among men, and shall assist the original investigations and efforts of those who may devote themselves to the pursuit of any branch of knowledge. (Quoted in Goode, 1901: 144)

This "copious storehouse" which, by the terms of this charter, the Smithsonian Regents were requested to erect and pay for, was then filled with the national collections, and the care of those collections was transferred to the Smithsonian Institution.

None of this was reached by way of a smooth road, and the power of the Smithsonian Regents would continue to be questioned and tested by Congress for years to come. This is important to mention since the role of Congress in such matters can change the role of the art museum in the American culture and the relationship established between the Congress and the Smithsonian impacts on the government's role with all museums. (The relationship between the Congress and the Smithsonian Regents in the 1840s and 1850s might be compared to the dilemma of the National Endowment for the Arts in the late 1980s and 1990s which will be addressed later.)

Congressional members did continue to interfere with the authority of the Board of Regents, suggesting how the act of Congress should be interpreted. This included lobbying for the bulk of the income to be devoted to a library; endeavoring to overthrow what had been established and substitute a Washington University; and returning the entire Smithson legacy to England to be given to anyone who could legally take it (Goode, 1901: 145–47).

The Regents boldly asserted through Senator Jefferson Davis that it was "improper for Congress to interfere with the administration of a fund which it has confided to a Board of Regents not entirely formed of members of Congress and not responsible to it" (Davis, quoted in Goode, p. 146). The conflict culminated in 1856 with a Congressional investigation. The Smithsonian Board of Regents was successful in maintaining the position that they were not amenable to the advice or instructions of Congress and were the only authorities qualified to interpret the act of incorporation and the intentions of James Smithson (p. 147).

The various art museums and galleries referred to earlier are considered units or bureaus of the Smithsonian Institution, and most were adopted during this century as generous gifts from American financiers and industrialists. The Cooper-Hewitt Museum, for example, was administered by the Cooper Union until 1968 and is housed in the Carnegie Mansion in New York City. The Freer Gallery was a gift of Charles Long Freer (1856–1919), and the Hirshhorn Museum was donated by the American financier John H. Hirshhorn (1899–1981). For the purpose of understanding the place of a government-funded art museum among all the art museums in America, the focus here will be on the National Gallery of Art, the gift made to the American people in the middle of the twentieth century by Andrew W. Mellon.

The National Gallery

Andrew W. Mellon (1855–1937) was a financier, an industrialist, a statesman, and a collector of fine art. He began his career in his father's banking firm in Pittsburgh, Pennsylvania, and later became president of the Mellon National Bank. He was involved in several industries, including coal, iron, steel, and oil, and was director of many industrial and financial corporations.

Mellon arrived in Washington, D.C. in 1921 as Secretary of the Treasury in President Warren Harding's Cabinet. He stayed to serve in this position for President Calvin Coolidge and President Herbert Hoover. It was during this period that the art collection Mellon had begun in Pittsburgh, under the guidance of a young Henry Clay Frick, would grow to become the nucleus of a national collection (Walker, 1984: 23).

With the assistance of the art dealer C. R. Henschel of M. Knoedler and Company, Mellon acquired Botticelli's *Adoration of the Magi*, Jan Van Eyck's *Annunciation*, Perugino's *Crucifixion*, Raphael's *Alba Madonna* and his *St. George and the Dragon*, Titian's *Venus with a Mirror*, Velazquez' study for his portrait of Pope Innocent X, and several paintings by Rembrandt, Van Dyck, and Frans Hals (Finley, 1973; Kopper, 1991). He purchased the famed Dreyfus Collection of Renaissance sculpture in 1936, which included works by Donatello and Verrocchio, and a number of Renaissance paintings, including works by Antonello da Messina, Lippo Memmi, Pisanello, and others (Finley, 1973; Kopper, 1991).

It was clear that Andrew Mellon was building a collection of master works and that his vision of a national art museum was influenced by the great museums of Europe: the Louvre Museum and the National Gallery in London. One problem, as Mellon saw it, was that America's National Gallery of Art at this point consisted of a collection that could not measure up to his standards. Mellon did not want his collection associated with the inferior works in the National Gallery. What he wanted from that institution was its name. The Regents of the Smithsonian Institution therefore agreed that the existing National Gallery of Art would henceforth be known as "The National Collection of Fine Arts" and the Andrew Mellon Collection would be called the "National Gallery of Art."

On December 22, 1936, Andrew Mellon made his offer to the President of the United States, Franklin D. Roosevelt.

> Over a period of many years I have been acquiring important and rare paintings and sculpture with the idea that ultimately they would become the property of the people of the United States and be made available to them in a national art gallery to be maintained in the city of Washington for the purpose of encouraging and developing a study of the fine arts.

Mellon goes on to explain that a Board of Trustees has been formed to carry out this purpose and that this Board has full power and authority to deed these works to a national gallery. In addition, these trustees have been given "securities ample to erect a gallery building of sufficient size to house these works of art and to permit the indefinite growth of the collection under a conservative policy regulating acquisitions."

Other regulations, restrictions, and conditions were also put in place. The letter discusses the architect Mellon employed (John Russell Pope of New York), the location of the gallery (the desired site had been promised as a George Washington memorial and excavations had begun, but funds were insufficient and Mellon was able to convince the Washington Memorial Association to evacuate the site), and the additional gift of an endowment fund, the income from which was designated to pay certain salaries (director and curators) and to provide funds for future acquisitions.

It is stated that future acquisitions be limited to "objects of the highest standard of quality, so that the collections to be housed in the proposed building shall not be marred by the introduction of art that is not the best of its type."

Mellon goes on to propose that the administration of the gallery be managed by a separate board of trustees and that they be empowered to make bylaws and regulations governing its operations. This request, along with the others, was granted, so that, although the National Gallery is in fact an integral part of the Smithsonian Institution, it is administered by a separate board of trustees patterned after a private corporation.

"If this plan meets with your approval," the letter continues, "I will submit a formal offer of gift stating specifically the terms thereof, and the erection of the building may proceed immediately upon the acceptance of such offer and the passage of necessary legislation by Congress."

A bill was therefore prepared and introduced to Congress as "House Joint Resolution No. 217." It stated that

> the faith of the United States is pledged that, on the completion of the National Gallery of Art by the donor in accordance with the terms of this Act and the acquisition from the donor of the Collection of works of art, the United States will provide such funds as may be necessary for the upkeep of the National Gallery of Art and the administrative expenses and costs of operation thereof.

The bill was passed by both houses with all the provisions Andrew Mellon desired, and signed into law by President Roosevelt on March 24, 1937. The National Gallery formally opened on the evening of March 17, 1941. By this time, two other important collections had been assimilated and a third collection was under negotiation.

The first collection was that of Samuel H. Kress of New York. Kress had created a huge mercantile business and with the fortune gained thus was able to build a collection of paintings and sculpture of the Italian school from the thirteenth to the eighteenth centuries. Some of the early examples included the *Madonna and Child* by Giotto and *The Calling of*

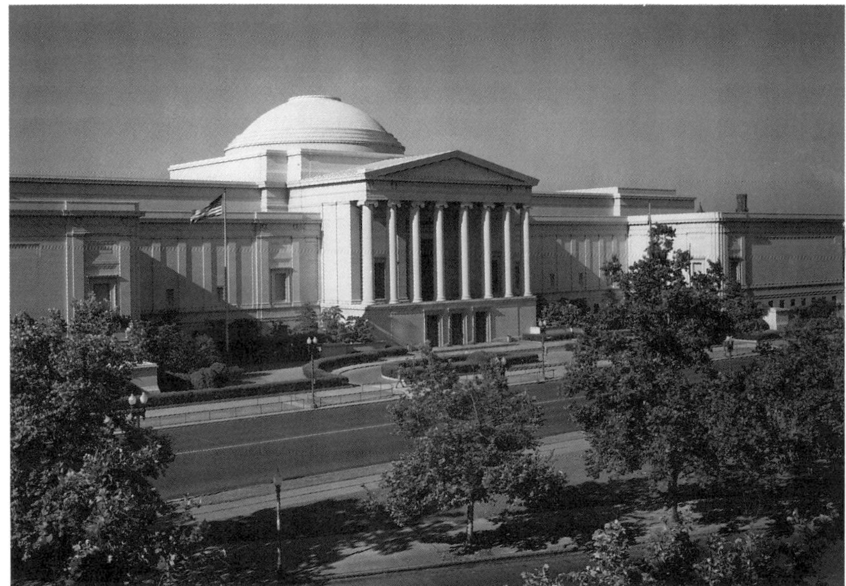

West Building of the National Gallery of Art, Washington, opened 1941. View from 6th Street and Constitution Avenue. John Russell Pope, Architect.
National Gallery of Art.

Peter and Andrew by Duccio. There were also paintings by Fra Angelico, Filippo and Filippino Lippi, Piero di Cosimo, and Perugino. Well-known paintings by Raphael, Titian, Tintoretto, Tiepolo, and Giovanni Bellini were also part of the Kress Collection. (Information on all collections is available in the National Gallery's catalogue of the collection.)

Later, Samuel Kress would broaden the scope of the collection given to the National Gallery to include French, German, Flemish, and Spanish art. He purchased the French works first: a distinguished group of paintings by Fragonard, Poussin, Chardin, Boucher, and others. Following this he bought others in the French School, the most famous being *Napoleon in His Study* by Jacques Louis David.

The German collection was developed next and included paintings by Holbein and Dürer and the famous *Small Crucifixion* by Grünewald. The Flemish paintings included works by Peter Paul Rubens, Van Dyck, and Hieronymus Bosch's *Death and the Miser*. Finally, there was the collection of Spanish paintings, paintings by Goya and Zurbaran and several canvases by El Greco, among them the *Laocoon*. Kress donated sculpture as well: groups of Italian Gothic and Renaissance, a group of 1,300 Renaissance bronzes, Hellenistic marbles, and important French works.

When the National Gallery opened in 1941 it contained an exhibition of American paintings donated by Chester Dale. Chester Dale was also interested in French Impressionist and Post-Impressionist paintings and assembled one of the most important collections of that genre, which he then donated to the National Gallery. The Chester Dale collection illustrates the development of French painting from David to Cézanne and includes works by Monet, Renoir, and Cassatt. With these paintings comes the introduction of modernist ideas to the National Gallery and the first twentieth-century paintings by modernists such as Picasso and Matisse. It is important to note that these paintings were recognized as master works and incorporated into the permanent collection at the very beginning.

Modern art was also part of the Widener Collection, which the National Gallery was awarded in August of 1942. The remarkable *Dead Toreador* by Manet hangs with paintings by Corot, Degas, Renoir, and other artists who signaled this major shift.

The collection also contains fourteen Rembrandts, two Vermeers, and works by Raphael, Bellini, El Greco, Titian, and the great English artists, Reynolds, Gainsborough, Turner, and Constable. But what is noteworthy is the fact that the National Gallery, dedicated to "collecting, preserving, and exhibiting the finest works of art obtainable," included modern art as part of its foundation. What will be considered now is the second part of the National Gallery's mission: "to make those works of art known and enjoyed by the people of this country and, indeed, by people everywhere to whom, in the larger sense, these and all works of art belong." (Finley, 1973: 180). How is the National Gallery fulfilling its promise? A comparison of acquisition records and exhibition records over a ten-year period, beginning in 1984 and moving through 1993, will offer some insight. This was a major growth period for the National Gallery and included both the tenth anniversary of the East Building and the 50th anniversary of the Gallery, events that stimulated gift-giving.

Acquisitions, exhibitions and public demands

The National Gallery is an institution rich in the objects of Western culture, and its collections include paintings, sculpture, drawings and prints, photographs, and decorative arts. In any given year the total number of acquisitions, according to the annual reports, might range from 500 to 1,500 objects. The 50th anniversary year, 1991, saw the collection increased by 2,444 acquisitions. At the heart of the National Gallery, however, is the painting collection; and so, to facilitate our purposes, we will consider only the painting acquisitions and, later, painting exhibitions.

In 1984, the National Gallery acquired a total of sixteen paintings, ten of which were by twentieth-century artists, including the American abstract expressionists, Jackson Pollock and Lee Krasner. (All statistics are compiled from the National Gallery Annual Reports; see Figure 4.1.)

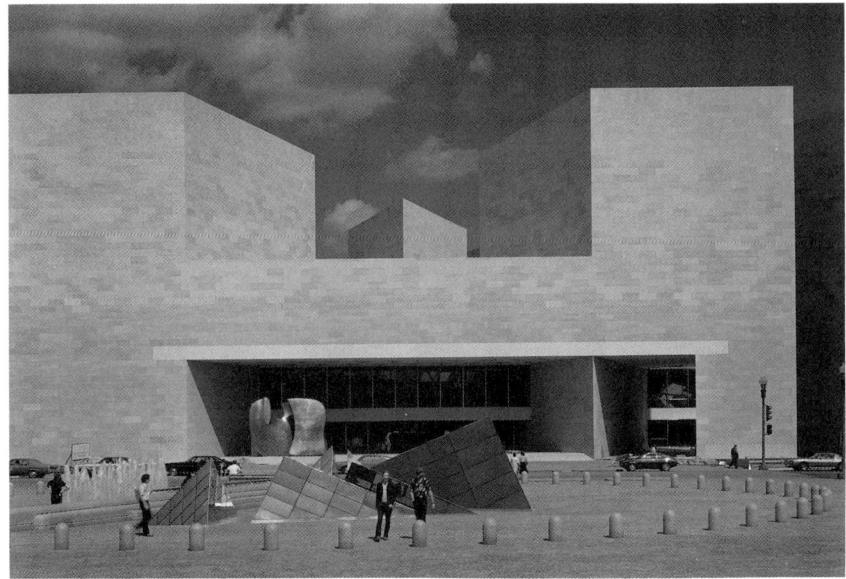

East Building of the National Gallery of Art, Washington, opened 1978. View from 4th Street Plaza. I. M. Pei, architect.
National Gallery of Art.

In 1985, the total number of painting acquisitions was fifteen, ten of which were twentieth-century and six of those being works by another member of the New York School, Mark Rothko. In 1986, the National Gallery scored a major win as it was awarded 174 by the Mark Rothko Foundation. The gift would eventually total 285 paintings and works on paper and more than 500 additional reference and study works, as the Mark Rothko Foundation designated the National Gallery the chief repository of its collection. That same year other painting acquisitions totaled 52, eighteen of which were twentieth-century, and twenty of which were late-nineteenth-century modern works.

In 1987, 50 of the 55 painting acquisitions were twentieth- century, with the New York School still dominating. That year saw a gain of fifteen paintings by Barnett Newman and fifteen paintings by Mark Rothko. In 1988, eleven paintings were acquired and ten of them were of the twentieth century (Figure 4.1).

In 1989 and 1990, ten out of sixteen and five out of the ten paintings acquired were produced in the twentieth century. The years 1991 and 1992 witnessed a tremendous growth in the permanent collection due in large part to the Gallery's 50th anniversary celebration. The number of new acquisitions of twentieth-century art during this period was very high: 31 of the 49 acquisitions reported in 1991 and 44 of the 57 acquisitions reported in the 1992 *Annual Report* were of the twentieth-century. In addition, over the course of those two years, six modern

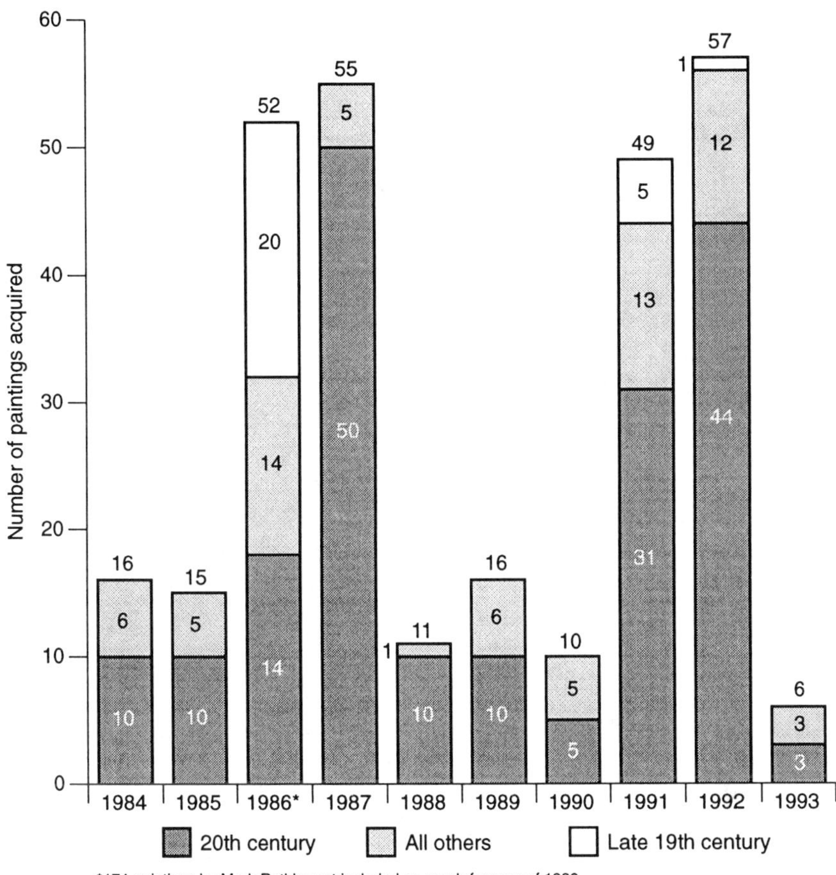

Figure 4.1 *National Gallery of Art, Washington, D.C. Painting Acquisitions, 1984–93.*

paintings of the late nineteenth-century entered the collection. The Gallery mounted an exhibition of some of these acquisitions in 1991. Almost 300 works of art from more than 220 donors were included in "Art for the Nation: Gifts in Honor of the 50th Anniversary of the National Gallery of Art." A second exhibition of anniversary gifts was opened in May, 1992. Some gifts involved private collections. The Dorothy and Herbert Vogel Collection of more than 2,000 contemporary paintings, drawings, and sculptures by more than 200 artists began to be transferred in 1992 to the National Gallery with an initial gift and partial purchase of 214 works by eleven artists. During the 1993 fiscal year, three of the six paintings acquired were twentieth-century works.

Certainly the availability of works of art explains in part the high percentage of twentieth-century acquisitions. There are simply more

Jackson Pollock paintings in the marketplace than there are works by Giotto. The point is, however, that the National Gallery is actively engaged in gathering the art of the twentieth-century, and since abstraction has been the dominant force of that art, it's safe to assume the National Gallery is actively engaged in preserving abstract objects and ideas.

The National Gallery is dedicated to "collecting, preserving, and exhibiting the finest works of art." Works of art from the permanent collection are continuously on view and are supplemented by temporary exhibitions which are curated from the museum's holdings and/or borrowed from other institutions. Let us now examine the exhibition program during this same period and compare it to the acquisition record. In order to maintain a consistency with the record of acquisitions, we will focus on exhibitions of painting and on exhibitions containing paintings along with other media. Exhibitions of prints, drawings, and sculpture only will not be considered here. (All information is compiled from the National Gallery *Annual Reports*; see Figure 4.2.)

In 1984 the National Gallery mounted fifteen special exhibitions, nine of which included paintings. Of the nine exhibitions containing paintings, three focused on the work of twentieth-century artists: "Mark Tobey: City Paintings;" "Modigliani: An Anniversary Exhibition" (the artist was born in 1884, died in 1920), which combined paintings, drawings, and sculpture; and a major retrospective of the cubist painter Juan Gris (1887–1920).

In 1985, 25 exhibitions were launched, eight of which included painting exhibits. According to the report of the department of installation and design, "The Treasure Houses of Britain" was the largest and most complex exhibition ever mounted by the National Gallery. It occupied 35,000 square feet of the East Building, space traditionally given over to twentieth-century art. (Selections from the twentieth-century collection were installed in the concourse.) There were, therefore, no special exhibitions of twentieth-century art during this period.

The 1986 schedule contained twelve exhibitions, eight of painting, one of which, "Seven American Masters," was of twentieth-century art.

In 1987, two of the six painting exhibitions were composed of art of the twentieth-century: Henri Matisse and Andrew Wyeth. "Henri Matisse: the Early Years in Nice 1916–1930" contained 171 paintings; "Andrew Wyeth: The Helga Pictures" presented 140 images in pencil, watercolor, and tempera of the artist's neighbor, Helga Testorf.

The eight painting exhibitions organized in 1988 included a show of paintings, pastels, and drawings by Georgia O'Keeffe and "The Flag Paintings of Childe Hassam."

The 1989 schedule of 21 special exhibitions included ten dedicated to paintings. Selections from the twentieth-century collection were installed in a celebration of the tenth anniversary of the East Building, the only exhibition of the year concerned with the art of the twentieth-century.

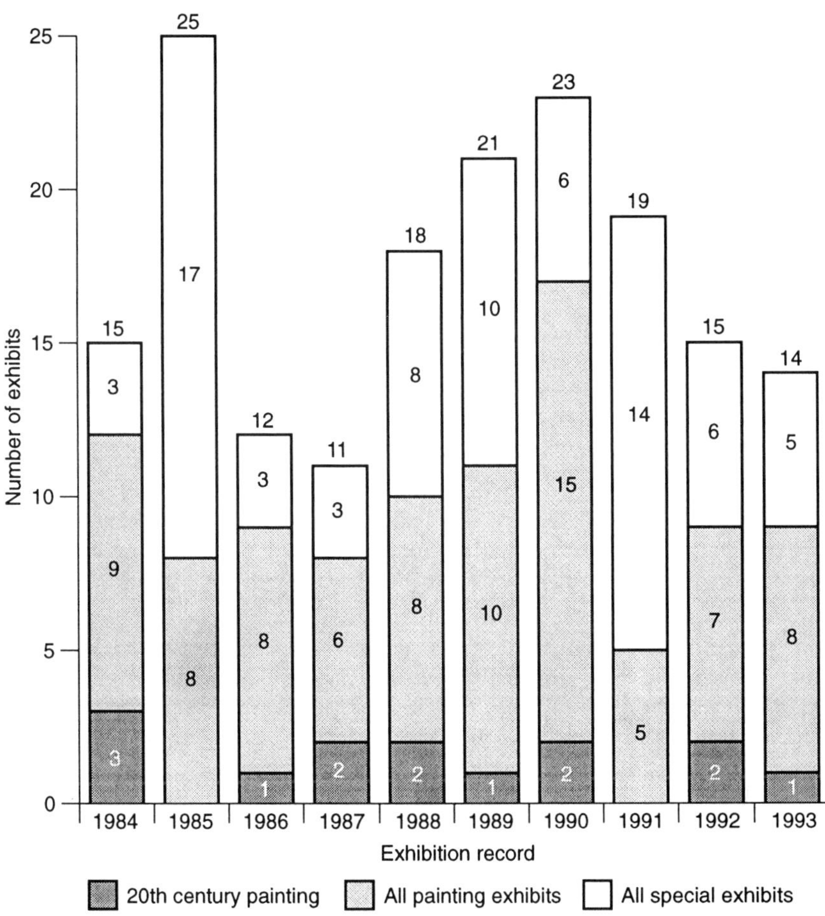

Figure 4.2 *National Gallery of Art, Washington, D.C. Exhibition Record, 1984–93.*

Of the fifteen painting exhibitions held in 1990, two involved twentieth-century artists: "Matisse in Morocco: The Paintings and Drawings, 1912–1913" and "Kazimir Malevich, 1878–1935." But in 1991, none of the five painting exhibits concerned recent art.

The 1992 schedule included a one-month show of work by the contemporary figure painter, Alice Neel, and a show of paintings, drawings, and prints by Ernst Ludwig Kirchner (1880–1938). There was a total of fifteen exhibitions, and the principal undertaking was "Circa 1492: Art in the Age of Exploration," in celebration of the Columbus Quincentennial. This complex exhibition looked at the world cultures of the late fifteenth and early sixteenth centuries through more than 600 objects from 33 countries.

Of the fourteen special exhibitions in 1993, eight included paintings and one focused on a contemporary artist: "Ellsworth Kelly: The Years in France." The blockbuster of the year was a painting show: "Great French Paintings from the Barnes Foundation: Impressionist, Post-Impressionist, and Early Modern," which featured 80 works by Renoir, Cézanne, Monet, Van Gogh, and others (Figure 4.2 and Table 4.1). (The exhibition record was compiled from information in the National Gallery *Annual Reports*.)

In summary, of the 461 painting acquisitions in this ten-year period, 365, or in excess of 79 percent, were twentieth-century works. By contrast, of the 84 special painting exhibitions during that same period, only fourteen, or 16.2 percent, dealt with the twentieth century, and of those fourteen exhibitions, only four could be considered "difficult" in their advanced visual concepts and degree of abstraction (see Table 4.1). Why does the National Gallery dedicate such a relatively small percentage of exhibitions to recent art? Part of the answer may be found in attendance figures.

Table 4.1 *National Gallery of Art, Washington, D.C.: Exhibitions of 20th-Century Painting 1984–1993*

1984	"Juan Gris, 1887–1927" "Modigliani, 1884–1920: Paintings, Drawings, Sculpture" * "Mark Tobey: City Paintings"
1985	
1986	* "Seven American Masters: Newman, Rothko, Held, Johns, Kelly, Lictenstein, Rauschenberg"
1987	"Henri Matisse: The Early Years in Nice, 1916–1930" "Andrew Wyeth: The Helga Pictures"
1988	"Georgia O'Keefe" "The Flag Paintings of Childe Hassam"
1989	"Selections from the 20th Century Collection" (10th Anniversary of the East Building)
1990	"Matisse in Morocco: The Paintings and Drawings, 1912–1913" * "Kazimar Malevich, 1878–1935"
1991	
1992	"Alice Neel" "Ernst Ludwig Kirchner (1880–1938)"
1993	* "Ellsworth Kelly: The Years in France"

* *Only four exhibitions over a ten-year period could be considered "difficult" in their degree of abstraction and advanced visual concepts.*

Two special exhibitions seem to have heightened the Gallery's awareness of attendance figures. Prior to 1986, attendance growth was generally consistent, showing small, healthy increases no doubt tied to increased leisure time and increased travel. In 1986, however, there was a sudden and striking increase in attendance as two of the special exhibitions offered proved to be highly popular. "The Treasure Houses of Britain" and "The New Painting: Impressionism" were responsible for increasing the number of visitors by 3.6 million over the 1985 fiscal year record of 5.1 million for a total of 8.1 million. (Attendance figures are taken from the National Gallery *Annual Reports.*) The Gallery had not calculated the unprecedented numbers and was forced to quickly hire and train more than 40 temporary employees to assist the education department in their responsibility of crowd control (National Gallery *Annual Report*, 1986: 70).

How temporary that new staff was is not clear, since the attendance figures remained quite high through 1987 and 1988. Almost 7 million visitors attended the Gallery in 1987 and slightly more than 7 million in 1988. The 1989 *Annual Report* notes the decline to 6.2 million visits, "a gratifying number during a year marked by a decline generally in Washington tourism" (p. 9). The numbers over the next four years range between 5 million and 5.6 million visits (Figure 4.3).

While the National Gallery is celebrated for its scholarly research,

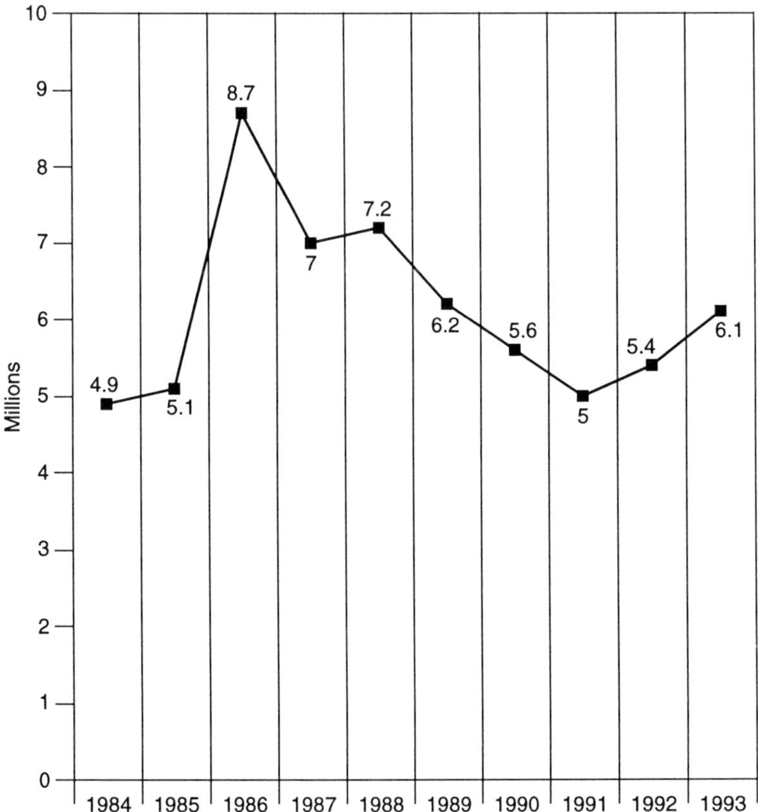

Figure 4.3 *National Gallery of Art, Washington, D.C. Attendance Figures, 1984–93.*

exhibitions, and publications, the concern for and benefits of drawing large numbers of the population cannot go unnoticed. The schedule of popular exhibitions, of exhibitions of realism as opposed to abstraction, greatly outnumber the art generally considered to be less popular, more difficult for the untrained eye to appreciate (Table 4.2). No one can dispute the level of the special exhibitions, which is certainly very high, but one must question the apparent neglect of a huge body of international art production, the prominent thrust of an entire century.

A government-funded museum has an obligation, some would argue, to address the common denominator and satisfy democratic taste. However, having assumed a position of authority from which it defines the standard by which all art can be judged, the National Gallery also assumes a responsibility to provide a basis for informed judgement. This can only happen through exhibitions.

The National Gallery, funded primarily by taxpayers' dollars, is free and open to the public every day of the year, except December 25. Since revenue from admissions is not an incentive as it is in other museums, what are the relevant considerations that should be noted?

The first is the importance of private funds and the role of corporations in Gallery financing. A review of financial records shows that most of the Gallery's operating budget (79–85%) comes from the federal government. The remaining 15–21 percent is supplied by endowments, gifts, and grants. Corporations contribute heavily to special exhibitions underwriting 50–70 per cent of the costs (Figure 4.4; all statistics are compiled from *Annual Reports*). Private companies also provide for opening receptions, brochures, films and other events related to special exhibitions. It is generally accepted, even with museums such as the Museum of Modern Art and the Metropolitan, that corporations fund exhibitions for the purpose of establishing a positive public image and good public relations. (The corporate/museum partnership is explored in Chapter 7.) The continuation of funding therefore depends greatly on the numbers of people reached by the museum. Corporations appreciate high attendance figures and wide dispersement of the brochures they fund.

The second consideration, reflecting attendance records, is income from museum shop sales. According to financial reports (National Gallery *Annual Reports*), in 1986, the year of special exhibits "Treasure Houses of Britain" and "The New Painting: Impressionism", revenues from sales of art books, posters, and prints reached $10.2 million, more than doubling the $4.3 million record set in 1985. Publication sales remained high at $8.8 million in 1987 and then increased by more than 40 percent in 1988 to $12.3 million. The sale of special exhibition catalogs increased 75 percent over the previous year for a total of 200,000 Gallery catalogs.

A new medium for the arts is the video cassette. The sale of these Gallery productions increased 75 percent in the course of one year (National Gallery *Annual Report*, 1988: 121). A survey published by the

Table 4.2 *Ten years of "blockbusters" at the National Gallery*

1984	**The Orientalists: Delacroix to Matisse: the Allure of North Africa and the Near East** "explored the fascination that these lands exerted on the European and American imagination in the later nineteenth century, ending with the continued treatment of this theme in the more abstract work of Matisse and Kandinsky" (National Gallery *Annual Report*, 1984, Director's Review, p. 25).
1985	**The Sculpture of India: 3000 BC–1300 AD** "fulfilled a dual purpose. It was conceived, from the outset, as a survey of masterpieces that would convey the richness and stylistic diversity of India's great old-master sculptural tradition. It was, as well, the first event of the Festival of India. This year-and-a-half-long, nationwide celebration of the many facets of Indian culture was endorsed by President Reagan and the late Prime Minister Indira Gandhi ..." (National Gallery *Annual Report*, 1985, Director's Review, p. 29).
1986	**The Treasure Houses of Britain: 500 Years of Private Patronage and Art Collecting** was "conceived and designed to illustrate the remarkable contribution that the British country house has made to Western culture, over eight hundred works of art were assembled in a series of rooms which made reference to country-house interiors without attempting to reproduce them. This large-scale undertaking was brought about by the cooperation of hundreds of people on both sides of the Atlantic. Ford Motor Company awarded the Gallery the largest exhibition grant it has ever received, and special funding from the 98th Congress, government indemnities from both countries, and help from the British Council also made it possible for the Gallery to mount 'The Treasure Houses of Britain' on the grand scale necessitated by its theme. Unprecedented cooperation on the parts of the more than 226 lenders enhanced the exhibition ... The lenders interest in and support of the project was measured not only in their generous sharing of their possessions but also in their attendance ... By its final day, 13 April, just short of one million visits had been made to it" (National Gallery *Annual Report*, 1986, Director's Review, p. 17).
	The New Painting: Impressionism 1874–1886 "During fiscal 1986 a total of 8,703,055 persons visited the Gallery. The increase of 3,623,197 visitors over fiscal 1985 can be attributed to 'The Treasure Houses of Britain' and 'The New Painting: Impressionism,' both very popular exhibitions" (National Gallery *Annual Report*, 1986, p. 126).
1987	**Henri Matisse: The Early Years in Nice 1916–1930; The Age of Sultan Suleyman the Magnificent**; and **Andrew Wyeth: The Helga Pictures** enjoyed the largest audiences and the best-selling exhibition catalog.
1988	**The Art of Paul Gauguin** "Opened after five years of planning. The most comprehensive Gauguin exhibition ever realized ... was jointly organized by the Gallery, the Art Institute of Chicago, and the Reunion des musées nationaux. One out of every ten paintings came from the Soviet Union ..." (National Gallery *Annual Report*, 1988, Director's Review, p. 20).
1989	**Japan: The Shaping of Daimyo Culture 1185–1868** "focused on the art of the daimyo, the feudal lords who ruled Japan for nearly 700 years. The largest exhibition of its kind ever presented in the West or Japan, the show brought together more than 450 Japanese-owned works of art ... Nearly one-third of the objects in the show were officially designated by the Japanese government as National Treasures, Important Cultural Properties, and Important Art Objects" (National Gallery *Annual Report*, 1989, Director's Review, p. 12). Supported by R. J. Reynolds Tobacco

Company, The Yomiuri Shimbun, Nomura Securities Company Ltd., and the Federal Council on the Arts and the Humanities.

1990 **Masterpieces of Impressionism and Post-Impressionism: The Annenberg Collection** and **The Passionate Eye: Impressionist and Other Master Paintings from the Collection of Emil G. Buhrle** "brought under the Gallery's roof a rich and beautiful concentration of French pictures from the end of the nineteenth and beginning of the twentieth centuries. The two collections allowed the Gallery to augment its own extensive holdings in this field with fifteen additional works by Cézanne, eleven by Van Gogh, ten by Monet, and nine each by Manet, Degas, Renoir, and Gauguin" (National Gallery *Annual Report*, 1990, Director's Report, p. 12).

1991 **Art for the Nation: Gifts in Honor of the 50th Anniversary of the National Gallery of Art** "exhibited a selection of nearly three hundred of the works of art given or pledged to the Gallery by over 220 donors from twenty-two states, the District of Columbia. and five foreign countries. It was generously supported by a grant from GTE" (National Gallery *Annual Report*, 1991, Director's Report, p. 9).

1992 **Circa 1492: Art in the Age of Exploration** "took visitors on a world wide voyage of discovery, 'horizontally', as it were, around the principle world cultures of the late 15th and early 16th centuries, a time that changed forever the world's perceptions of itself. The theme was globalism, and the exhibition was, in fact, made possible by a global consortium of sponsors, in addition to a special appropriation from the U.S. Congress." (National Gallery *Annual Report*, 1992, Review of the year, p. 14). Organized by a team of 30 scholars, the exhibit included more than 600 objects from 33 countries.

1993 **Great French Paintings from The Barnes Foundation: Impressionist, Post Impressionist, and Early Modern** began its world tour at the National Gallery. "Featuring 80 works from the pioneering collection of the late Alfred C. Barnes, which now belongs to the educational institution he established in Merion, Pennsylvania, in 1925, the show included such icons of modern art as Cézanne's *Card Players*, Seurat's *Models*, and Matisse's *Joy of Life* (National Gallery *Annual Report*, 1993, p. 14.

American Council for the Arts, conducted by the National Research Center for the Arts, and sponsored by Philip Morris Companies, reports video cassettes as the most promising medium of growth for the arts, a potential annual market of billions of dollars.

Examining the National Gallery figures for these three areas (corporate contributions for special exhibits, annual attendance figures, and income from museum shop sales) shows a close correlation between the three (see Figure 4.4).

In 1984, annual attendance exceeded 4 million visitors, and the budget for special exhibits was about $3 million. When, in 1986, the budget for special exhibitions moved to $8 million, attendance figures broke all records at 8.7 million visitors. Museum shop sales rose proportionately from $3.6 million in 1984 to $10.2 million in 1986. Even as attendance figures stabilized between 5 and 6 million into the 1990s, the profits from publications sales remained high, ranging from $9 million to $11.7 million.

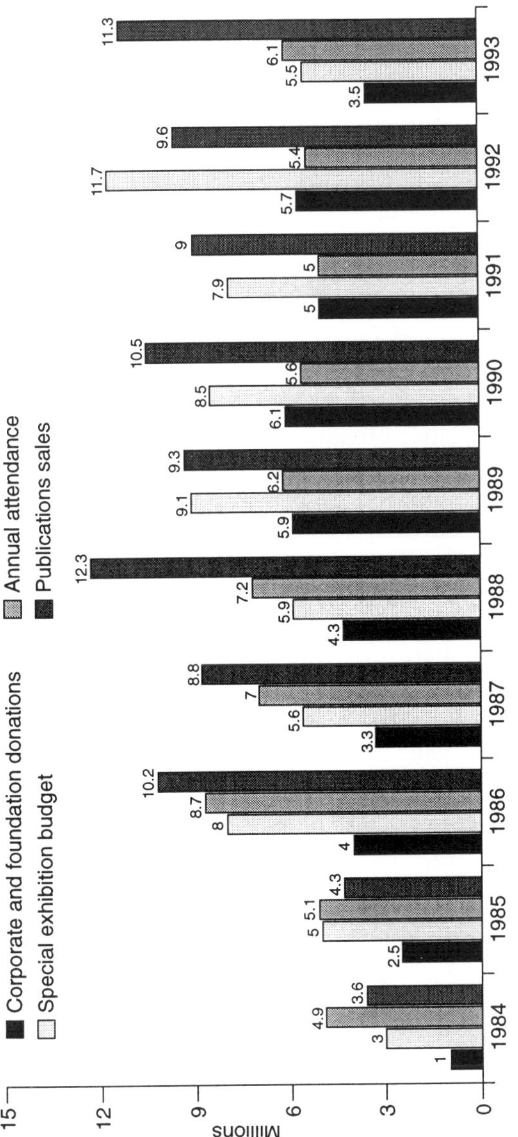

Figure 4.4 *National Gallery of Art, Washington, D.C. Attendance and Sales Figures Relative to Special Exhibitions Budget.*

Museum shop sales shot up to an unprecedented $12.3 million in 1988 due, in part, to a reorganization of the museum store. "During the year the publications service made changes in the West Building sales shop. Two seating areas and one area of under-used selling space were converted to efficient self-service selling areas, with video cassettes, note cards, posters, and calendars" (National Gallery *Annual Report*, 1988: 121).

The museum shop in fact sold more than 2.3 million postcards, prints, note cards, greeting cards, and posters that year. The sale of items such as calendars and address books exceeded 220,000 units. The National Gallery then made plans to expand its mail order market. The museum adopted the corporation's marketing techniques, and the result was a great sales success. Museum attendance, stimulated by popular special exhibits, boosts museum shop business and also generates income from corporations wishing a broad audience for programs they sponsor.

In 1989, the publications service experienced its fourth highest year in sales with the special exhibition catalog of "Japan: The Shaping of Daimyo Culture" as the bestseller. A total of 100,000 catalogs were sold. As reported in the National Gallery *Annual Report* (p. 73), temporary sales areas were opened to offer, as the Report indicates, "convenience, service, and a selection of focused materials. . ." (p. 57). These areas are set up at the exits of special exhibitions in order to promote the exhibition catalog. It is also noted that while 600,000 visitors were served in person, another 7,000 were served through the mail. In 1990, these numbers would grow to over 700,000 visitors and 7,500 mail orders. In 1991, the bestselling catalogs were "Titian" and "Van Dyck," and the grand total of books and catalogs sold was over 200,000. These numbers remained constant in 1992 as "Circa 1492" proved to be a very popular exhibition catalog. Although the number of visitors served in person by the bookstores dropped to 500,000, the total number of books sold remained at 200,000. This may have been due in part to the expansion of children's books which, the Report noted, "increased sales of these books by 20 percent" (p. 68).

The popularity of the "Barnes" exhibition and accompanying catalog resulted in an increase in sales in 1993. Visitors purchased 268,880 catalogs and books and more than 2 million printed reproductions. The Report for 1993 celebrates that the Board of Trustees approved of a "line of products being offered by the Gallery's sales shops" which includes sculptural reproductions and jewelry related to the collections.

The Gallery continues to pursue distribution and licensing agreements in commercial markets throughout the world as a way to provide broad exposure to the Gallery's collections and, of course, to generate additional revenue. It is important to note that all revenue from publication sales is used to support publications.

The third major influence to be considered when analyzing the seemingly conservative special exhibition schedule of the National Gallery is the watchful eye of the Congress of the United States. As has been noted, most of the Gallery's operating budget (79%–85%) comes from the federal government, a government that in recent years has become more watchful of taxpayers' dollars.

As political and economic tensions heighten, museum exhibits funded by the federal government are likely to be more closely scrutinized and more openly criticized. The National Gallery has no record of exhibition alteration or cancellation under pressure (real or imagined) from Congress. But on record and in the press other noteworthy institutions have not been as fortunate. Perhaps the first major blow-up came in 1989 when the Robert Mapplethorpe exhibition was canceled by Washington's Corcoran Gallery. A detailed discussion of that decision and its connection to the National Endowment for the Arts will come later. First, let us review briefly recent actions within the Smithsonian Institution.

The National Museum of American Art, a division of the Smithsonian, caused a debate with the exhibit "The West as America: Reinterpreting Images of the Frontier." When the curators matched favorite American paintings of the old west with revisionist interpretations which cited the paintings as propaganda for the nineteenth-century concept of Manifest Destiny, the exhibit generated great controversy. Much discussion took place both in art and history circles, in and out of museums, and in and out of the United States Congress, members of which threatened the museum with economic penalties. Senator Ted Williams called the exhibition perverted and criticized the Smithsonian for having a political agenda.

The Air and Space Museum, also part of the Smithsonian, planned an exhibition to mark the 50th anniversary of the flight of the *Enola Gay*, the plane used in 1945 to drop the atomic bomb on Hiroshima. The exhibition, which intended to examine the decision to use the atomic bomb from different perspectives, was challenged by veterans' organizations, the Air Force Association, and members of Congress. This resulted in the cancellation of the exhibit as planned. The Smithsonian chose instead to simply exhibit portions of the plane without question or comment. This approach, according to Smithsonian Secretary, I. Michael Heyman, would create an exhibit "every American can be proud of" instead of one distorted, as charged by House Speaker Newt Gingrich, by left-wing ideologies.

The attempt to satisfy democratic demands may call into question the entire definition and role of interpretation in America museums, especially when the interpretation risks challenging those things, as discussed in Chapter 1, that American museums were built to promote: prestige, patriotism, and moral elevation.

What at first glance appears to be a situation where a guaranteed, secure income provided by Congress allows the freedom to pursue scholarly research and exhibitions, may have complications resulting in a downside. Is the special exhibition schedule determined, not solely by research on the collection and the charge "to make those works of art known and enjoyed by the people of this country," but also by populist pressures? Has the corporate underwriting of special exhibits exerted influence on curatorial decisions? (see Chapter 7.) Has the museum, through the corporate presence and influence, developed a marketing strategy that is driven as much by commercial concerns as educational ones? Have the very recent developments, such as the populous events of 1988, and the outspoken anger of congressional leaders, altered museum practice and policy in a way that is in conflict with the museum's mission?

While the Smithsonian Institution contains the nation's federally funded art museums, other American museums and art institutions are touched by the federal government because they receive federal funding through the National Endowment for the Arts.

The National Endowment for the Arts: control and controversy

The National Endowment for the Arts was established as

> an independent agency of the Federal Government, created in 1965 to encourage and assist the nations' cultural resources. The Endowment is advised by the National Council on the Arts, a presidentially appointed body composed of the Chairman of the Endowment and 26 distinguished private citizens who are widely recognized for their expertise or interest in the arts. The Council advises the Endowment on policies, procedures, and programs, in addition to making recommendations on grant applications.
> (National Endowment Act, 1965)

The statement of mission for the Endowment as described in the literature speaks in lofty language of man's desire to create and his need to express his perception of the world.

> It is through art that we can understand ourselves and our potential and while the arts in America have always been supported directly by the people, it is also an appropriate matter of concern for the Federal Government. The government recognizes that man's need to make, experience, and comprehend art is as profound as his need to speak and thus wishes to foster the arts and to broaden their availability.
> (National Endowment for the Arts Guidelines)

The potential for government support to slip into government interference was addressed from the beginning, and all N.E.A. materials had references to this. America's governance is based on freedom; freedom of thought, freedom of action, freedom of expression. In setting up the National Endowment, a commitment to these freedoms was reinforced.

> In implementing its mission the Endowment must exercise care to preserve and improve the environment in which the arts have flourished. It must not, under any circumstances, impose a single aesthetic standard or attempt to direct artistic content. (National Endowment Act, 1965)

Livingston Biddle, in his book about the birth and growth of the National Endowment for the Arts, *Our Government and the Arts: A Perspective from the Inside*, writes in optimistic tones of how the new endeavor "fostered a belief that the arts are of central importance in our lives." Biddle drafted the original legislation and served first as deputy chairman of the N.E.A. and in 1977 was appointed chairman (Biddle, 1988).

In July 1989, the former director acknowledged to the *New York Times* that circumstances had made it clear that Congress wanted more accountability on the part of the Endowment and that he considered their recent actions "overly punitive" and "a very dangerous precedent" (Gamarekian, 1989c).

Twenty-five years after the founding of the National Endowment, the United States Senate voted to restrict N.E.A. funds from use "to promote, disseminate, or produce obscene or indecent materials, including but not limited to depictions of sadomasochism, homoeroticism, the exploitation of children, or individuals engaged in sex acts, or material which denigrates the objects or beliefs of the adherents of a particular religion or nonreligion." The bill, sponsored by Senator Jesse Helms of North Carolina, would also bar grants for art work that "denigrates, debases or reviles a person, group or class of citizens on the basis of race, creed, sex, handicap, age or national origin."

The events that brought this bill to Congress raised issues about artistic freedom and censorship in America and the influence of the government on art museums.

The controversy began in June, 1989 when, at the prospect of congressional disapproval, Christina Orr-Cahall, then Director of the Corcoran Gallery of Art in Washington, D.C., canceled a touring show of photographs by the late Robert Mapplethorpe. (Mapplethorpe died of AIDS in March of 1989.) The exhibition was a retrospective of the artist's work that contained, as described in the *New York Times*,

> images depicting homosexual and heterosexual erotic acts and explicit sadomasochistic practices in which black and white, naked or leather-clad men and women assume erotic poses. Along with these photographs are fashionable portraits of the rich and trendy, elegant floral arrangements and naked children—images that might not necessarily be considered indecent if viewed singly but that in this context seem provocative. (Signs accompanying the show on its tour suggested that it might be unsuitable for children.)
> (Glueck, 1989a: 1)

The touring show, organized by the Institute of Contemporary Art in Philadelphia, was funded by a grant from the National Endowment for the Arts. The show was seen in Philadelphia, at the Museum of Contemporary Art in Chicago, and at the Whitney Museum in New York without incident. Its viewing in Washington, D.C., however, was to coincide with a congressional review of the N.E.A. budget. The House Appropriations Committee had already approved a proposal to make the

N.E.A. "more accountable for all the work they support" (Gamarekian, 1989a) as a result of criticism of the Mapplethorpe show.

"We had the institutional responsibility to decide if this was the right environment in which to present the show," said Dr. Orr-Cahall in a *New York Times* interview in July.

> There would have been a lot of folderol about it, with attention directed away from substantive issues, such as the effort in Congress to emasculate the endowment. It would be a three-ring circus in which Mapplethorpe's work would never be looked at in its own right. We knew that certain Congressmen were just waiting for us to open the show, and we felt we shouldn't bow to that pressure. It was a no-win situation. We decided we wouldn't be anyone's political platform. (Glueck, 1989a: 9)

Dr. Jacob Neusner, Brown University Professor and Reagan-appointed member of the National Endowment's advisory council, the National Council on the Arts, disagreed with Dr. Orr-Cahall. He felt the cancellation of the Mapplethorpe exhibition was

> pusillanimous and dishonest in the extreme. There was absolutely no pressure on them from the endowment, and to say they were defending us is ridiculous. It is our job to take the heat, and our process knows how to deal with controversy. But they betrayed the process by acting as censors. In doing so they raised the stakes. Had they not, the whole thing would have gone away. A Congressman or two might have visited the show and complained, and that would have been the end of it. Now it will never go away. (Glueck, July 9, 1989a: 9)

On July 12, the House of Representatives administered a carefully designed punitive message to the National Endowment when they voted 361 to 65 in favor of an amendment that reduced the Endowment's 1990 budget by $45,000. Although that $45,000 was a small part of the Endowment's $171.4 million appropriation for the 1990 fiscal year, it represented the exact amount of Endowment-related funding for the Mapplethorpe exhibit and one other controversial show involving a photograph by Andres Serrano depicting a plastic crucifix submerged in the artist's urine. It was a clear message and followed hours of congressional debate over the art projects and the proper use of taxpayers' money (Gamarekian, 1989b). On July 25, the Senate Appropriations Committee took the controversy a step further when they voted for a five-year ban on N.E.A. grants to the two museums, the Institute of Contemporary Art in Philadelphia, and the Southeastern Center for Contemporary Art in Wiston-Salem, North Carolina, that had originated the exhibitions of Mapplethorpe and Serrano photographs.

The cancellation of the exhibit at the Corcoran Gallery along with the measures on the part of the House and the Senate were viewed by artists, museums, and arts advocates as a threat to the arts and to the first amendment guarantee of free speech. The actions taken by the Congress, in particular the move to ban N.E.A. funding to the two organizations that had supported the exhibitions, were viewed as "shocking." Hugh Southern, then acting director of the endowment, called the action "a dangerous precedent which goes against the long and widely respected system of Federal support for the arts through a competitive peer-review process" (Gamarekian, 1989c). The Corcoran's cancellation was viewed by many as a form of self-censorship by a museum. It seemed a direct challenge to the symbolic role of both the artist and the museum in America. Grace Glueck of the *New York Times* wrote:

> Artists are important to us, among other reasons, because of their ability to express what is deep or hidden in our consciousness, what we cannot or will not express ourselves and museums are traditionally the neutral sanctuaries—entered voluntarily by the public—for this expression.
> (1989a: 9)

It is understood that what the public encounters in the museum may not always please, but that is the privilege we give to the museum and the museum in turn gives to art. For a museum to censor itself cuts this trust and alters the understanding.

While the majority of the Corcoran's board supported the decision to cancel, some viewed it as wrong. Robert Lehrman, a Corcoran board member, expressed his disappointment to the *New York Times* when he said that external pressures should not impact on the museum's judgement. "We have relinquished our responsibility to be, as is carved in stone over the entrance, 'Dedicated to Art'" (quoted in Glueck, 1989a: 19).

Lehrman's view of the role of the museum was affirmed when, in September, following two months of protests by artists in the form of canceled shows and boycotts, the Corcoran issued a statement of regret for the cancellation. At the same time, some members of the staff proposed that the museum present an exhibit on censorship that might include the work of both Mapplethorpe and Serrano in an effort to restore the museum's reputation (*New York Times*, September 9, 1989, Section 1: 11).

The apology of the board and director was not enough to mend the broken ties to the art community, and artists who had canceled their exhibits in protest refused to reinstate them. The boycott continued, making contemporary exhibits and programs impossible. The boycott was accompanied by staff resignations and outcries for the director's resignation.

As Tom Armstrong, then director of the Whitney Museum, observed, "When an art museum reverses a decision based on professional judgement because of outside pressures, the integrity of the museum is severely impaired" (quoted in Glueck, 1989a: 9). The resignation of Christina Orr-Cahall came in December, six months after the controversy began.

In the midst of all this furor several arts advocates, beginning with the

American Association of Museums, expressed their views on the role of government in subsidizing the arts. The American Association of Museums issued a background paper for members of Congress which stated that

> while some works of art or ideas seeking public funding may be offensive, the greater risk is a restriction of freedom of expression and individual judgement that would compromise the necessary openness of a democratic society. The test of a democracy is not that the majority gets its way, but that the minority's free access to the full choice of ideas is protected along with its ability to express those ideas.
>
> (American Association of Museums, 1989)

The American Council for the Arts released a position paper that declared:

> The American people have no need for the government to screen or edit art for them. Each adult American has an inalienable right to choose . . . which art to view . . . In a society that is as broad and as free as ours, a society with so many differing voices and opinions, we are not only tolerant of various artistic and political expression, we take great pride in that tolerance . . . There will always be art that offends some taxpaying Americans some of the time. Censorship, however, offends Americans all of the time. Traditional American values are opposed to a society speaking with one government-authorized voice. (American Council for the Arts, 1989)

The College Art Association provided guidelines for members concerned with the issues.

> Art must not be equated with entertainment. Society assigns to art an important purpose: to keep our citizens in touch with their past, to define the present, and to consider the future. Serious art explores new frontiers, celebrates individuality, and mirrors the diverse ideas and values that characterize American society. Art can be controversial and confrontational, and can reflect elements of our society that are offensive to some. Art, by its very nature, involves risk if it is to succeed and grow. The climate of freedom prescribed by the Endowment's authorizing legislation must continue. (College Art Association, 1989)

Compromise legislation and political fallout

After months of debate, a House–Senate conference committee reached a compromise agreement on the amendment that would severely restrict projects eligible for N.E.A. grants. The agreement retained a portion of the Senator Jesse Helms amendment "to prohibit the use of N.E.A. funds to promote, disseminate or produce materials which in the judgement of the Endowment may be considered obscene." What was struck from the amendment was the provision banning funds for "indecent" material that denigrates a religion, a person, or a group or class of citizens on the basis of race, creed, sex, handicap, or national origin. The conferees also borrowed language from a Supreme Court decision on obscenity standards (*Miller* vs. *U.S.*, 1973) and tacked that to the amendment prohibiting funding of materials which may be considered obscene and "which do not have serious literary, artistic, political, or scientific value."

Following the adoption of the revised legislation by Congress came an incident that stunned the arts community. "We could see immediately that the compromise arts funding bill passed by Congress was a hunting-license for the ultra-conservatives," said Ted Potter, director of the Center for Contemporary Art in Winston Salem, "but we didn't expect the first shot to be fired by the N.E.A." (Honan, 1989a).

The National Endowment for the Arts withdrew its sponsorship of an exhibition about AIDS to be held at a nonprofit gallery in New York City. On November 8, John E. Frohnmayer, the newly appointed chairman of the Endowment, announced that he had suspended a $10,000 federal grant which had been approved by an Endowment panel in May, and asked that the Endowment not be listed as a sponsor. Mr. Frohnmayer said he took the action against the exhibition, "Witnesses: Against Our Vanishing," because of derogatory references in the show's catalog to political and religious figures.

The host of the exhibit, a nonprofit gallery called Artists' Space, then located in the Tri-Be-Ca section of Manhattan, had an excellent reputation as an alternative museum devoted to contemporary art. Founded in 1973, the organization had a 1989 annual budget of $725,000. Roughly 40 percent of that came from public grants by the National Endowment, the New York State Council on the Arts, the New York City Department of Cultural Affairs and the Institute of Museum Services (another federal agency). In other words, Artists' Space was the kind of program that could not exist without public money. Yet, it had proven its value, providing first showings to artists such as Scott Burton, Jonathan Borofsky, and Barbara Kruger. In short, Artists' Space was respected and had built and maintained an excellent relationship over the years with government groups that support art, including the National Endowment.

As the N.E.A. withdrew its sponsorship of "Witnesses: Against Our Vanishing," Susan Wyatt, director of Artists' Space denied that the exhibit was political, saying it was an attempt to depict the emotions and spirituality felt by AIDS patients and their friends. She said she notified the Endowment in advance about the contents of the AIDS exhibit because

> I was concerned that the N.E.A. not be blindsided and that Artists' Space not be blindsided. I never anticipated all this would happen. Artists' Space is a cultural organization, not an activist organization. I have nothing against activism, but that is not our goal. It's important to point out that I don't consider the N.E.A. an adversary. I've always considered it a part of the art world, at least until now. (Kimmelman, 1989)

The protests against the action taken by the National Endowment were immediate and strong and included the American Arts Alliance, PEN American Center, the College Art Association, and many prominent individuals. Joseph Papp, producer of the New York Shakespeare Festival, called the action "an assault on the principles we think of as fundamental in our society." Leonard Bernstein, nominated for the prestigious National Medal of Arts, declined to accept the award in protest. In Washington, the Endowment's visual arts panel, the panel which decides on Endowment grants, expressed their "disappointment and distress" over Mr. Frohnmayer's decision and urged him, "make public your commitment to the peer panel process and the Endowment's original mandate to foster the excellence, diversity, and vitality of the arts in this country" (Honan, 1989a).

It was all more than Frohnmayer anticipated or could stand against. On November 15 he flew to New York City to visit Artists Space and to announce the restoration of the grant. "After consulting with members of the National Council on the Arts, several of whom have seen the show, I have agreed to approve the request of Artists Space to amend the fiscal '89 grant and will release the grant" (Honan, 1989c).

"We are feeling our way along in a situation which none of us really wanted, under a law which none of us think is necessary" (quoted in Honan, 1989b).

"Not necessary" and also "ambiguous" were the terms used by many. Representative Pat Williams of Montana, when addressing the House subcommittee that oversees the National Endowment, asserted

> It may well be that in responding to recent Congressional language the N.E.A. has begun to have a chilling effect on art in the United States and it may be entering the quicksand of censorship. This committee must thoughtfully consider whether the Federal Government can maintain an environment necessary for artistic creativity to flourish while fulfilling the recent Congressional mandate that bans assistance to certain art based on content, not quality. Congressional pressure has placed N.E.A. on a slippery slope. The Endowment's authorizing language prohibits it from interfering with the content of the art it subsidizes but Congress is demanding more restrictions on the Endowment's grant making.
>
> (Quoted in Gamarekian, 1989d)

Looking back on the Congressional interference with the Smithsonian Institution of 150 years ago, one recognizes that the autonomy of the museum system was saved by the Smithsonian Regents. The conflict today with Congress over N.E.A. funding of controversial art was deepened by the actions of the Corcoran Gallery and the Endowment itself. The rescue of the National Endowment and the restoration of its original mission statement which demands that the Endowment "must not, under any circumstances, impose a single aesthetic standard or attempt to direct artistic content" was left to independent arts advocacy groups. Some believed the effort of Senator Jesse Helms was not directed at legislating art but rather at the reduction and, eventually, total dissolution of federal funding for the arts.

The National Endowment for the Arts was given life every five years through Congressional legislation and 1990 was one of those years. The debate over the restrictive language introduced and the debate over the very existence of federal funding for the arts became intense during that period.

Arts advocacy groups rallied for insurance that no form of censorship or restriction of content be allowed to become part of the reauthorization legislation under which the life of the Endowment is extended.

Representative Pat Williams prophetically referred to this as "a critical time in the history of federal support of the nation's cultural life. A small minority who oppose Federal support of the arts are on a war footing and are intent on killing or crippling the arts endowment" (quoted in Gamarekian, 1990). In each successive review of the endowment, funding would be further reduced and the authorization period shortened. The orchestrated demise of the National Endowment was under way.

Conclusion

The National Endowment for the Arts and the National Gallery of Art were both founded by an Act of Congress and financially supported by American taxpayers, yet designed to be independent of Congressional influence. The founders of these institutions sought to insure the institutions' autonomy in order to insure the institutions' standards. The National Endowment confirms its belief that "man's need to make, experience, and comprehend art is as profound as his need to speak," while guaranteeing that Congress will never "under any circumstances, impose a single aesthetic standard or attempt to direct artistic content." Such judgements were to be left to the panel of art experts.

The National Gallery, which is the property of the people of the United States and is supported by their tax dollars, exists as specified by its founder, Andrew Mellon, for the "purpose of encouraging and developing a study of the fine arts ... art of the highest standard of quality." When Andrew Mellon first proposed the idea of a National Gallery to the President of the United States, he stated clearly his wish to have the gallery administered by a "competent and separate board of trustees" in order to safeguard that the "highest standard of quality will always be maintained in the art to be displayed in the gallery."

While the founders sought to control the democratic influences on these two institutions, the safeguards established early on have proven vulnerable. The blatant disciplinary actions by the Congress against the National Endowment were efforts to impose aesthetic standards and to direct content. The possibility of Congressional influence on exhibition programs at the National Gallery should be viewed with clear and discerning perceptions and a reckoning of history. The schedule of popular exhibits draws large crowds which pleases Congress and the corporate sponsors of the special exhibits, but apparently ignores the huge body of abstract, more difficult art produced in this century and held in the Gallery's collection. Government funding of art institutions appears to bring with it democratic influences which may be in conflict with the higher institutional goals. These influences have the potential to change the role of the art museum in the American culture in ways our forefathers tried to guard against.

5

The development of American modernism and its influence on the American art museum

Introduction

The Museum of Modern Art in New York City opened its new building at 11 West 53rd Street in November, 1939. This modern structure designed by Philip Goodwin and Edward Durell Stone is considered to be the first truly modern museum. What is meant by the concept of modernism as it applies to art and architecture and how modernism has impacted on the American art museum are the issues to be examined in this chapter.

The term "modern" as used here refers to the modern period as defined by the Museum of Modern Art, that is the period since 1880. It also refers to a particular use of formal elements as described in the writings of Alfred Barr. (Barr and the Museum of Modern Art are discussed in Chapters 8 and 9.) When linked with art and architecture it refers to a multiplicity of styles and schools of thought which parallel changes in the industrial, technical, political, economic, social, and spiritual conditions of the twentieth-century. Modernism developed in Europe and was first introduced to the American art world through the Armory Show, the exhibition of modern European art held in a New York City armory in 1913 (Association of American Painters and Sculptors, 1913: 11–13). This exhibit had a major impact on working artists of the period.

At that point, a few American artists were experimenting with variations of cubism, which resulted in the development of American abstraction. (For example, see the work of Arthur Dove in the collection of the Whitney Museum of American Art.) Artists focused on the expressive potential of the elements of art such as rhythmic lines and vibrant colors. Even much of the realism of the day emphasized abstract composition. Alfred Stieglitz exhibited the work of John Marin, Georgia O'Keefe, Arthur Dove, and other innovative painters in his New York City gallery early on (Lynes, 1989: 5). It was, however, the influx of European artists and architects during World War II that etched the lasting mark of modernism on American art and architecture and allowed the development of the first truly American art movements.

The artists fleeing Paris for New York in the wake of the Nazi's rise to power transmitted the principles of modernism through America's system of higher education as well as in New York's cafés. At the same time American collectors began to establish museums dedicated to modern art. (The development of the first Museum of Modern Art is covered in Chapter 8.) All of this resulted in the creation of a New York avant-garde which quickly began to replace Paris as the dominant center for art.

We will examine first the informal means of influence on the American culture exerted by European artists through personal contact with American artists in New York City cafés and through public exhibitions, in particular by the artists affiliated with the Surrealist movement. Secondly, we will look at the formal means of influence exerted through the American system of higher education, especially by transplanted Bauhaus faculty. These two influences, the philosophy of Surrealism and the Bauhaus philosophy, can be viewed as the two parallel yet opposing approaches to the making of American art and architecture that would dominate and define the American modernist movement. American modernism would in turn determine the architecture of the American museum, an architecture that would provide the practical, systematic, instructional space demanded by a democratic society.

Surrealism made its impact first, while the Bauhaus influence would be somewhat delayed. Coming through the educational system, the Bauhaus philosophy was felt in the next artistic generation and was felt most profoundly by architects of the day. The Surrealists' contact was directly with young working artists hungry for new ideas from Paris and so its impact was immediate.

The influence of Surrealism

Surrealism was recognized as the most widely influential aesthetic movement between World Wars I and II. Its impact was due in part to the movement of artists as a result of the war and also to the attitude that held Surrealism to be not just an art movement, but a philosophy of life (Barr, 1936b: 8). Basically, Surrealism looked to the subconscious, dream world as a means to discover and express truth. It depended on intuition and instinct rather than rational, logical thought processes. André Breton, the poet and Father of Surrealism, defined it as the "belief in the higher reality of specific forms of associations, previously neglected, in the omnipotence of dreams, and in the disinterested play of thinking."

The Surrealist artists settling in New York City included Marcel Duchamp, Yves Tanguy, Roberto Matta Echaurren, André Masson, Max Ernst, and Man Ray. For the most part they were a congenial group willing to share their ideas and methods within the Parisian mode of the café or the salon.

One very important meeting ground was Peggy Guggenheim's gallery,

Art of This Century. Peggy Guggenheim described the gallery as "a center where all the artists were welcome and so they treated it as a sort of club" (Guggenheim, 1979: 317). It was in this gallery that the first American Abstract Expressionists exhibited their work. One-person shows of the paintings of Jackson Pollock, Robert Motherwell, William Baziotes, Hans Hoffman, Mark Rothko, Clifford Still, and David Hare were presented. Another important salon was Roberto Matta Echaurren's Ninth Street studio, where a number of artists, Europeans and Americans, gathered weekly to view each other's work and analyze the images.

One of the first exhibits to bring Europeans and Americans together was the "First Papers of Surrealism" held in 1942 at the Whitelow Reid Mansion on Madison Avenue. The exhibition included works by Masson, Matta and Ernst along with the young Americans Baziotes, Gorky and Motherwell (Jean, 1967: 312–13). Organized with the assistance of the French artist Marcel Duchamp, the exhibition succeeded in closing the gap of colonial modernism and rooting Surrealist concepts in American soil.

Duchamp installed at this exhibition his *Mile of String*. The string crisscrossed the gallery space, looped over the exhibition panels and clustered in tangles in front of the paintings. Photos documenting the event show that the string kept the visitor from entering the gallery and made viewing the works of art impossible but it also defined the gallery space in a way in which it had never before been defined and ultimately transformed it into a work of art.

Duchamp addressed the modernist sensibility in the literal use of the material and the simplicity of the gesture. He also, in an immediate and powerful way, commented on the effect of context on art. The *Mile of String* functioned like a spider's web to catch and hold the paintings on the gallery walls, trapping them in a specific moment, and rendering them unapproachable and obsolete. Duchamp was commenting on art exhibitions and on the context in which we view art. The context within which we view the work of art can alter, diminish or intensify the meaning the object carries.

Duchamp was born on the outskirts of Rouen to a cultured bourgeois family who loved chess and music and art. Early on he worked as a printer and also did cartoons for the *Courrier François* and *Le Rire*. His early work seems influenced by Cézanne, but he quickly came to know and imitate Fauvism, and by 1911, at the age of 24, the influence of Cubism can be seen (D'Harnoncourt and McShine, 1973: 12–13; Moure, 1988: 11–13).

Duchamp was known for his tendency to take a very detached view of things (including the professional art world) and he was a master of irony (Breton, 1972: 86–8). He had the ability to deliberately exploit the absurd while appearing completely serious. These traits can be seen as contributing to the development of Dada, and later to Surrealism.

Nude Descending a Staircase (Collection of the Philadelphia Museum of Art) was painted in 1912 and exhibited the following year in the

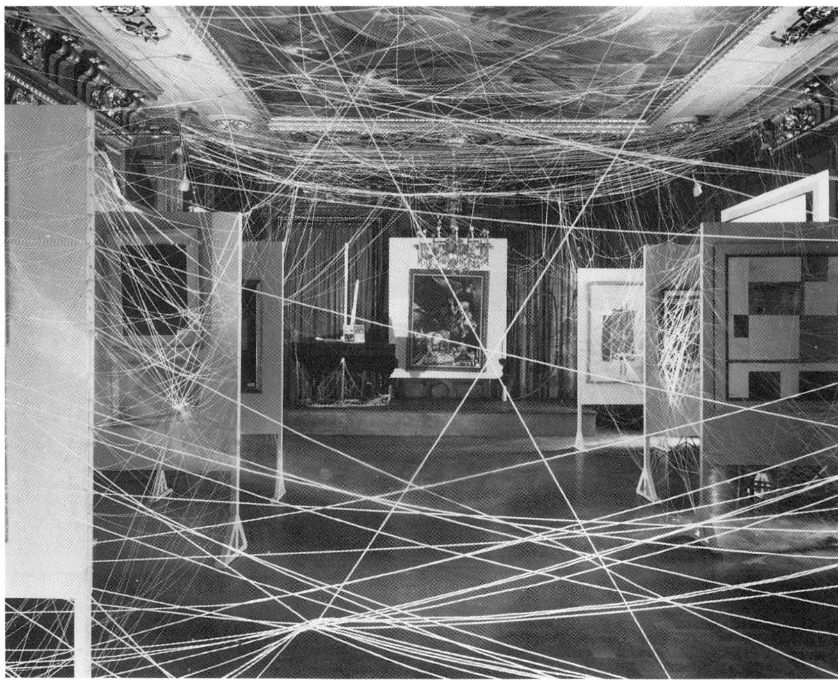

Mile of String by Marcel Duchamp, installation view at First Papers of Surrealism, 1942, New York.
John Schiff Archives, F-M Campus Library, Fairleigh Dickinson University, Madison, NJ.

Armory Show. It aroused immense curiosity and outrage and placed Duchamp in a position of influence among American painters (Hamilton, Richard, in D'Harnoncourt and McShine, 1973: 63). When the artist arrived in New York in 1914, fleeing from the war in Europe, he found that he was already famous, and reporters came to interview him. Duchamp returned to New York, again to escape war, in 1942. It was at this time that he helped organize, along with André Breton, the "First Papers of Surrealism" exhibition (Jean, 1967: 312–13; 1980: 403–4).

Another important art hypothesis was instigated by Duchamp with the invention of the "readymade". The "readymade" was a manufactured object assigned the dignity of an art object through the context in which it was placed. Duchamp appropriated a urinal and, placing it atop a pedestal, assigned it the title *Fountain* (Collection of The Museum of Modern Art, NYC). With this gesture he asserted the belief that art can be created through the power of context. A bicycle wheel mounted upside-down on a wooden stool is another example of a Duchamp readymade (Collection of The Museum of Modern Art, NYC). He was in many ways the ultimate Surrealist, maintaining his freedom, holding nothing sacred. His readymades call into question our ideas concerning value in art. They were a way to separate art and money. "In art and only in art," said Duchamp, "the original work is sold, and it acquires a sort of aura that way. But with my readymades a replica will do just as well." Duchamp's influence was wide-ranging because he did not hold to a particular style but connected the making of art to the living of life (Andrews, 1990: 31–3), a philosophy essential to the formation of American modernism.

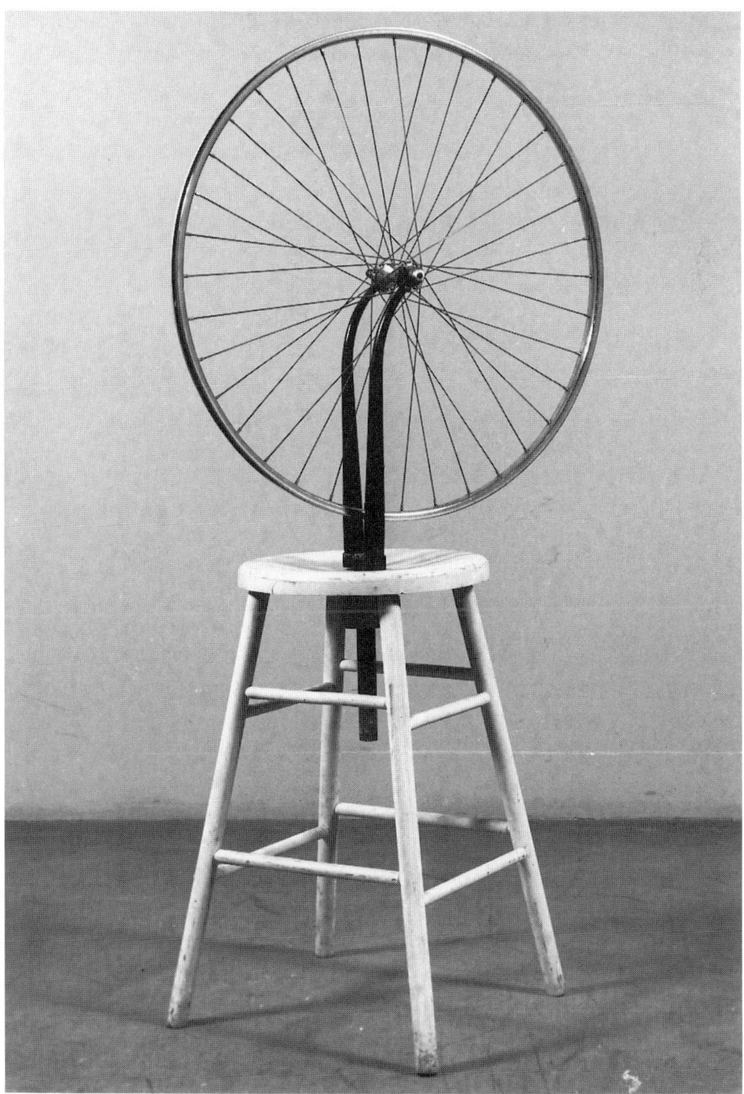

Bicycle Wheel by Marcel Duchamp, 1951 (third version, after lost original of 1913), New York. Assemblage: metal wheel, 25½ in. (63.8 cm) diameter, mounted on painted wood stool 23¾ in. (60.2 cm) high; overall, 50½ × 25½ × 16⅝ in. (128.3 × 63.8 × 42 cm).
The Museum of Modern Art, New York. The Sidney and Harriet Janis Collection.

This philosophy would be adopted by the young Americans and would include an intense interest in psychology and psychoanalysis, especially an interest in the role of the unconscious in the making of art. Seeking a means to express certain universal truths, the American artists employed symbols and signs and myths, in methods similar to those of the Europeans. What evolved at this point was a new process for the making of art, a process that was based on personal expression and personal experience voiced within a universal concept.

Surrealism and Jackson Pollock

The artist who best exemplifies this aesthetic impulse is the American Abstract Expressionist, Jackson Pollock. Pollock's painting had a strong emotional content from the start. Although he began his career under the influence of the American scene painters, in particular Thomas Hart Benton, Pollock's work was never a commonplace interpretation. (See Pollock's works on paper, *circa* 1935, Collection of The Museum of Modern Art, NYC). He quickly discovered the Mexican muralists Orozco and Siqueiros, whose expressionism touched him. By the late 1930s Pollock was ripe for the Surrealist aesthetic and connected both with the symbolic imagery and with the methods of automatism (Naifeh and Smith, 1989: 426). He, along with the other New York painters Rothko, Motherwell, and Baziotes, used the automatic painting techniques of the Surrealists to reveal what they believed to be universal symbols that inhabited the inner mind.

Pollock took the Surrealists' automatic techniques to an extreme and by 1947 was producing his "drip" paintings. Pollock would place the unstretched, often unsized, canvas on the floor of his studio and, with paint in hand, he would move around and even across the canvas dripping, flinging, spotting the pigment in great gestures that involved his entire body.

> When I am in my painting, I'm not aware of what I'm doing. It is only after a sort of 'get acquainted' period that I see what I have been about. I have no fears about making changes, destroying the image, etc., because the painting has a life of its own. I try to let it come through. It is only when I lose contact with the painting that the result is a mess. Otherwise there is pure harmony, an easy give and take, and the painting comes out well.
>
> (Pollock, 1947–48: 79)

The images were therefore produced by the movements and gestures of his entire body, not just his wrist and elbow. This method emphasized the process of painting as opposed to the finished product (Sandler, 1970: 102). It registered the energy, drama, passion of the moment and forced the viewer to respond actively rather than as a passive observer. These paintings appeared revolutionary to the art public of the day, for not only were they completely non-objective but they seemingly defied even the

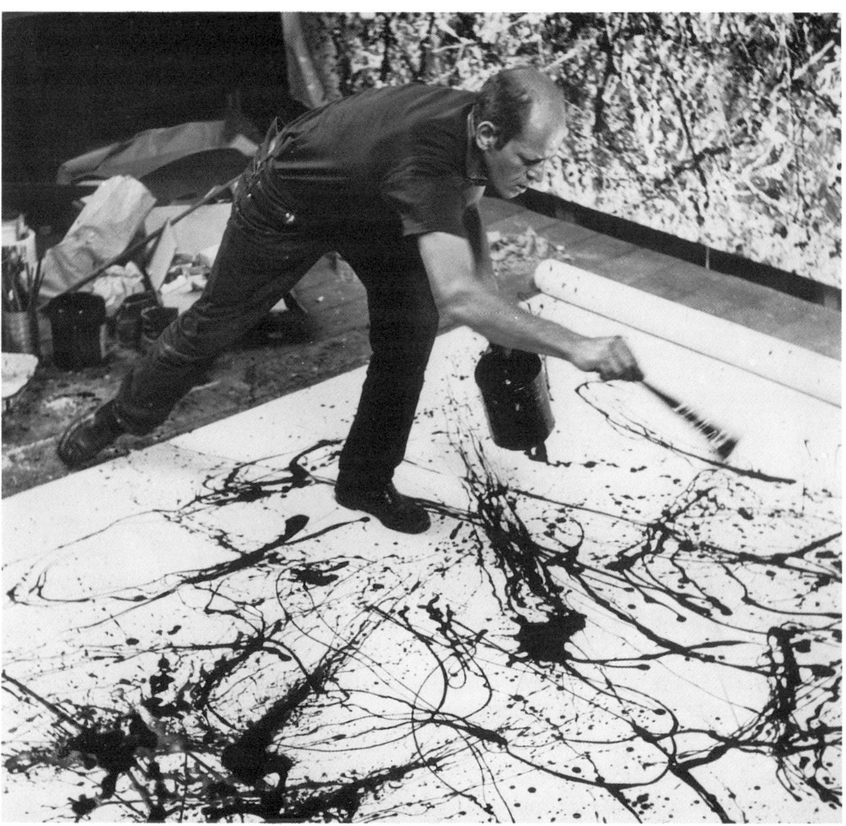

Jackson Pollock at work, 1950.
Hans Namuth photographs, Archives of American Art, Smithsonian Institution.

formal elements of art since there was no focal point, no apparent structure, and no planned composition. (For example, *Autumn Rhythm*, 1950, Collection of The Metropolitan Museum of Art.) They required the viewer to possess information about and understanding of the painting process.

Pollock's interest in myth stemmed from the Surrealist aesthetic also and, like the emphasis on process, required the viewer to approach the painting informed. Pollock said in an interview in 1944

> I accept the fact that the important painting of the last hundred years was done in France ... the fact that good European moderns are now here is very important, for they bring with them an understanding of the problems of modern painting. I am particularly impressed with their concept of the source of art being the unconscious. (Pollock, 1944: 14)

Pollock's friend John Graham, while exploring the role of the unconscious in art, identified two factors in primitive art: first, "the degree of freedom of access to one's unconscious mind in regard to observed phenomenon," and second, "an understanding of the possibilities

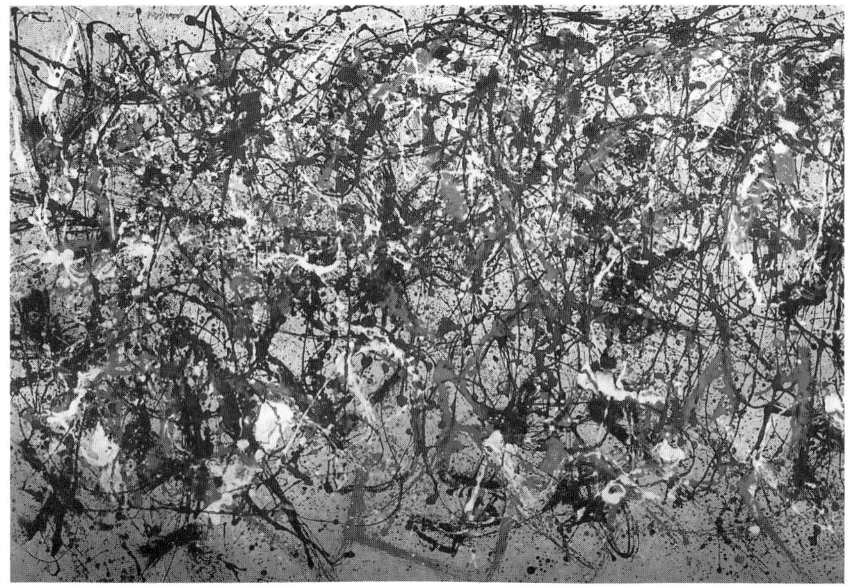

Autumn Rhythm by Jackson Pollock (1912–56), oil on canvas, 105 × 207 in.
The Metropolitan Museum of Art. George A. Hearn Fund, 1957 (57.92).

of the plain operating space" which would permit "a spontaneous exercise of design and composition as opposed to the deliberate which is valueless" (Graham, 1937: 236–7). Clearly, Jackson Pollock's methodology related to both of these factors. Pollock's ideas about primitive art and mythology were influenced also by Carl Jung, and in fact Pollock was in therapy with a Jungian analyst from 1939 on (Naifeh and Smith, 1989: 327–38).

Pollock and the other Americans differed from the European Surrealists in their orientation to Jung rather than Freud. Jung's publication, *Symbols of Transformation* (1956), for example, described close parallels between ancient myths and psychotic fantasies. Jung developed his theories through the use of history and mythology, especially the history and mythology of primitive cultures. He made the distinction between the personal unconscious and the collective unconscious, which he defined as being those thoughts, feelings and memories shared by the group and which manifest themselves symbolically in myths. Jung explained human motivation in terms of a larger creative energy.

Aware of these ideas, Pollock used psychotherapy toward the invention of a new visual language (Schimmel, 1986: 26). He lifted symbols and signs from other cultures and employed myths as a means to enter into deeper preconscious realms. Eventually the references became less specific and he came to depend on the act of painting rather than on the iconography to express these ideas. Painting became for Pollock a ritualistic act so that he illustrated, interpreted, and symbolized myths through the process rather than the image. The content was mythic in spirit and intended to provoke in the viewer either ecstasy or anxiety. Pollock conceived the content of a painting as being action, free and dramatic.

These factors, the technical and poetic information contained in pure painting and the use of psychology, mythology, and history in the making of art, resulted in work that was very difficult for the public to understand. The new art often demanded specific knowledge such as a knowledge of Freudian or Jungian concepts as they were applied to visual art, a knowledge of mythology, an understanding of the poetry inherent in the painting process, an understanding of the basic elements of art and how they might be interpreted within the visual language. (The role of museum education in American modernism is addressed in Chapter 6.)

In sum, American modernism required the viewer to be intellectually, sensually, and emotionally cognizant of visual language. The new art forms being produced were not accessible on other levels, not accessible without specific knowledge and therefore potentially selective in audience. The regionalism that had dominated American art thus far in the century provided, through its narrative element, a point of entry for the man on the street, and provided also, through the realist style, a basis for judgement for even the untrained eye (i.e. Does the cornfield look like a cornfield?). Now Americans were faced with unrecognizable images executed in a fashion that had no relation to ordinary experience and were expected to respond, if not intellectually, at least on a gut level. The reaction of the average American to modern art was often imbued with suspicion and, in some instances, with hostility (*Life*, August, 1949: 42–3).

While the new art posed problems amidst the American democratic culture because of its inaccessibility, it also satisfied certain democratic longings. This kind of painting focused on the individual, on the emotions and ideas of the maker. It was a celebration of American individualism, and its practitioners became culture heroes (Naifeh and Smith, 1989: 595).

Again, Jackson Pollock is an excellent example of this phenomenon. Pollock had come out of Wyoming, he was strong and tough and projected the spirit of an American cowboy. His paintings referred to the rituals of American Indians and he compared himself to the sand painters of the West. The process he employed was athletic, it was far from any effeminate image Americans held about easel painting but appeared, on the contrary, quite masculine, vigorous, even wild.

Jackson Pollock's technique of painting was recorded both in still photographs and on moving film and was presented to the American people through the popular press. Pollock became a kind of culture hero and an American success story, an unusual situation for an American artist. Millions of Americans who would never actually see his paintings, nor understand fully their history or inspiration, were nevertheless moved by the activity of this rebel *Time* magazine labeled "Jack the Dripper" (Eliot, 1949).

The photographs taken by the artist Hans Namuth capture Pollock in his studio. We see the artist holding not a palette but a can of house paint in one hand while with a brush or stick in the other he applies the paint. The canvas is spread on the floor in front of him and he moves around it and across it in an aggressive manner. He is fully absorbed in the activity, not as a contemplative artist but as a man of action (see plate 15). In another Namuth photograph we see Pollock alone, a huge canvas serves as backdrop. He is dwarfed by his own creation and appears alienated.

These images succeeded in conjuring up in the American imagination a poignant vision of the artist as existential hero. "It seems to me," said Pollock in a 1951 interview with William Wright, "that the modern painter cannot express this age, the airplane, the atom bomb, the radio, in the old forms of the Renaissance or of any other past culture ... the modern artist, it seems to me, is working and expressing an inner world ...."

Pollock as offered up by the media satisfied the yearnings of a postwar generation who sought spontaneity and rebellion in a repressed, gray-flannel world. The media had discovered the world of high art and had found the means of digesting it and converting reality into myth. By focusing on the activity of painting, the press avoided serious analysis of the finished product, they avoided addressing the role of the objects in the history of Western art. Furthermore, the photographs emphasized the artist more so than the art. Since the paintings reveal so little through reproduction, losing the qualities of color and texture, the personality of the artist was allowed to dominate. Pollock became a media hero, his image took on a dimension greater than that of his work, and the first lessons in the business of marketing art were learned.

The influence of the German Bauhaus

The second influence on the development of American modernism was exerted by those transplanted artists, designers, and architects from the German Bauhaus. During World War II the Nazis forced the closing of the Bauhaus School of Design and this key faculty emigrated to the United States. This period of emigration is, in general, considered to be significant because, unlike the mass emigrations of the nineteenth century, it did not consist of representatives of politics, business or unskilled labor. Those entering the United States during the 1930s were the representatives of cultural life—humanists, scientists, and artists.

It was in 1937 that Walter Gropius, Herbert Bayer, Josef Albers, Marcel Breuer, Mies van der Rohe, and others from the Bauhaus arrived in New York City. Walter Gropius was made head of the school of architecture at Harvard University and Marcel Breuer joined him there. Josef Albers began teaching at Black Mountain College in North Carolina and later moved to Yale University, where he became chairman of the department of art. Mies van der Rohe accepted the position of dean of

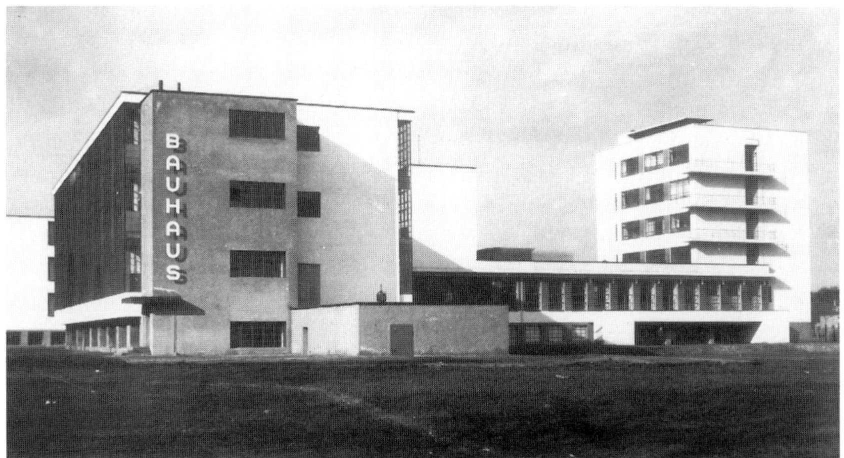

Bauhaus Building at Dessau, Germany (1925–26). Walter Gropius, architect.
The Museum of Modern Art, New York.

architecture at the Armour Institute in Chicago, which merged with the Lewis Institute to become the Illinois Institute of Technology (Hahn, 1990: 7).

Within a short period of time the course of architecture and design in the United States would change, due in part to the buildings these men designed, but mainly to the educational impact they exerted. In his introductory essay to the catalog of the Bauhaus collection at the Busch–Reisinger Museum, Harvard University, Charles Kuhn writes:

> For a brief period there were plans to devote a section of the collection to the influence of Bauhaus instruction concepts on American institutions. It was soon realized that Bauhaus influence was so widespread that it would be out of the question to document it completely. (Kuhn, 1971: 8)

The influence of the Bauhaus on American design began with Walter Gropius, the architect, influencing other architects. Gropius came from a family of artists and architects and stands as a leader in the modern movement. He brought architecture into the twentieth-century through the use of industrial materials and techniques. This influence produced designs that were austere, rational, and intelligent (Whitford, 1988: 33).

Gropius also wished to see architecture play a part in resolving social needs, and to this end he designed numerous working-class housing complexes (Gropius, 1984: 126). He promoted standardization and prefabrication and the adaptation of modern materials to modern social needs.

Gropius called for a unity of the visual arts, crafts, and design under the primacy of architecture in his *Manifesto* of April, 1919. Painters, weavers, ceramicists, graphic designers, all artists and craftsmen alike were taught to engage the problems of architecture. Architecture was for Gropius "the ultimate art form in which beauty and utility, design and structure could be combined. Buildings were conceived not merely as functional necessities but as experimental answers serving psychologically based needs" (Kuhn, 1971: 14). The idea of controlling an environment through an understanding of the psychological impact of color, light, form, and space, and integrating that environment through the implementation of those simple elements is the essence of Bauhaus design.

As the founder and director of the Bauhaus School of Design, Gropius made his influence felt on the broad scale. Architects Louis Skidmore, Louis Kahn, and Edward Durell Stone all made the pilgrimage to Germany early on, as did the Museum of Modern Art director, Alfred Barr (see "Barr as modernist" in Chapter 8). The Museum of Modern Art's 1932 "International Exhibit of Modern Architecture" featured photographs and models of the work of Walter Gropius and essays by Henry-Russell Hitchcock, Philip Johnson, and Louis Mumford. Before World War I, Gropius had executed key works in which skeleton and skin were separated into the curtain wall formulation and aesthetically exploited for the first time. The Bauhaus building at Dessau, designed in 1925, was a classic example of the new aesthetic, with rectangular forms and flat roof. Constructed in steel and glass, it was the pure expression of modernist thought.

Gropius wielded influence as an educator and a man of ideas. Because the Bauhaus was a philosophy and not simply a building, an institute, an art school, it could be transported to American soil and planted in American minds. As Alfred Barr wrote in the preface to an exhibition catalog of Bauhaus design:

> In America, lighting fixtures and tubular steel chairs were imported or the designs pirated. American Bauhaus students began to return; and they were followed... by Bauhaus and ex-Bauhaus masters ... In this way ... Bauhaus designs, Bauhaus men, Bauhaus ideas ... have been spread throughout the world. (Barr, 1938: 5–6)

Because the Bauhaus philosophy emphasized the design of the total environment, the building, the interior space, and all the objects, both functional and aesthetic, it touched many aspects of American design. Philip Johnson, who studied with Gropius at Harvard University stated in the 1933 exhibition catalog "Objects: 1900 and Today" that the discipline of modern architecture had become so broad that there were no longer subcategories such as decorative arts or what Johnson called "the minor arts." He also believed that all design should follow the principles of modern architecture, that it should be objective and logical, that it should employ geometric simplicity in line and form, and that the materials used should be appropriate and true to their nature. Surfaces should be smooth, ornamentation should be avoided, form should be determined by the function.

> In 1900 the Decorative Arts had a style independent of the architecture of their day, based on imitation of natural forms and lines which curve,

diverge and converge. Today industrial design is functionally motivated and follows the same principles as architecture: machine-like simplicity, smoothness of surface, avoidance of ornament.

The principles of modernism were taught by the Bauhaus faculty now in residence in America's art schools and universities. At Yale University, Josef Albers continued his *Vorkurs* (preliminary course). Albers conducted experiments with various materials. "We have first to investigate what a material can do ... economy of form depends on the material we are working with ... notice that you will often have more by doing less" (Kuhn, 1971: 30). Reduce and simplify and let the material reveal itself and preserve its inherent qualities.

An understanding of the nature of materials was coupled with an understanding of the form they might assume, and economy was stressed all around. Clean lines, no frills and appropriate materials would provide the best design. Perhaps the most obvious example of this is the now classic Breuer chair (Collection of The Museum of Modern Art, NYC). Marcel Breuer epitomized Bauhaus design by rethinking the common chair in the light of new materials and technology (Whitford, 1988: 173). Breuer's chair is practical, comfortable, and light, with an economy of material and line. A salute to the Gropius slogan "Art and Technology—A New Unity."

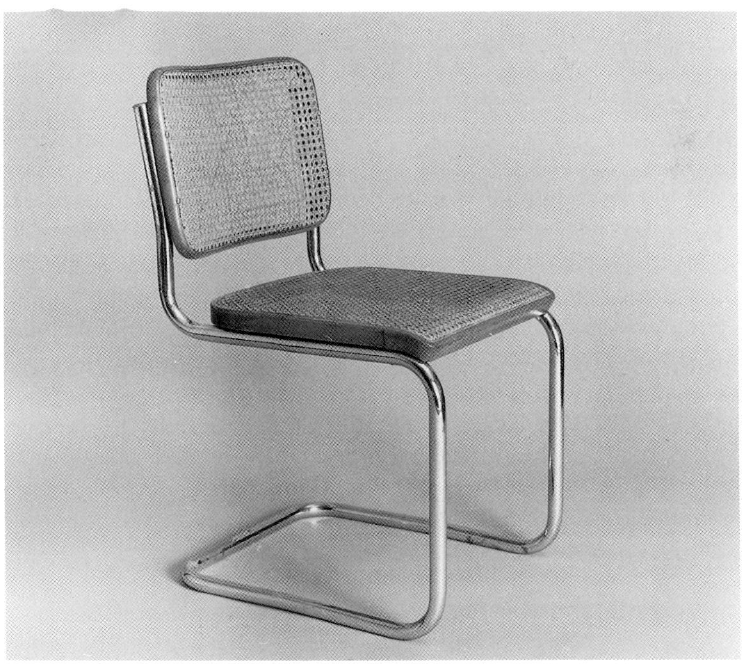

"Cesca" Side Chair by Marcel Breuer, 1928. Chrome-plated tubular steel, wood and cane, $31\frac{1}{2} \times 17\frac{1}{2} \times 18\frac{3}{4}$ in. (80 × 44.5 × 47.6 cm).
The Museum of Modern Art, New York. Museum Purchase.

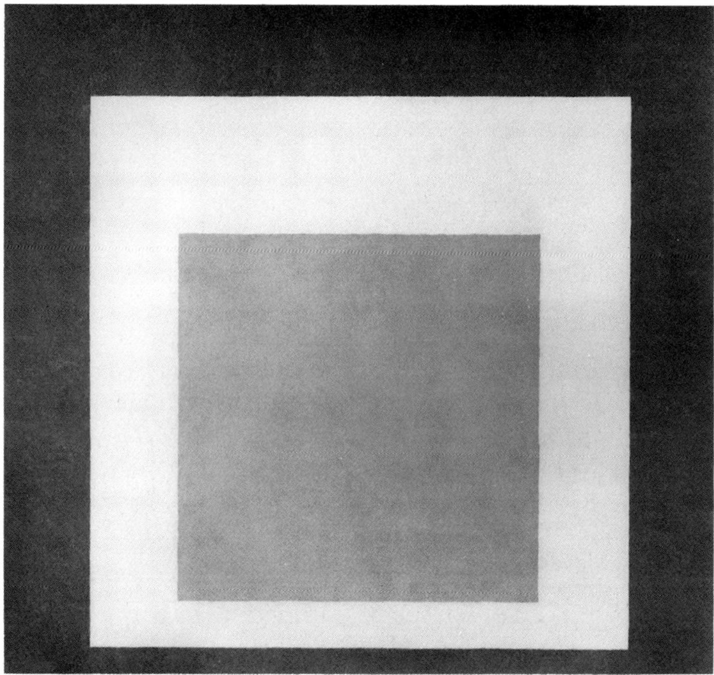

Homage to the Square: "Ascending", 1953, by Josef Albers (1888–1976). Oil on composition board, $43\frac{1}{2} \times 43\frac{1}{2}$ in. (110.5 × 110.5 cm). Purchase, 54.34. *Whitney Museum of American Art, New York.*

Gropius himself stated shortly before his death that the importance of the Bauhaus could be found in the "attitude intended to provide the art forms of our environment with an objective method of work and thought developed from elementary roots" (Kuhn, 1971: 25). Elementary roots: art and design reduced to their basic elements of line, form, and color and these elements then analyzed and categorized. Albers' color theory is an excellent example of the reductive, analytical process. In his own paintings, *Homage to the Square* series in particular, we see rigid geometric compositions investigating color relationships. The structure is composed of three or four squares superimposed upon one another with the bottom, side and top margins in a 1:2:3 ratio. Each color reacts with the others affecting spatial relationships, hues, and sizes. Albers' color theory is still the predominant method of instruction today in American art schools.

The reductive trend in American art

The principles of Bauhaus modernism became pervasive in the American art world, in the classrooms, and in the artists' studios; in the galleries and in the museums. Bauhaus faculty and their disciples dominated the

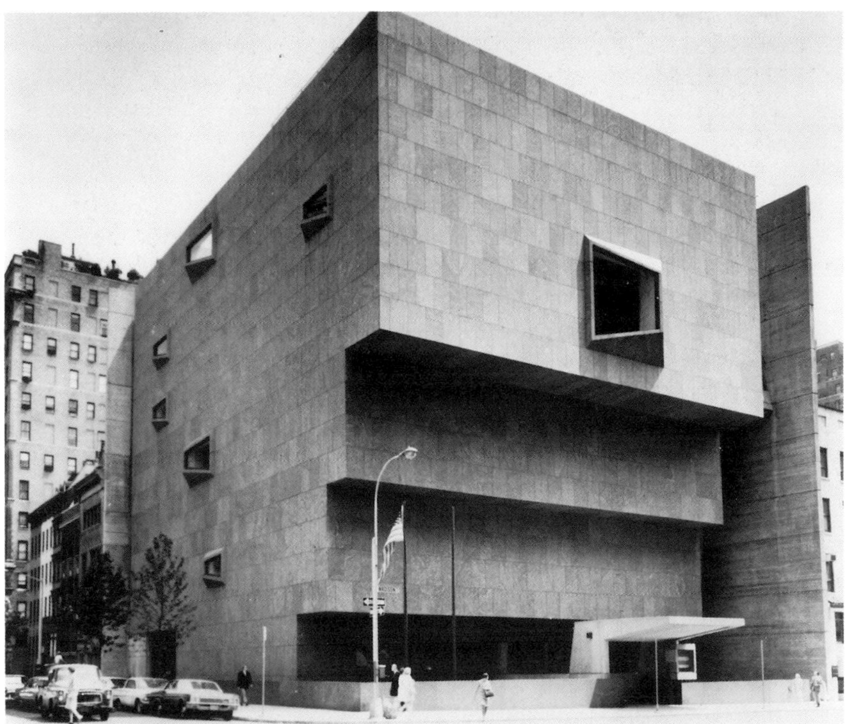

Exterior view of the Whitney Museum of American Art designed by Marcel Breuer, 945 Madison Ave., New York City. Opened September 27, 1966.
Whitney Museum of American Art, New York.

1960s art world inside and out. On the "outside," Marcel Breuer designed the new Whitney Museum of American Art in New York City. The exterior design is not in the International Style, but in keeping with modernist taste, Breuer's design provides a vertical stack of loft-like spaces, pure white and unobstructed, ideal for viewing works of art. This was the perfect gallery, the pristine space that shut out worldly distractions.

On the "inside" or private world where the individual artist resolves the problems of personal concepts, expressions, and aesthetics, the principles of Bauhaus modernism began to shape the forms of painting and sculpture. Considering the major art "movements" of the period (geometric and "hard-edge" painting, minimalist sculpture and Pop Art) we can see the trend toward the reductive, the "truth in materials" dictum, and the logical, objective approach to creating art.

The American painter, Frank Stella, is said to have been influenced early in his career by the Abstract Expressionist Hans Hoffman. In 1958, however, Stella turned from Abstract Expressionism to a drastically reduced and severely ordered style that remained at the forefront of American painting through the 1960s. Adopting an uncompromising approach to abstraction, he first painted concentric rectangles of white line that echoed the frame of the canvas against a black background (for example, *Die Fahne Hoch*, 1959, enamel on canvas, Collection of The Whitney Museum of American Art). When questioned about this shift by Bruce Glaser in a WBAI-FM, New York broadcast in February, 1964, Stella replied:

> There's always been a trend toward simpler painting and it was bound to happen one way or another. When painting gets complicated, like Abstract Expressionism, or Surrealism, there's going to be someone who's not painting complicated paintings, someone who's trying to simplify ... You're always related to something and I'm related to geometric, simpler painting. (Battcock, 1968: 149)

Fellow artist and friend Donald Judd participated in the same radio interview. While his art took a sculptural form and fell neatly into the newly defined category called "Minimalism," Judd shared with Stella the same concern with simple, geometric forms and reductive tendencies. "We're getting rid of the things that people used to think were essential to art" (p. 159).

Minimalism was the first sculptural movement to exclude all excess and redundancy, creating some of the most austere work in the history of art. The Minimalists used industrial materials and processes (art and technology) and paid special attention to the physical properties of materials and the materials' expressive, inherent qualities. This emphasis on industrial materials and techniques produced an art that was objective, logical, and intellectual, an art that responded to the urban industrial environment.

Donald Judd, who wrote art criticism prior to devoting himself completely to the making of art, composed a widely circulated essay on "Specific Objects" in which he expressed his preference for a literal use of materials, space, and concepts. Judd's forms were concepts such as "cube;" his materials were industrial steel and aluminum and were machined to perfection leaving no indication of the human hand; his art occupied real space, deliberately dividing and compartmentalizing the exhibition room (for example, *Untitled*, 1965, galvanized iron and aluminum, Collection of The Whitney Museum of American Art). This literalism was clearly influenced by the Bauhaus philosophy, which demanded truth and pragmatism.

The greater emphasis on the intellectual content of art can also be viewed as a Bauhaus influence, since the new generation of American artists were trained, not in technical art schools, but in universities. Many of these artists were both writing and talking about their work and collaborating with critics who could articulate the new ideas. (Carl Andre, Mel Bochner, Dan Flavin, Brian O'Doherty, Robert Smithson, Robert Morris, and Sol Lewitt are a few artists who published their ideas.) Attempting to force the art audience to an awareness beyond the

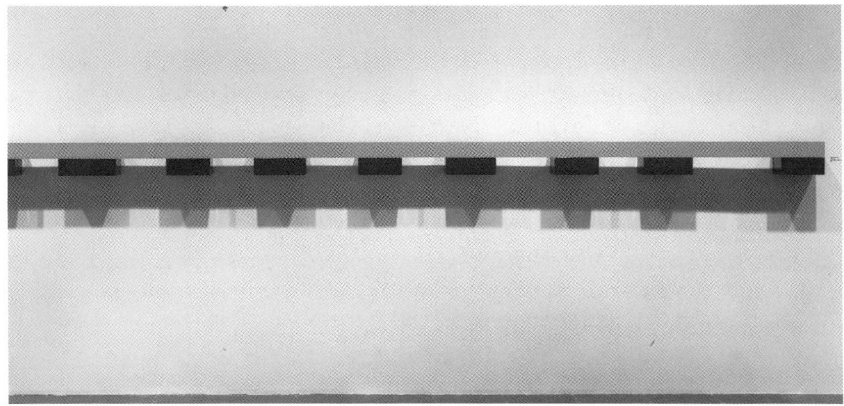

Untitled, 1965, by Donald Judd (1928–1994). Aluminium, $8\frac{1}{4} \times 253 \times 8\frac{1}{4}$ in. ($21 \times 642.6 \times 21$ cm). Purchase, with funds from the Howard and Jean Lipman Foundation, Inc.
Whitney Museum of American Art, New York.

particular art object and to obliterate confusion and misunderstanding about their work, the Minimalists wrote at length about their ideas, their influences, and the forms they found. Here was a difficult, highly intellectual, not particularly charming form of art.

Minimalism proved to be even less accessible than Abstract Expressionism, even with the volumes of essays published regarding it. These obscure references to Gestalt psychology and the writings of the German philosopher Ludwig Wittgenstein were lost on the average American. Furthermore, unlike Abstract Expressionist paintings, Minimalist sculpture did not translate well to the popular press. Even heroes like Jackson Pollock were hard to find since most of the work was conceived by the artist and then fabricated by a hired craftsman.

The literal trend in American art

Another art movement coming at about the same time satisfied the needs of the mass media and in fact mirrored the images created by and for that culture. Pop Art held as its main protagonist the media manipulator and star personality, Andy Warhol. Working in both painting and sculpture, Warhol lifted his images from the commercial world of newspapers, magazines, advertising. There is in the imagery of Pop Art a simplicity necessary for the quick communication required by the commercial world. Warhol was a master of the quick fix, applying the techniques of the advertising industry to the making of high art. He related to Marcel Duchamp's readymades as he appropriated the images of Campbell's soup cans and Brillo boxes to make paintings and sculpture (Collection of The Whitney Museum of American Art). He well understood the success

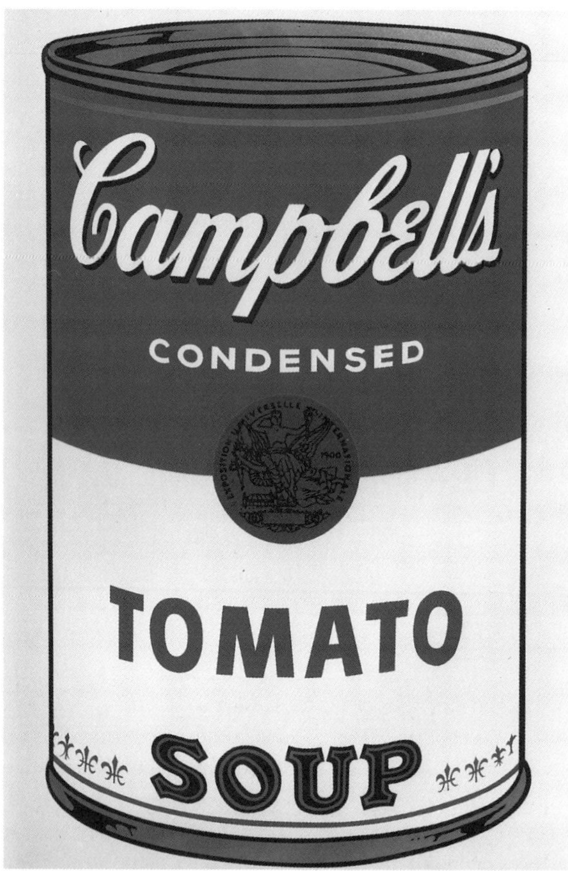

Tomato, 1968, from the portfolio *Campbell's Soup* by Andy Warhol (1925–87). Colour screenprint. Sheet: 35 × 23 in. (89.1 × 58.6 cm). Image: $31\frac{7}{8}$ × $8\frac{7}{8}$ in. (81 × 47.9 cm). Frame: 37 × 25 × $1\frac{1}{2}$ in. (94 × 63.5 × 3.8 cm). Purchase, with funds from the Friends of the Whitney Museum of American Art.
Whitney Museum of American Art, New York.

Jackson Pollock achieved as an art celebrity in the popular journals, and therefore orchestrated for himself a public life akin to that of a movie star seen at all the "right" parties and openings (Warhol and Hackett, 1983). If Americans viewed his art with suspicion and stood convinced that he was exploiting the galleries, museums, and collectors, that was, in the end, acceptable. It made Warhol one of the people, and they smiled while he took the money from the rich, from the fools who praised the emperor's new clothes.

What ties the work of Warhol to that of Stella and Judd is first of all the objective approach and secondly the need for an art context. The paintings of readymade images and machinelike reality were appropriated from mass culture and produced by commercial silk-screening techniques.

These depersonalized works needed to be removed from the commercial world in order to convey their full impact. It was in that white-walled haven for art exhibition that Campbell's soup cans became art.

The literal qualities shared by Pop Art, Minimalism and the "new" geometric painting caused this art to require a segregated space, away from the urban environment that produced it.

> The ideal gallery subtracts from the art work all cues that interfere with the fact that it is "art". The work is isolated from everything that would detract from its own evaluation of itself. This gives the space a presence possessed by other spaces where conventions are preserved through the repetition of a closed system of values. Some of the sanctity of the church, the formality of the courtroom, the mystique of the experimental laboratory joins with chic design to produce a unique chamber of aesthetics. So powerful are the perceptual fields of force within this chamber that, once outside it, art can lapse into secular status. (O'Doherty, 1986: 14)

Minimalism, Pop Art, and Sixties geometric painting were vulnerable to a decline to worldly or secular status once removed from the gallery space because of the literal qualities they shared. In the case of Pop Art the imagery was literally that of the world of commerce and advertising. Geometric painting addressed the literal qualities of abstraction. Stella's

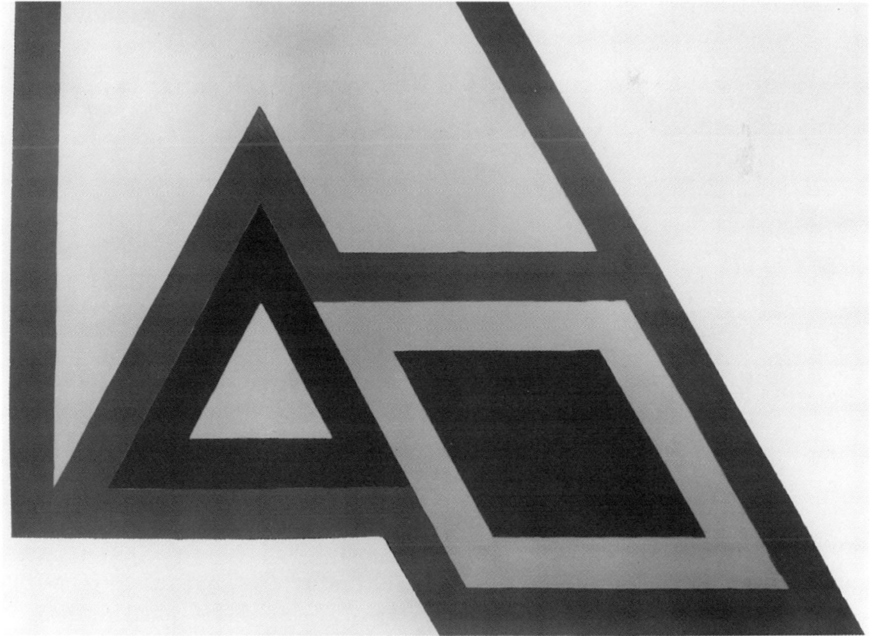

Sanbornville III, 1966, from the *Irregular Polygon Series* by Frank Stella (b. 1936). Fluorescent alkyd and epoxy paint on canvas, 104 × 146 in. (264.2 × 370.8 cm). Gift of Joseph A. Helman, New York.
Collection of Whitney Museum of American Art, New York.

shaped canvases (*Sanbornville III*, 1966, fluorescent alkyd and epoxy paint, Collection of The Whitney Museum of American Art) bent or cut the painting's edge according to the internal logic of the composition, making the viewer keenly aware of the painting as a real object with no illusion of space or depth. Minimalist sculpture was exactly what it appeared to be and made no reference to anything outside itself. Judd's aluminum cubes were actual aluminum cubes, containing no illusion or metaphor. Placed in a secular environment they would easily have been absorbed by that world.

Conclusion

So it would be that the art propagated by modernism would require a museum designed by modernists. The philosophy of modernism produced, in high art, work that was visually difficult, intellectually demanding, and, for the general public, inaccessible. That same philosophy, when applied to solving the problems of exhibiting this art, found solutions that aided the population. The same demands of truth and pragmatism that removed the art from the public realm provided, when applied to architecture and design, democratic solutions. In other words, while modern art was elitist, modern architecture was really democratic. Modernist architecture and design as it was applied to the American art museum was meant to provide a setting for the art and to provide a practical, systematic, instructional space that would, according to Bauhaus law, fulfill its function. (For the development of the first Museum of Modern Art building, see "Barr as modernist" in Chapter 8.)

The result was a building that considered practical issues such as traffic flow and lighting; considered human requirements such as restaurants and rest rooms; considered what had become the principal concern, the principal function of the American art museum: the education of the masses. Modernism's architects, teachers, and artists, through an analysis of form, material, and structure, had altered the art America produced and altered also the context in which it was viewed.

The exhibitions of modernist art strove to be informative and interesting and were frequently coupled with publications explaining the work and its historical precedents (for example, see "Barr as populist" in Chapter 8). Designers tried to attract and hold the attention of the general public through the pre-exhibition publicity as well as the actual installation. The museum hoped to sustain that interest by way of related lectures and tours and related publications available in the museum shop. (See also "Barr as capitalist" in Chapter 8.) They also hoped to sustain the visit by supplying the comforts afforded by restaurants and members' lounges. All this grew from the conviction that the art museum was not intended for the few but for the enlightenment and education of the masses.

In America, where democratic ideals were held high and education was not only every person's right but also a necessity for the country's cultural and technological advance, the potential of the museum as a center for the enlightenment of the general public was being recognized. The American art museum began to adopt service to the broad community as a goal, and modernist design could provide a logical, instructional focus for the entry of the public into the esoteric world of modern art.

Edward Larrabee Barnes, the architect of numerous American art museums including the Carnegie Institute in Pittsburgh and the Dallas Museum of Fine Arts, spoke to this issue as he discussed his design for the Walker Art Center in Minneapolis:

> The problem in museum design, I feel, is to focus on the art, and on the way people go through the museum, and not on making an architectural monument ... I was dedicated to the idea of anonymous white spaces ... The question was how to arrange these spaces so that the galleries themselves could become a procession. Usually you think of museums like the Metropolitan, with an enormous Grand Central Station hall, with no art in it—a sort of stage for pomp and circumstance—and then galleries beyond it. At the Walker, you are immediately caught up in a succession of white rooms ... The idea is to get people involved immediately with whatever the museum has ... Once in the building, you're immediately caught up in it, and are thinking of the art ...
>
> I feel very definitely that the rooms themselves have to represent calm, well-proportioned spaces. The sequence and the sense of flow must work, and the way you move through it must be graceful. I think it's a very difficult thing to explain how you can do architecture with a strong central idea, with just as self-centered an idea as any building, and at the same time have that idea opt for this function of bringing out these various shows which go through it. It's not just an anonymous building ...
>
> (Diamonstein, 1980: 17–18)

In conclusion, we see that the modern art museum and the modern art object came to exist in a symbiotic relationship. Most of American modernist art is dependent on the context of the gallery space to fully realize its meaning. Growing out of the philosophies of European Surrealism and the German Bauhaus, much of the art produced since World War II required the viewer to possess information about psychology, mythology, art history, and a specific knowledge of visual language. Because of its literal quality, its reductive tendencies, and its basic abstract nature, it also required the modern gallery space for exhibition. The exhibition space as designed by the modern architect is, in turn, dependent on the art to fulfill its function. The modern art museum cannot stand like a palace of culture, aloof and passive, but rather is charged with a very specific task. The modern art museum in a democratic society is charged with the pragmatic presentation of the enigmatic object.

6

Art for the masses: a study of educational practices in American art museums

Most of what is shown in any museum is incomprehensible and uninteresting to most of its visitors ... A museum that will truly unlock its treasure to the world must maintain in its service ... men who have studied its possessions sufficiently exactly and deeply to have laid hold of the recognized reward of all study of art—the full pure enjoyment of the individual work ...
Benjamin Ives Gilman, *Museum Ideals of Purpose and Method*

Introduction

Education, as viewed by Americans, is a pillar of democracy, the means to opportunity and advancement for the general population, advancement on intellectual, economic, and social levels. American museums have long been involved in educational pursuits, and many were established with the education of the public as a main mission. (For the historical overview, see Chapter 2.) Art museums in particular were viewed as a means to better citizens: uplifting morals, communicating history, and teaching aesthetics. Key people in key museums wrote and taught their ideas regarding the educational mission of American art museums. John Cotton Dana, director of the Newark Museum in New Jersey from 1909 to 1929, was a firm believer in the museum as an institution of learning, an institution with exhibits and programs made available to all the people. His ideas were widely published, studied, and practiced (Alexander, 1983: 379–406). Benjamin Ives Gilman is generally considered to have invented the gallery talk at the Museum of Fine Arts in Boston, a method now standard in art museums (Gilman, 1918: 312). Thomas Munro, Curator of Education at the Cleveland Museum of Art during the 1930s, 1940s, and 1950s, conducted research regarding learning in museums and was known for his concern for teaching the general population while maintaining high standards (Munro, 1940: 18–19).

Whether by chance or by design, American art museums took the lead in educational theory and techniques (Wittlin, 1970: 150–1). Whole departments for education sprang up in museums across the country.

Perhaps more than any other internal force in museum administration, the growth of educational programming reflected the democratic concerns of the museum staff. Education was seen as necessary for the fulfillment of the art museum's democratic mission. As a way to understand the role of education in the art museum in the American democratic culture, we will look first to the general art museum and then examine one educational program for modern art.

We will begin with a brief history of education at the Cleveland Museum, considered a pioneer in this field, and then look to a recent survey of four general art museums in the North-East. The comparative survey includes a questionnaire, site visits, interviews, and a review of museum records, including budgets. Education at the general art museum can then be compared to education at the modern art museum by a close look at one contemporary art exhibition at New York's Museum of Modern Art and the educational effort which accompanied it.

Model: the Cleveland Museum

The Cleveland Museum of Art has long been recognized for its educational programs, which are considered a benchmark for American art museums. From the time of its founding in 1916, the Cleveland Museum, reviewing the art of all ages and cultures, had an educational department and a method for reaching the community (Munro, 1940: 2–7).

The collections of the Cleveland Museum include one of the finest oriental collections in the Western world; a medieval collection that ranks with the leading museums of Germany, France, and England; an excellent assemblage of European and American paintings from the Middle Ages to the present, including outstanding collections of Renaissance, Baroque, and seventeenth-century Dutch painting, nineteenth-century American landscape, and Impressionist and Post-Impressionist works.

Today the Cleveland Museum offers studio and art history classes for young people and adults, and lectures for the public by museum curators and visiting scholars. The museum also offers advanced placement courses to Cleveland area high school students and, in conjunction with Case Western Reserve University, undergraduate and graduate courses in art history. (Unless otherwise noted, all data is compiled from the Cleveland Museum *Bulletin* and *Financial Reports*.) All of this is in addition to the regularly scheduled gallery talks and tours. The museum also publishes many books and catalogs, slides and reproductions. The scholarly *Bulletin* was published ten times a year up to January of 1995. It has been replaced by the Members Magazine plus an annual scholarly journal, *Cleveland Studies in the History of Art*.

The Cleveland Museum set down a plan of action beginning with the children and moving on to various educational levels (secondary school, university, graduate) and to adults seeking a serious study of art or a casual "cultural experience."

In a 1952 publication on the museum's educational programs, Thomas Munro, then Curator of Education, wrote:

> The department of education is charged with carrying on a complex program of instruction and guidance throughout the year. This includes work with children and adults; with schools, organized groups, and individuals. Some of it is on a popular, elementary level, to convey the fundamentals of art appreciation to a large public; some is on a level of more advanced study, research, and scholarship through post-graduate courses and publication. A constant effort is made to preserve high standards, even while reaching a large audience, and thus to show that mass education does not have to involve a lowering of quality.
>
> (Munro, 1952: 5)

The museum's conscious desire to make art available to a large public, and its concrete commitment to this principle through the development of programs early on, resulted in a highly developed education department by 1952, including 23 full-time staff members, 30 part-time, and eleven volunteers (Munro, 1952: 73, 74).

It is important to note that the education department was aware, from the very beginning, of the possible pitfalls inherent in a program geared toward a wide and diverse audience. The danger in developing a program so democratic in its scope was that the content would be reduced to the lowest common denominator. One way Thomas Munro found to help insure a maintenance of high standards was the two-track system of the popular program (the fundamentals of art appreciation) and the scholarly program (advanced research and publication) (Munro, 1952: 33–4). This was based on the belief, or at least the hope, that the staff would constantly be reminded of the true mission of the education department, which was to educate, not entertain, the public and always strive to raise the level of understanding of art.

Munro acknowledged that a visit to the Cleveland Museum was, for most people, a "leisure activity," but one, he maintained, which could be rendered permanently valuable.

> In learning to perceive a great variety of complex forms and subtle qualities of line, shape, and color, one acquires visual powers which carry over into daily life. They intensify awareness and enjoyment, not only of art itself, but of nature and of life. (Munro, 1952: 8)

And on a broader historical note he added:

> A study of the visual arts contributes greatly to the general education of the student. They are one of our principal means of understanding the civilizations of the past and the cultural trends of our own day. It is well known that art expresses its age as well as the personality of the individual artist. But it is not an easy task to interpret the different attitudes, beliefs, and interests which are thus expressed—those, for example, which distinguish the Greek or Chinese culture from our own.
>
> (Munro, 1952: 8)

The task of interpretation would be aided by the education department because, as Munro pointed out, the casual observer could not grasp the complex, subtle, or deeper meanings of art without guidance.

Track two, the scholarship within the museum, mainly involved the curatorial staff. According to Munro's plan the curators and librarians would communicate their knowledge and judgement to the education department, which would, in turn, communicate with the public. The curatorial research might also result in publications which would reach a wide audience.

In addition to this, the Cleveland Museum established a relationship with Case Western Reserve University and its art department which allowed for university students to conduct research within the museum and provided classrooms for courses conducted by the university. Also, some members of the museum staff served as members of the university faculty. Munro urged the further development of joint publications on art: "through articles, monographs, and books of discussion and scholarship on the highest level, of a permanent value commensurate with that of the museum's tangible possessions" (1952: 16).

Another noteworthy development was the affiliation at that time of the *Journal of Aesthetics and Art Criticism* with the Cleveland Museum. Although the publication was owned by the American Society for Aesthetics, and the museum had no legal or financial connection to the publisher, the journal was edited at the museum.

All of this, plus a flow of visiting scholars invited to use the collections in research and present their findings in public lectures, contributed to the image of an institution filled with great cultural wealth in the form of objects and knowledge. Combined with the more popular programs of the education department, the image of the Cleveland Museum was that of a dynamic and beneficial agency in the cultural life of the community, reaching out to provide understanding and enjoyment of the permanent collections and special exhibitions (Lee, 1983: 110).

The Cleveland Museum's reputation as a leader in art museum education was founded on a strong philosophical base and implemented by a large staff whose programs were generously funded. The Cleveland Museum recognized the importance of education from the beginning, articulated it better than any other museum by mid-century, and thus became the benchmark by which other programs might be measured. With this brief history in mind, let us now consider current educational efforts at other art museums.

Education in the general art museum: a comparative survey

Four general art museums located in the North-East were surveyed in an effort to determine the developments in public education programs over a 25-year period, including the relationship between these programs and the size of museum staff and budget. The Worcester Art Museum in

Worcester, Massachusetts; the Philadelphia Museum of Art; the Herbert F. Johnson Museum of Art at Cornell University in Ithaca, New York; and the Whitney Museum of American Art in New York City were selected to represent a broad range in size, staff, holdings, budget, and public served.

The survey commenced with a questionnaire mailed in January, 1990. This was followed by site visits, a review of budgets, and interviews.

Worcester Art Museum, the collections of which span 50 centuries of art, was incorporated in 1896 as a private nonprofit institution. Egyptian, classical, Far-Eastern, and Renaissance art are represented. European paintings range from fourteenth-century Italian to seventeenth-century Dutch and twentieth-century Cubism. There are pre-Columbian art and American paintings and a substantial collection of Japanese prints. The collection of contemporary works of art is growing steadily.

In 1970, a major addition to the museum, the Higgins Education Wing, was built to house studios for students of all ages. The school also offers classes for college credit in conjunction with the Quinsigamond Community College, the Massachusetts College of Art, and the College of Professional and Continuing Education at Clark University. Another addition provided 20,000 square feet of space for the museum. Between 1970 and 1990 the museum staff grew from 66 to 135 (full- and part-time). The museum reported in the questionnaire 25 full-time employees holding B.A. degrees, eight with M.A. degrees, and three with Ph.D. degrees. Personnel are reported to belong to all professional organizations, to attend professional conferences, and to continue professional training through workshops and courses since, as the then Deputy Director commented in the questionnaire, the museum "continues to provide and maintain a commitment to professionalism."

One striking statistic at the Worcester Art Museum is the dramatic increase in volunteers (Table 6.1). The museum reported a volunteer force of 175 in 1970 and 500 in 1990, an increase of 188 percent. The museum budget leaped from $677,850 in 1970 to $4 million in 1990, approaching $6 million in 1995. With the increase in staff, space, volunteers and budget, it is surprising to note the decrease in the public served (Table 6.2). Attendance declined from 150,000 in 1970, to 120,000 in 1980, and to 110,000 in 1990. This situation may be the result of shifting demographics since, as we shall see, the museum is making a serious effort to "diversify" its audience. While much of the budget, space, and staff increases go toward the support of the museum school, the volunteer force is within the museum itself. The museum now has an outreach program servicing local schools which is largely volunteer and also offers more tours of the museum guided by volunteers. While the number of tours increased, however, the total number of people remained substantially the same. In other words, the tours contained fewer participants. For example, the number of school groups increased 152 percent from 254 in 1970 to 640 in 1990, but the number of schoolchildren serviced within those groups

Table 6.1 *Museum survey: comparative growth patterns in budget and staff, 1970—1980—1990*

	1970	1980	1990
Worcester Art Museum			
Budget	$677,850	$1,356,000	$4 million
Staff (Full/Part-Time)	66	102	135
Volunteers	175	N/A	500
Philadelphia Museum			
Budget	$3.3 million	$7 million	$16 million
Staff (Full/Part-Time)	N/A	181	211
Volunteers	150	180	410
Whitney Museum			
Budget	$1,377,392	$4,868,512	$11,087,102
Staff (Full/Part-Time)	114	135	179
Volunteers	N/A	39	81
Herbert F. Johnson Museum			
Budget	$300,000	$750,000	$1.5 million
Staff (Full/Part-Time)	22	45	41
Volunteers	0	1	2

Table 6.2 *Museum survey: comparative growth patterns in exhibition space, budget, attendance 1970—1980—1990*

	1970	**1980**	**1990**
Worcester Art Museum			
Space	70,000 sq.ft.	70,000 sq.ft.	90,000 sq.ft.
Budget	$677,850	$1.3 million	$4 million
Attendance	150,000	120,000	110,000
Philadelphia Museum			
Space	259,000 sq.ft.	268,000 sq.ft.	268,000 sq.ft.
Budget	$3.3 million	$7 million	$16 million
Attendance	783,562*	405,691	667,997
Whitney Museum		23,100 + 5,000	23,100 + 19,100
Space	23,100 sq.ft	(branch)	(4 branches)
Budget	$1.4 million	$4.9 million	$11 million
Attendance	N/A	514,413	983,997
Herbert F. Johnson Museum			
Space	N/A	22,000 sq.ft.	22,000 sq.ft.
Budget	$300,000	$750,000	$1.5 million
Attendance	23,757	80,086	77,656

*This figure reflects attendance at the Van Gogh exhibition: 410,000 visitors, the highest attendance ever recorded.

increased by less than 2,000 over the same period, just 2 percent of the total attendance. The number of adult groups being served increased by 138 percent, going from 99 groups in 1970 to 236 groups in 1990, but the actual number of individuals in those groups increased by less than 700.

In 1994, Worcester Art Museum received the largest grant in the history of the museum: $1.36 million from the Lila Wallace—Reader's Digest Fund for the support of an education project aimed at increasing and diversifying their audience. The "Art of Discovery" project was designed to achieve a "more effective orientation (to the museum) and interpretation (of its collections) created for and with input from a broad group of participants," specifically the ethnically diverse lower-income urbanites and the economically diverse suburban population.

The museum chose its Greek and Roman collections for the project and is focusing on the everyday cultural lifestyles of the period. The program includes collaborations with public schools and special lectures for individuals.

At the same time, the museum's 1995-adopted long-range plan includes the goal of 200,000 visitors by the year 2000. In pursuit of this goal the museum has introduced programs targeted at specific ethnic groups, (e.g. the Puerto Rican Film Festival) launched exhibitions such as "Heritage of the Land" (the art and culture of native Americans) and "Mexico: A Landscape Revisited" (in which the wall labels were bilingual); and established a Diversity Committee composed of representatives from the museum and the community. This committee, according to Museum Director James A. Welu, "is charged with helping our institution achieve diversity among its staff, governing board, programming and audience. In addition, Museum staff and volunteers will participate in diversity awareness training in order to become better informed about potential biases concerning gender, race, ethnicity, disabilities and other issues" (Welu, 1995: 2).

Another dramatic increase in the number of volunteers occurred at the Philadelphia Museum of Art. Like Worcester, the Philadelphia Museum's treasures come from all parts of the world and range in time from the first century to the twentieth. Its collections of Far-Eastern and Italian Renaissance art are particularly strong. Medieval European art occupies the second floor, and there is an Armory of fifteenth- and sixteenth-century German, Italian, and English arms and armor. The museum is rich in modern works, thanks in part to the Arensberg collection, which includes the largest group of Brancusi sculpture in America, and galleries of master works by Marcel Duchamp. Philadelphia is a large museum with 250,000 square feet and a 1990 budget of $16 million, up from $3.3 million in 1970. The 1995 budget approached $25 million, a $5 million increase over 1994 due to the exhibition "From Cézanne to Matisse: Great French Paintings from the Barnes Foundation." Philadelphia's exhibition space, personnel, and annual attendance figures reflect a slow, steady growth over the twenty years from 1970 to 1990 as might be expected.

The extreme increase in the 1990 budget should therefore be explained. In 1986, the Philadelphia Museum undertook a major capital campaign, the Landmark Renewal Fund, with the ambitious goal of raising $50 million in private support over a five-year period. Of this amount, $30 million will be allocated for endowment, to build a capital base capable of generating income for operations. Another $15 million will go toward building repairs and improvements, and the remaining $5 million will assist with "increasing operating costs during the campaign period." In other words, it costs money to raise money. A review of the *Annual Report* shows increases in gifts, endowment and trust fund income and an increase in revenue from the sale of art objects amounting to $1,393,928 in 1989 over the $47,496 gained two years earlier.

The dramatic increase in volunteers at Philadelphia can be compared to Worcester (Table 6.1) and, as at Worcester, these new forces are used in educational programs. The number of volunteers is recorded as 150 in 1970, 180 in 1980, then more than doubling to 410 by 1990. This dramatic increase of 173 percent is comparable to Worcester's 188 percent increase between 1970 and 1990. And, as at Worcester, the volunteer force provides lectures and tours of museum exhibits. Over the twenty-year period examined, lectures increased 900 percent, tours increased 79 percent. Also, as at Worcester, the number of individuals being served is not in proportion to the phenomenal increase in lectures and tours (Table 6.2). The Philadelphia Museum reports the number of individuals being served by these services as increasing from 8,181 in 1970 to 9,680 in 1990. The numbers reported by both the Worcester Museum and the Philadelphia Museum indicate more and more volunteers presenting more and more lectures and tours for basically the same size audience. This curious development will be further addressed later.

These two museums, Philadelphia and Worcester, can be seen in sharp contrast to two other large museums in the North-East, the Whitney Museum of American Art in New York City and the Herbert F. Johnson Museum of Art at Cornell University in Ithaca, New York.

The Herbert F. Johnson Museum recorded in the 1990 survey only two volunteers assisting a paid staff of 41 (Table 6.1). Shortly after the survey was conducted, the museum initiated a volunteer docent program and, as we shall see later, greatly expanded its educational offerings. To begin the program review, we will consider the 1970 to 1990 period and then examine the more recent developments.

The museum, named after its prime supporter Herbert Johnson of Johnson's Wax, was designed by I. M. Pei and is a bold construction of rectangular forms built high on a rise with spectacular views of Lake Cayuga. The poured concrete building houses a broad collection particularly strong in nineteenth- and twentieth-century American painting, and Asian ceramics from China, Japan, Korea, and Southeast Asia. The museum exists primarily as a cultural resource for the Cornell University students but does offer lectures and tours for visitors from the community. These were limited between 1970 and 1990, as one might expect, knowing there was virtually no use of volunteers. The lack of a volunteer force should be viewed as a significant indicator because, as we have seen at both Philadelphia and Worcester, volunteers are often synonymous with educational programs.

Educational programs at Cornell's museum during this period were in the hands of the professional staff, and traditionally the university museum staff's main focus has been on research. The museum is, however, a cultural center for Ithaca, an upper New York State town containing no other art museum and with no art resources in the greater region. The annual attendance at the Johnson Museum was reported at a healthy 77,656 for the 1989–90 season (Table 6.2). The 1994–95 *Annual Report* notes attendance at 74,000 which, although down from the 1980 and 1990 numbers was, according to Director Franklin Robinson, up 10 percent from the previous year. The introduction, therefore, in 1991 of a docent program has had no major impact on attendance figures.

The Whitney Museum of American Art is comparable in size, at 23,100 square feet, to the Herbert F. Johnson Museum of 22,000 square feet. Designed by the renowned Bauhaus architect, Marcel Breuer, the Whitney is located on a prime corner in Manhattan, Madison Avenue at 75th Street. One should not be deceived by its diminutive size, for the Whitney Museum has been a powerhouse of influence on and beyond the world of American art. Although its physical size is comparable to the Herbert F. Johnson Museum, its 1990 budget was almost ten times that museum's amount. Compared to the Philadelphia Museum, the Whitney building is less than 10 percent the size of Philadelphia, but its 1990 budget was 67 percent that of Philadelphia and its staff was almost 75 percent of the number of personnel at Philadelphia (Table 6.2).

The Whitney was founded in 1930 by Gertrude Vanderbilt Whitney, the daughter of the railroad magnate Cornelius Vanderbilt. It has been at its present location since 1966. Dedicated to American art of all periods and in all media, the Whitney has paid special attention to contemporary American art as its Biennial Exhibition and Lobby Gallery shows attest. It also runs an active film and video program.

As a way of expanding its exhibitions and influence, the Whitney, during the decade of the 1980s, moved beyond the museum walls to "branch" museums set up in the lobbies of corporations. Since 1990, major changes have occurred in both staffing and programs at the Whitney. These will be reviewed in Chapter 7 as we address the role of the corporation in the American museum. For now we will focus on the period from 1970 to 1990.

The Whitney Museum established the first corporate branch by 1980, and by 1990 the museum could boast four branches funded by corporations for a total of 19,100 additional square feet: the Whitney Downtown at Federal Reserve Plaza (funded by IBM and Park Tower Realty); the Whitney at Equitable Center (funded by Equitable Insurance

Co.); the Whitney at Philip Morris (funded by Philip Morris); the Whitney at Fairfield (headquarters of Champion International).

These four branches, while expanding the exhibition space by 19,100 square feet, resulted in a meager show of increase in personnel, from 135 in 1980 to 140 in 1990 (Table 6.1). This is explained in part by the fact that the corporations supplied the maintenance and security for these spaces, and also by the museum's use of graduate student interns in curatorial roles. It should also be noted here that the educational programs at the branch museum sites were not comparable to the usual museum offerings.

The Whitney Downtown, for example, provided a gallery talk only on Monday, Wednesday, and Friday at 12:30. The same was true of the Whitney Museum at Philip Morris, which presented changing exhibits in both its indoor sculpture court and adjacent gallery, and the Whitney in Fairfield County, which also presented changing exhibits. The Whitney Museum at Equitable Center consisted of two galleries, one for long-term installations of works from the permanent collection, the other for temporary exhibits. Equitable offered a gallery talk each weekday at 12:30. All four branches, with their midday lectures, appeared to be providing a service for the host corporation employees rather than an aggressive outreach program to educate the community.

As a means of surveying the educational relationships of art museums to their public and assessing the meaning and motivation of such relationships, two indicators have been identified. The first indicator is the number of people served by a museum. Is the museum fulfilling its democratic mission to provide educational opportunities to the general population? The second indicator is the number and role of the volunteers in the museum because the strength of the volunteer staff is often indicative of the breadth of the educational program.

The research conducted in the four museums profiled indicated a steady attendance or a slight increase in attendance in three of the four museums between 1970 and 1990. Only the Whitney Museum indicated a dramatic increase in attendance, (from about one-half million visitors to almost one million visitors per year over a ten-year period) and this was clearly due to the development of four branch museums housed at four corporate sites. What is of importance, or at least interest, is the unprecedented increase in educational program offerings at both the Worcester Museum and the Philadelphia Museum. While Philadelphia reported a 75 percent increase in tours, and Worcester reported more than doubling its number from 353 tours to 876, neither museum showed a comparable increase in the number of visitors served. So while the research showed increases in the museums' budgets, staff, and educational programs, no remarkable increase in the number of public served by these programs can be documented.

The second indicator selected is the number of volunteers. Volunteers are traditionally employed within educational programs and, in fact, the numbers cited here reflect increases in educational staff. Of the four museums profiled in this report, two were using volunteer docents extensively. Philadelphia and Worcester reported increases by 173 percent and 188 percent respectively in the number of volunteers over a twenty-year period (1970–90). These figures reflect the increase in programs, lectures, and tours, while underscoring the question of numbers of visitors served. What we see connected to the increase in volunteer and paid staff is a growth in educational programs, and in overall operating budget.

The prime motive for educational programming must be viewed as a didactic, democratic impulse set in motion by the museum's mission. It seems evident, however, that there are at least two ulterior motives for museums' educational programs. The first is the relationship between educational programs and admission charges for a museum.

The Philadelphia, Whitney, and Worcester Museums each have an extensive volunteer educational staff and also charge admission. In all three cases, a substantial percentage (usually 25 percent) of the museum's operating budget comes from admission charges and educational programs. The Johnson Museum at Cornell University is not dependent on admission fees (there is no charge for admission) and only recently began to develop a volunteer staff, and outreach programs. The implication here is that educational programs help to establish a relationship between the museum and the visitor, and that the growing importance of that relationship to the budget may increase the museum's need for educational programs. It is in the interest of the Philadelphia, Worcester, and Whitney Museums to draw visitors and to try to encourage return visits. Their budgets require this. The university museum traditionally has had a different priority (Table 6.3).

Table 6.3 *Museum survey: comparison of income from admission; percentage of volunteer staff (1990)*

	Percentage of budget from admission	Percentage of volunteers within total staff
Worcester Art Museum	Approximately 25%	89.2%
Philadelphia Museum	Approximately 25%	66%
Whitney Museum	Approximately 25%	31.1%
Herbert F. Johnson Museum	0%	4.6%

One additional note is that five other university museums were surveyed, and each of these reported few volunteers, feeble educational endeavors, and budgets not dependent on earned income. University museums, generally subsidized by the university, exist for the cultural enrichment of their students and as a teaching resource for the faculty. In a sense, they are a single track in the Cleveland two-track system. They provide a place for scholarship but have little need to appeal to a broad population.

Another indication that there is a relationship between educational programs and admission charges can be found in a comparison between the Whitney Museum and both Philadelphia and Worcester Museums. The fact that the educational programs at the Whitney Museum branches were so limited may be because those branches were underwritten by the corporations and did not charge for admission. As with the university museums, there is no incentive for drawing large crowds nor for cultivating a steady audience.

The second ulterior motive for the development of a museum's educational program is the involvement of the volunteers. We can look at the volunteer as being an individual interested in the museum and knowledgeable about art, who donates a few hours each week in service to the museum. The volunteer might also be a huge multinational corporation donating money and services to the museum for a complex set of reasons ranging from a desire to improve the corporate image in the community, to the fulfillment of a plan for investment in a corporate art collection.

Individuals who volunteer in art museums proceed through a comprehensive training program that includes research, reading, lectures, discussions, and hours of observation of practicing docents. All this is no doubt preceded by several months, or perhaps years, on a waiting list. Upon completion of the training program, a docent must usually commit to at least two hours' service per week for a minimum of two years. Since money is not an incentive, these people are clearly dedicated to art and to the museum. (Part of the incentive also is the status attached to the art museum.)

A typical profile of the individual who volunteers in the art museum reveals a white female, well-educated, and wealthy, with a broad circle of friends within the same affluent class structure. It is possible that the volunteer's sphere of influence is as valuable as her contributions of time and money.

If we consider the corporation as volunteer, we may recognize that it too has a sphere of influence. The corporation's role will be examined more thoroughly in Chapter 7, but let us note here the corporate relationship to the Whitney Museum. The Whitney Museum was limited to 23,100 square feet and an annual attendance of 514,413 people in 1980. The size of the building precluded any substantial increase in attendance. When the corporations volunteered their 19,100 square feet for Whitney Museum exhibits, they also volunteered their sphere of influence and immediately doubled annual attendance figures.

What this study, limited though it is, indicates is that a museum's educational outreach may be dictated by the financial needs of the institution. Those needs are satisfied in part by the hundreds of thousands of $7.00 admission charges collected from individuals, itself an argument for the democratization of the art museum. The survey also poses the possibility that art museums may reach a visitor saturation point, in particular those museums not situated in major tourist centers. The increase in volunteers and programs serving basically the same visitor pool will no doubt result in a very well informed audience for art. But museums should be wary of the expansion of exhibits and programs for the purpose of enlarging their audience.

The museums surveyed, all general art museums, have educational programs which are also general and follow the traditions established by leaders in the field, such as the Cleveland Museum. Methods for teaching art history, art techniques, and interpretation, were tried and agreed upon over the years. Modern art, however, posed a different set of problems, and the nation's premier modern art museum would face the challenge of how to lead a nation to an understanding of and appreciation for the new art forms.

Education in the Museum of Modern Art

Modern art in the modern art museum: art without recognizable imagery or with imagery distorted; art inspired by mythology or psychology and dependent on a knowledge of the field of inspiration for full understanding; art resulting from process and demanding knowledge of the elements of visual language for comprehension. (The development of American modern art is examined in Chapter 5.) Modern art in the modern art museum is not democratic. It requires the viewer to be intellectually, sensually, and emotionally cognizant of visual language, information the average person does not possess. Americans were faced with this new art form, with unrecognizable images executed in a fashion that held no relation to ordinary experience, and the response was generally negative. This was the challenge faced by the new art museum, the Museum of Modern Art.

When The Museum of Modern Art opened its doors in 1929, the established American art museums rarely showed any late-nineteenth- or twentieth-century art. As Paul J. Sachs observed: "We were all, as a matter of course, reading modern literature; we were listening to modern music; but in spite of the excitement engendered by the Armory Show of 1913, our country was, on the whole, antagonistic to modern art" (Sachs, 1954: 27). As a matter of fact, at this time not one museum in the City of New York owned a single canvas by Van Gogh, Gauguin, Picasso, Miro, or Klee.

The Museum of Modern Art was chartered "for the purpose of encouraging and developing the study of modern arts," so its educational purpose was established at the outset. Exactly how the study of modern art would be conducted resulted in a course quite different from that of the Cleveland Museum, a course set down by the Modern's first director, Alfred H. Barr, Jr. (see Chapter 8, "Alfred H. Barr, Founding Director").

As an undergraduate at Princeton University, Alfred Barr studied with Charles Rufus Morey, who taught medieval visual arts as a record of that civilization, combining painting and sculpture with architecture, murals, illuminated manuscripts, and crafts. Barr used Morey's idea as a model when he developed, at Wellesley College, the first undergraduate course in modern art offered in American higher education. The course included painting and sculpture and also architecture, film, photography, industrial design, music and theater. This concept was reinforced by a visit to the Bauhaus at Dessau, Germany, where Barr discovered "a fabulous institution ... painting, graphic arts, architecture, the crafts, typography, theater, cinema, photography, industrial design for mass production ... all were studied and taught together in a large new modern building" (quoted in Hunter, 1984: 11).

Upon his acceptance of the directorship of the Modern, Barr proposed the museum be organized according to a multidepartmental plan based on his Wellesley course in modern art. It was a radical plan, for it included, not just the fine arts, but the practical, commercial, and popular arts as well. The fine arts, of course, would lead the way, and the museum opened with an exhibition of paintings by the modern masters Cézanne, Gauguin, Seurat, and Van Gogh. The show was accompanied by a catalog which marked the beginning of the Museum's publication program, a program envisioned as a way to spread the modernist message (see Chapter 8, "Barr as populist").

Barr moved on the implementation of the departmental plan and established the Department of Architecture in 1932 with the exhibition "Modern Architecture: International Exhibition" curated by Henry-Russell Hitchcock and Philip Johnson. There was also established at this time a Department of Circulating Exhibitions, and the international architecture show traveled throughout the United States.

In 1934, the "Machine Art" show initiated the Design Collection, and in 1935 the Film Library was established, the first department in any museum in the world devoted to this twentieth-century art form. The Department of Photography was founded in 1940, the first curatorial department dedicated to photography. The Museum of Modern Art was the first museum to present photography as art when, in 1932, it presented the exhibition called "Murals by American Painters and Photographers." It was also the Museum of Modern Art which organized the first comprehensive photography exhibition in 1937 called "Photography 1839–1937."

So, in a little more than a decade after its founding, the Museum of Modern Art had reached the goal of being a multidepartmental arts museum. As the critic John Russell described it:

> The Museum of Modern Art covers not only painting and drawings, but photography, prints and drawings, architecture, design, the decorative arts, typography, stage design, and artists' books. It has its own publishing house, its own movie house, and its own department of film and video. It has a shop in which everyday objects of every kind may be on sale, provided they pass the Museum's standard of design. It is a palace of pleasure, but it

> is also an unstructured university. You don't get grades for going there, but in a mysterious, unquantifiable way, you become alert to the energies of modern art. (Quoted in Hunter, 1984: 11)

The structure Alfred Barr had devised for the museum fostered education by its very nature, it was part school and part entertainment. People would visit to study architecture and then look at paintings; stop to examine a toaster design and stay for a film preview. Somehow the magic combination worked to draw the public in, and Barr worked to keep them intrigued. In museum publications he talked to them about modern paintings sometimes considered "puzzling, difficult, incompetent or crazy." He expressed his intention, through these printed materials, to "undermine prejudice, disturb indifference and awaken interest so that some greater understanding and love of the more adventurous paintings of our time may follow" (Barr, 1943: 2).

Barr's methods for converting the skeptics included a catalog published in 1932 called *A Brief Survey of Modern Painting*. While it may have been written for people who had little experience looking at paintings, especially modern paintings, it was appreciated also by the more sophisticated museum visitors. Barr took the reader from familiar, recognizable imagery to more abstract paintings, all the while suggesting meanings and emotions which might be attached to the work. The catalog was clear, concise, to the point, and, as Barr called it, "propaganda in the original and best sense of the word" (Marquis, 1989: 216).

This little booklet was considered by many to be the most important tract for modern art ever written. Up to this point, no one in the museums or in education had considered converting the masses to modern art. The huge new audience was touched by Alfred Barr's simple but persuasive prose. In explaining the paintings of Manet ("pronounced 'Manay'") Barr wrote: "He tried to simplify what he saw so that one, large, flat brush stroke might do the work of five. This made the public of the 1860's laugh at his work which they disliked because . . . he didn't paint in every detail" (Barr, 1932). So while learning the correct pronunciation of artists' names (Ma-tees, Say-zanne) they were also instructed: "To enjoy the work of these artists it is well to forget prejudices, both modern and old fashioned. Give the picture, itself, a chance to live!" (Barr, 1932).

Barr believed that the painting collection was the museum's principal collection and also the most frequently misunderstood. Painting was to be placed in a broader context, was to be viewed with period architecture and design, and with music and poetry, in order to be understood. This special context supplemented by educational material such as *A Brief Survey of Modern Painting* would be the path to enlightened seeing.

So the Museum of Modern Art differed fundamentally at the beginning in its approach to education from general American art museums, in that education was viewed as a curatorial function rather than, as we saw at the Cleveland Museum, a separate endeavor. Education was built into the structure of the museum by Alfred Barr, and was viewed as a natural outcome of exhibits supplemented by publications and gallery talks. This approach was a result of the multidepartmental structure of the museum, which was a result of *modernism* being the subject of the museum, not only art as we think of it in the context of the general art museum.

As the Museum of Modern Art developed its Department of Education, it did so as a separate enterprise with separate goals and objectives. The Department of Education began as a pilot project in 1937 for the purpose of providing visual teaching materials to high schools in New York City. This was accomplished by one part-time employee (MOMA *Annual Report*, 1938: 4).

By 1951, the program had expanded from supplying ten high schools with materials to supplying 50 high schools. There was also established a People's Art Center, where children and adults could attend classes in painting, ceramics, jewelry, and woodworking. By this time the staff included a full-time director, six assistants and 24 full- and part-time instructors, still a small department compared to Cleveland. But the purpose of the Museum of Modern Art's Education Department was quite separate from exhibitions. It provided "creative opportunities to help in the general growth of the child and to satisfy the leisure time interests of the adult," objectives which could be accomplished independent of the museum (D'Amico, 1951: 4, 7).

Late in 1960, there was established the Institute of Modern Art for the purpose of conducting the art classes formerly sponsored by the Museum. In May, 1984, the Museum opened the Edward John Noble Education Center, which provides, among other things, a videotape introduction to the Museum and the *Guides to the Collection*, a series of loose-leaf cards highlighting individual works in the permanent collection which allow the visitor to create a self-guided tour of the Museum.

The education department also sponsors gallery talks, study tours, adult surveys of modern art, lectures in conjunction with special exhibitions, and of course the public school programs.

The 1994 *Annual Report* of the Museum of Modern Art lists a staff of twelve, including the Director, plus five assistants. This can be compared to the Cleveland Museum's education department, which lists in the 1994 *Annual Report* a staff of nineteen plus 224 volunteers in education.

The Cleveland Museum reported serving 70,615 students in 1994, while the Museum of Modern Art reported serving 20,000 students. The Modern's Education Center reported 22,000 visitors in 1988 (more recent data was not available), while the Cleveland Museum reported 140,374 visitors for education programs in 1988 and 154,384 in 1994.

Considering the total operating budget of both museums ($25.8 million at Cleveland in 1994, and more than twice that at the Modern, clearly these two museums have different priorities and different approaches. The Museum of Modern Art, continuing in the tradition of Alfred Barr, assumes a role in directing the public's interaction with the art which is different from "the benchmark" and will now be examined more closely.

Vito Acconci at the Museum of Modern Art: a study

A major exhibition of the work of Vito Acconci was held at the Museum of Modern Art in 1988. Curated by Linda Shearer, the show contained sculptural works which are as difficult as any art created in this century. A close look at the ways and means of presenting this art to the public will provide insight into the Modern's philosophy of education. This will be achieved through an interview with the artist in his studio, an analysis of his work in the studio and in the collection of the Museum of Modern Art, and an analysis of the exhibition catalog essay by curator Linda Shearer.

Vito Acconci has been a controversial artist since the beginning of his career in 1969. Trained as a poet, Acconci first combined photographs with words, and then used video and film in more ambitious works in which he manipulated his body as a performance artist. By 1971, at the age of 31, sculptural elements were combined in installations with audio- and videotapes. The notorious 1972 installation called *Seedbed* at the Sonnabend Gallery in New York City is an example of his method, materials, and message. A huge ramp, occupying most of the gallery space, was constructed so that the viewer would ascend automatically upon entering the space. The artist lay, unseen, under the ramp and carried on a monologue while masturbating.

Some gallery visitors were shocked and angered by the content of this and other pieces by Acconci and also confused by the forms the artist invented. Deprived of the familiar categories of painting or sculpture, viewers had no frame of reference for the work. and some thus felt uncomfortable with it. The artist has continued in this vein, attempting always to involve the viewer but at the same time resisting categorization and analysis. He admits to strong democratic tendencies which are invoked in the work, yet the references resulting from his education and intellect are obscure for the average person. Work filled with paradoxes and contradictions presents a great challenge to a curator with an educational mission. We will look first at what is perceived as the problem, that is, the inaccessible nature of the work, and then at the attempted solution, that is, the democratization of the objects. This analysis, like the artist, the art, and the American modern art museum, will hopefully reflect the elitist/democratic paradox.

Vito Acconci says his work is more about culture than it is about art. "As soon as something is called 'art', people who aren't involved in the art world feel very very left out. They immediately feel this is part of a realm they don't understand." (From an interview with Nancy Einreinhofer, January 9, 1990. Unless otherwise noted, all quotations of Vito Acconci are from this interview.) This is why Acconci incorporates in his art images and conventions he considers familiar to the average person. The images are constructed with materials which are readily available and are constructed in an ordinary manner with ordinary tools. Acconci acknowledges that not everyone will understand all the elements of a piece, but hopes they will at least know the meaning of the prime images and therefore feel familiar with the work and willing to explore it.

One example of such an effort is the sculpture, or "self-erecting architectural unit" entitled *Instant House*. Built in 1980, the piece consists of four eight-feet-by-four wood panels, lying on the floor, one on each of the four sides of a swing. Acconci invites the viewer to participate in the piece by sitting on the swing. Pulleys attached to the swing, the panels, and the ceiling raise the panels, which become walls that enclose the individual in a house-like structure. So it is that the viewer, not the artist, constructs the piece. The interiors of the walls are plastered with American flags, but the person operating the work cannot see that the sign of the hammer and sickle of the former Soviet Union has also been raised, attached to the exterior side of the sculpture's panel. Enticed by something akin to playground equipment, the participant becomes, in one sense, a victim, trapped in the home he has built, unaware of the secret agenda—propaganda. At the same time, Acconci renders the national symbols of the USSR and the USA interchangeable, therefore neutralizing the symbolic language of political institutions.

The piece indicates Acconci's reluctance to adopt an ideological orthodoxy. It also points to the contradictions the artist attaches to the house image. The house is private on the inside, public on the outside. The flags may represent an "us" and "them" mentality. The house means security, shelter, protection, but it is also restrictive. As long as the participant sits on the swing, he is closed off from the rest of the world.

Linda Shearer, curator of the exhibition, believes *Instant House* manifests the acknowledged influence of the architect Robert Venturi, who "favors signage of modernist forms because it is 'explicit, denotive communication'. Venturi observes that, in Las Vegas, architecture and signs are often combined, with the facade of a casino acting as one big sign" (Shearer, 1988: 5).

So we have in *Instant House* the ordinary images of a swing, a house, and flags, the images Acconci believes "anybody in a particular culture knows. They might not know what it all leads up to, the way things shift or collide, but they know what a house is, they know what a window is, they know all the elements, so at least they're on familiar ground." We also have the everyday materials the artist feels so strongly about. "I admit this is real important to me. It's important that the materials used are conventionally available." Available and able to be assembled by an average carpenter. Acconci detests the notion of the artist as priest, a special person removed from the crowd, chosen to perform a special task. "I think that's why it is important to me not to emphasize the artist's hand. The artist's hand means that this object is something particularly valuable, something that separates the artist from the non-artist. I believe the artist is simply a person who decides to organize certain things." Acconci, in fact, does not actually build any of his art works. Everything is fabricated by workers.

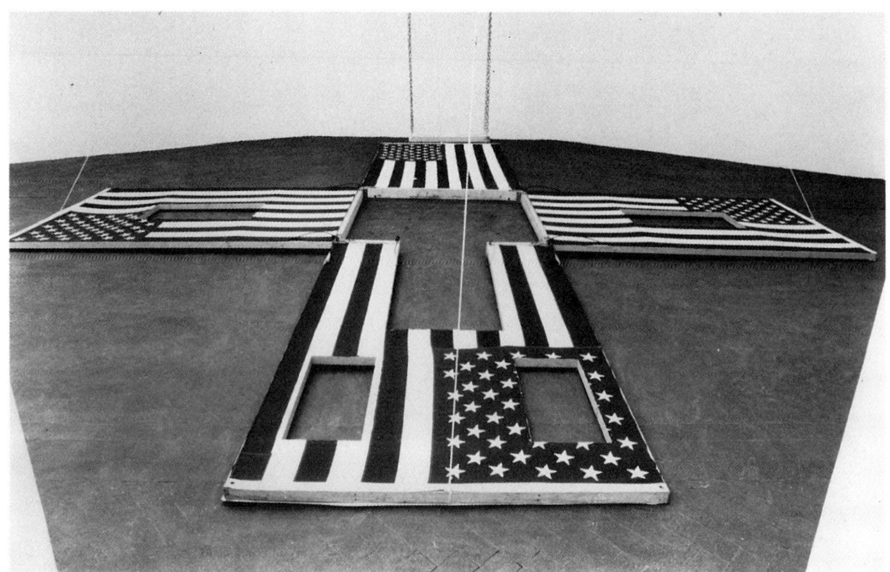

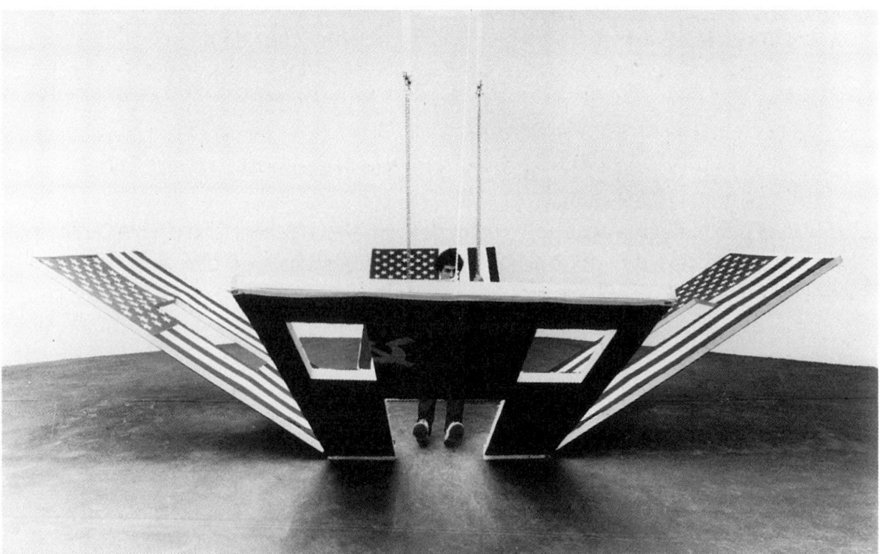

Instant House, 1980, by Vito Acconci. Flags, wood, springs, ropes, and pulleys, 8 × 5 × 5 ft. (243.8 × 152.4 × 152.4 cm), two views.
Collection of the San Diego Museum of Contemporary Art, California.

"I'm more interested in popular art, popular music, popular movies, than I am interested in high art. High art is about something hidden. I really want everything to be accessible. When museums say 'Do not touch', they place the viewer in a lower position. The function of 'Do not touch' is to make you feel that you don't own this and somebody else does. If you can only look at something, you're in the position of mere desire. You can never have it in your hands, you can only stand apart and wish for it. You are never quite good enough for originals. I think for me those 'Do not touch' signs in the museum were a major reason why I started making art. I want my stuff to be touched." Finally, we have in *Instant House* the participatory factor. The sculpture actually needs the viewer's interaction to be what it was meant to be.

Vito Acconci thinks through the issues of contemporary art, its content, materials, and presentation. He is, in his heart, a democrat and strives to engage the public. At the same time, the message he sends is not straightforward nor easily explained. He thrives on ambiguity and is willing to undercut social and political conventions as quickly as artistic ones. Faced with a gallery full of works by Vito Acconci, the public is likely to feel angry, challenged, insulted, entertained, or some other mix of confused emotions. As the artist himself admits "I really don't know how to be interested in any relationship that doesn't cause trouble for me and potentially for another person" (Shearer, 1988: 5).

Linda Shearer, in the catalog which accompanied the exhibition, takes up the difficult task of guiding the audience toward a more complete understanding of the artist and his work. She confirms that Acconci's work is subjective, and subversive: "In his attempt to rid himself, and us, of the constraints of social and aesthetic conventions, he remains an antagonist, an outsider, an eternal wanderer." Then cleverly adds that "The resulting sense of alienation is essential to the experience of his work" (Shearer, 1988: 5).

Throughout the catalog essay, Shearer refers to things outside the world of visual art. There is not a single reference to an art historical influence nor to any visual artist past or present. The influences, comparisons, references are all to be found elsewhere. Politics, architecture, history, philosophy, religion and sports, all find a place in the essay. Influential people range from the French philosophers, Roland Barthes and Michel Foucault, to the American filmmaker John Ford, and the comic Lenny Bruce.

"Of interest to Acconci has been the theorist Michel Foucault's identification of the body as a primary metaphor for power. Foucault cited the physical presence of the king's body in the seventeenth century, and the idea of a social body constituted through a universality of wills in the nineteenth century, as indicating the significance of this concept" (Shearer, 1988: 8).

"Humor ... has been a persistent element in his [Acconci's] work. His early monologues recall the blunt, aggressive wit of the late standup comic Lenny Bruce, as does Acconci's choosing to behave as transgressor; as with Bruce, what some saw as obscene was meant as social satire. Few of Acconci's recent works attempt the sheer preposterousness of such earlier pieces as *Trappings*, (1971), wherein he talked to his penis, which was dressed in doll clothes, and *Gang Bang*, (1980) in which huge inflated penises mounted on the roofs of cars chased an inflated breast through Spoleto, Italy" (Shearer, 1988: 7).

Virtually every theme developed in a work by Acconci finds a reference outside the art world. Game-playing, for example, is "according to Jacques Derrida, associated with anxiety, since it implies that the world does not have a stable, fixed structure. Acconci toys with shifts in meaning and the sense of instability and tension they generate" (Shearer, 1988: 8).

When Acconci uses, in an installation piece, mirrors in the shape of body parts, Shearer explains that, according to Jacques Lacan, the mirror stage "represents the child's first articulation of the concept 'I'. At this stage the child, frustrated with its limited motor capacities, believes its likeness to be more perfect than itself. So begins the life-long struggle between image and self-image; and the early fight for control over oneself also foreshadows a later struggle for power over one's environment. The mirrors in the forms of parts of dismembered bodies serve as reminders of the underlying violence of these struggles" (Shearer, 1988: 9).

There is no doubt that Vito Acconci would approve of this attempt to elucidate his art work. As he noted in the interview: "There is this notion that art is pulled out of nowhere. In fact, if you trace the history of an artist you see that the artist exists in a particular time, in a particular place. I might be influenced by something from a movie and then maybe I'll play around with it. I take ideas from lots of places. Electronics, for example, has something to do with television, something to do with light, something to do with past cultures. So that might be research but it's still research based on a particular, historically determined, material condition. It's not pure abstraction."

For Acconci, a large part of the problem with museums and education is the fact that the museum system is built on the idea of the supremacy of the artist. "It seems that there has to be the notion of the artist as some kind of specialized being to allow for the passage from one artist to another and from one group of artists at one time to a group of artists in another world. If the artist was just ordinary, then why is the museum preserving all this work?"

It is this elevated, elitist position of the artist and the art that, according to Acconci, intimidates people and triggers in them certain expectations. "People's taste in music might be much more adventurous than their taste in art. Why is that? It's because they're not afraid of music, they don't see it as something that's supposedly above them. As soon as they think of something as art, we're in trouble. Then they want it to be this way instead of that way."

Acconci looks forward to a time when art might be considered "not as a separate category, in its own arena and with its own products, but as an atmosphere instilled, almost secretly, within other categories of life" (Shearer, 1988: 20).

In the meantime he says, "A real educational system in a museum should talk about the art of a certain time in relation to the architecture of a certain time, the music of a certain time, the theater of a certain time. There should be a mix of categories. It seems that art history should be culture history." Alfred Barr would have agreed.

Conclusion

The education of the public has always been the democratic mission of the American museum, regardless of its discipline. The general art museum led the way in educational theory and practice as demonstrated in the profile of the educational programs at the Cleveland Museum. The Museum of Modern Art, under the direction of Alfred Barr, developed a very different approach to informing its visitors, alerting them to modernism in all its forms through a cross-referencing of painting to cinema and sculpture to architecture.

Through a comparative examination of four general art museums over a 25-year period, growth patterns and economic trends in educational programming were revealed. Huge increases in budgets and staff were not necessarily matched with comparable increases in visitors served. Likewise, increases in the number of programs offered did not result in increases in the total number of participants. This points to the danger that the museum may be hampered on its present course in fulfilling its mission of education for the masses. If a primary mission of the American art museum is education in a democracy, critical dialogue and alternative views must be offered.

The alternative path taken by the Museum of Modern Art and demonstrated here in the review of the exhibition and catalog of the work of Vito Acconci, offers different possibilities to the general art museum and to museums in general.

7

Capitalism and the American art museum: an analysis of the corporate influence

They have to raise the funds, they have to create their own identity, they want to be important. Every part of the fabric of the museum is geared toward expansion. The idea is that if we are successful, then we have to grow. And if we grow we need even more money. It is very self-absorbed and self-consuming."

Frank Stella, *Museum News*

Introduction

The American art museum born in the nineteenth century was the child of capitalists (See Chapter 3). This historical fact may account for the ease with which the American art museum of the twentieth century adopted corporate tactics. America's first museums were founded with private money, and their boards, composed mainly of wealthy capitalists, were modeled after corporate boards. Museums founded in the twentieth century would follow what was by then an American tradition. Even Andrew Mellon, with his great gift to the nation of a National Gallery of Art to function under the umbrella of the Smithsonian Institution, a federal agency, prescribed a private board for his museum, modeled after the private corporate board and different from the organization of other national museums (see Chapter 4).

The corporate–museum relationship manifests itself, not only in the profile of the museum board of trustees, but also in the sponsorship of special exhibitions, in the commercialization of those exhibitions and in the production and marketing of their related materials such as books, posters, catalogs, and videos.

An examination of the corporate influence and the particularly rapid growth of that influence during the 1970s and 1980s will be reviewed beginning with the Metropolitan Museum under the directorship of Thomas Hoving, whose revolutionary adoption of corporate money-generating methods came to be known in the museum world as "Hovingism." This will be followed by an analysis of the work of artist Hans Haacke, who, because of his tenacious investigations of museum practices, has gained the recognition in the art community as the conscience of the American art museum in its corporate dealings. Case studies of two American art museums closely associated with corporate tactics, the Whitney Museum of American Art and the Guggenheim Museum, will be reviewed as a way to identify the benefits and possible pitfalls in the museum–corporate partnership.

Thomas Hoving and the corporate–museum partnership

The peak post-war year for the American economy was 1968, when American industrial production was more than one-third of the world total. It was also the year that marked the beginning of serious spending by American corporations on the arts, spending that increased in an unprecedented manner through the 1980s. Thomas Hoving began his position as director of the Metropolitan Museum of Art that same year and thrust that museum into the age of corporate sponsorship, sponsorship which would result in the museum's subsequent adoption of certain corporate policies, techniques, and procedures. Beginning at the Metropolitan with Hoving, the corporate–museum partnership soon spread to other museums. In order to begin to understand this relationship and its implications, we must understand its genesis.

Thomas Hoving, director of the Metropolitan Museum of Art from 1967 to 1977, adopted the ways of the corporate world and instituted programs with a keen eye toward the art museum visitor as consumer. More than any other director in the history of American museums, Hoving revolutionized museum operations and the public's perception of the museum and turned the Metropolitan into New York City's premier tourist attraction. Under Hoving, the Metropolitan developed a master plan (MMA, 1968: 55) which included building five new wings, enlarging exhibition areas by one-third; planning special exhibitions promoted among the masses through popular appeal devices; and hosting gala parties attended by movie stars and rock stars along with the more usual celebrities, another publicity ploy to catch the national headlines. This new director soon became a household name, no small feat for a museum director, and "Hovingism" came to be identified with a specific set of operational policies.

Thomas Hoving was the son of the Swedish immigrant Walter Hoving, chairman of Tiffany's. A graduate of Princeton University, where he received his doctorate in 1959, Hoving specialized in medieval studies. That same year, at a symposium on art history held at the Frick Collection, Hoving met James J. Rorimer, then director of the Metropolitan. Rorimer recruited Hoving as an assistant curator, and in time Hoving became his protégé, succeeding to Rorimer's former position as chief curator of The Cloisters. In 1965, Hoving's good friend John V. Lindsay was elected mayor of New York City. Hoving had prepared Lindsay's campaign paper on city park policies and so the mayor-elect invited him to assume the position of parks commissioner. Surprising

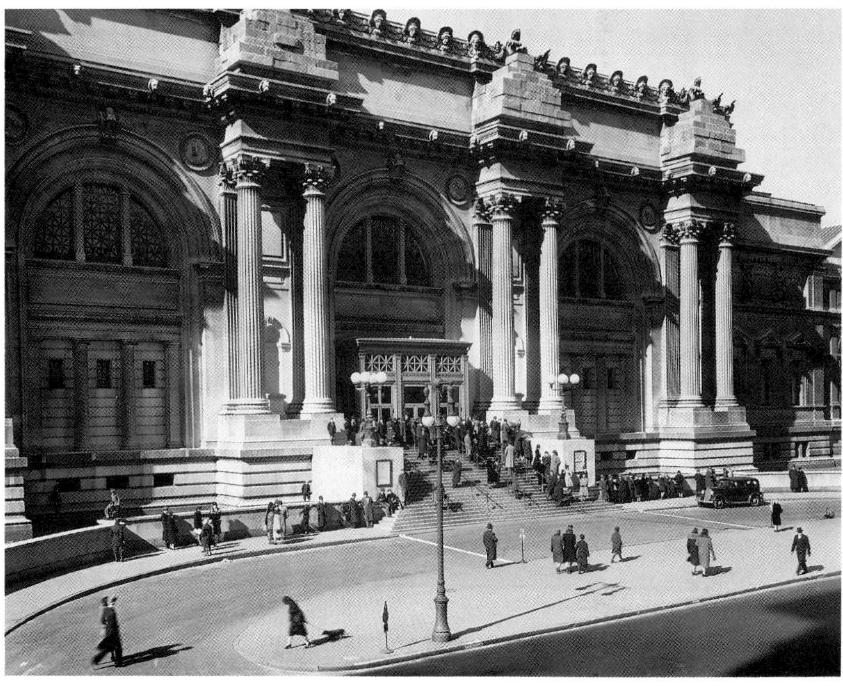

The Metropolitan Museum of Art, Fifth Avenue facade, 1939.
The Metropolitan Museum of Art, New York.

most people and disappointing his mentor Rorimer, Hoving accepted the appointment (Tomkins, 1989: 346–50).

Hoving served as commissioner of parks for only one year, but during that brief time his populist approach delighted the media. Hoving closed off Central Park to automobiles on weekends and staged "happenings" which filled the park with exuberant crowds, with cyclists, food fairs, music festivals, sporting events, and public "paint-ins" on a mile-long roll of paper. Hoving, as park commissioner, generated more excitement and publicity than anyone else in the Lindsay administration.

As park commissioner, Hoving served as an *ex-officio* trustee on the Metropolitan's board. In his nine months at that post, he missed only one meeting and understood, therefore, the workings, problems, and plans of the museum. When James Rorimer died suddenly in 1966, Thomas Hoving was prepared to present to the trustees' search committee something no other candidate for the job had: a long-range plan for the Metropolitan Museum and an outline of solutions to the museum's immediate problems (Hoving, 1993: 32). On December 28, 1967, at the age of 36, Thomas Hoving was introduced to the staff of the Metropolitan Museum as the newly appointed director.

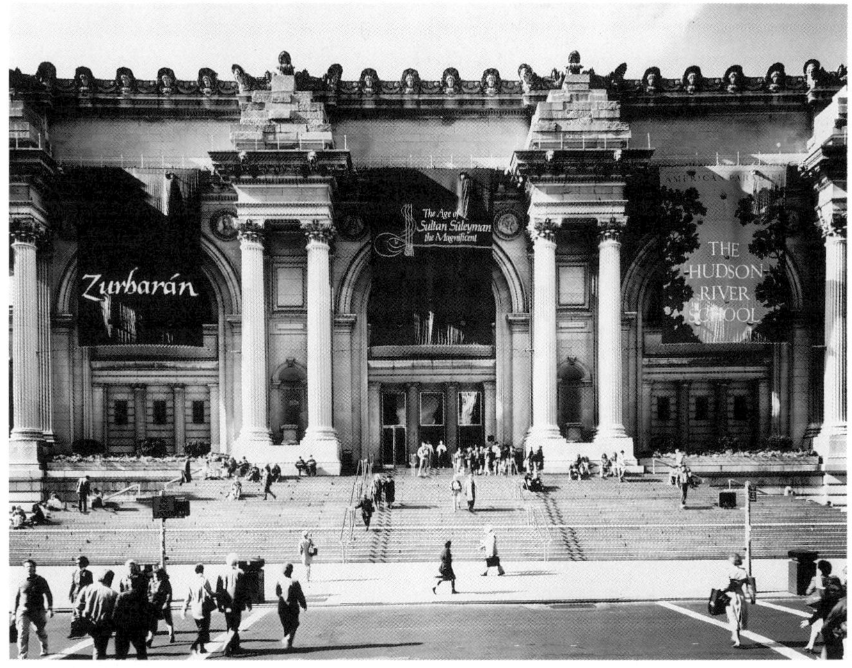

The Metropolitan Museum of Art, Fifth Avenue facade, 1987.
The Metropolitan Museum of Art, New York.

Hoving's influence on exhibition policy became immediately apparent. Special exhibitions were events to be promoted in the press, thus increasing museum attendance. The more exhibitions the museum could mount, the better. By 1972, Hoving had tripled the number of exhibitions presented under the directorship of James Rorimer, to a grand total of 62 shows for the 1972–73 season (MMA, 1973: 17–22). The pace was frantic, with short lead-times resulting, by some accounts, in sloppy scholarship. The cost was unprecedented, but so were the revenues generated. For example, the 1965 *Annual Report* cites two major sources of income for the museum: the New York City contribution of almost $1.4 million toward guarding and maintenance (25 percent of the total income) and the income from the museum's endowment, $3,883,873, which constituted 66.9 percent of the total. By 1976, "Hovingism," taking the form of admission charges, museum shop sales, restaurant and parking charges, and membership dues, had generated $16,334,000, or 58.9 percent of the operating budget of $27,777,000 (MMA, 1976: 81–91). Less than 10 percent ($2,678,000) was contributed by the city and 17.7 percent ($4,929,000) came from the endowment.

This $16,334,000 annually was dependent on the blockbuster shows which were the centerpiece of Hovingism. They were the grand and brilliant invention of Hoving because, not only did they generate this huge income by attracting hordes of people to the museum, but they were also substantially self-supporting ventures because they attracted support from corporations, foundations, and arts councils. The museum's 1976 annual financial report indicates that every special exhibition was supported by endowment grants or corporate money, usually corporate money.

The corporate sponsors wanted the world to know about their good deeds and inserted their publicity methods into the museum. Hoving, of course, adopted them happily, referring to his middle initials, P. F. (Thomas Pearsall Field Hoving) as standing for "Publicity Forever" (Hoving, 1993: 26).

The hectic pace, the changing exhibitions, the crowds and commercialism, disturbed more than a few people. Hilton Kramer, art critic for the *New York Times* during this period, wrote that

> In everything from the creation of overglamorized installations to the actual manufacture of reproductions, the Metropolitan in the Hoving era has led the way in erasing a precious distinction—the distinction, after all, that is the museum's very reason for being—between the authentic and the unauthentic in art. This is what Mr. Hoving has taken away: our confidence that the museum can be completely trusted to defend the interests of high art. (Kramer, 1985: 322)

Dissent grew within the museum as well and finally became public in 1975 when the head of the department of European paintings, Anthony M. Clark, resigned his post. His letter of resignation charges that Hoving's exhibition policies and "frantic loans" placed the museum's permanent collection at risk. Clark refers to Hoving's regime as one of poor reputation, big on "hucksterism" and lacking in honesty, simplicity, professional grace and skill (Meyer, 1979: 116).

In the professional museum world there was also great concern and seemingly endless debates at professional meetings and in professional journals regarding the role of the art museum in society. A 1989 *Museum News* article by Lawrence Wheeler, for example, refers to "Club Met," a nickname earned by the venerable Metropolitan since it made both its reputation and its facilities available to corporations willing to pay the price. The Whitney, with branch museums in corporate headquarters, "sometimes is chided as the 'McDonald's of the museum world'." As far back as 1972 Sherman E. Lee, then director of the Cleveland Museum of Art, expressed his concern in *Museum News*. He warned that art museums may be compromised or adulterated by their eagerness to please the public. In an obvious reference to Hoving and the Metropolitan, Lee writes: "If an 1870 charter, written with solid Victorian moral uplift, mentions the elevation of public taste, it does not necessarily follow that abortive, yet symbolic, attempts at mass education in 1970 can be really achieved by an art museum rather than other, larger and more pervasive institutions or processes. Playing at education may well be worse than no education at all."

In spite of debate, dissent, and criticism, Thomas Hoving and his "corporate tactics" changed forever the public face of the American art museum. Thomas Hoving and the Metropolitan were perhaps the first to travel the corporate route, but that move quickly became a trend pursued by museums across the country. American art museums founded by America's wealthy industrialists, merchants, and bankers, were amenable to that world and willingly assumed the corporate mantle. The influence resulted in profound changes both in the organization of the museum and in its function.

The 1970s witnessed major changes in board profiles and in the character of museum directorships. The apparent ease with which the shifts occurred can perhaps be attributed to the capitalistic mark left by the likes of Morgan, Frick, Carnegie, Rockefeller, and Guggenheim. American capitalists fashioned their museums, to some extent, after a corporate structure.

An examination of the corporate influence will demonstrate how that influence can manifest itself in the profile of the museum board of trustees, as well as in the corporate sponsorship of special exhibitions and also the more recent development of corporate headquarters as museum outposts. The close working relationship between corporate people and museum personnel in all of the above designations has caused the transfer of corporate management techniques and corporate thinking to the museum staff. This is surely a mixed blessing for while, on the one hand, it seems to provide balanced budgets and fiscal responsibility, it may also threaten the integrity of the art museum.

Hans Haacke and the corporate–museum partnership

The museum and the corporation, two very important institutions in the world of art, institutions wielding significant social, political, and economic influence, captured the attention of the artist Hans Haacke in the 1970s and have provided the grist for his mill ever since. No discussion of the relationship between the American art museum and the corporation will have credibility without the input of Haacke. Haacke's art work functions as a critique of these institutions and hopefully, as a catalyst for change. The following analysis is based on the artist's work as a primary source and an interview with the artist in his studio in February of 1991.

Haacke, a recipient of fellowships from the Fulbright and Guggenheim foundations and from the National Endowment for the Arts, has been an exhibiting artist since the 1960s. His early work focused on processes, situations, and open systems which communicated with their environment. He expanded his interest to social and political systems because of a belief in his artistic responsibility to engage the world as a whole. His early work in systems theory provided a theoretical base for this new direction. The work explores the relationship between the art world and the larger economic and political community because, as Haacke expressed in the interview, the social atmosphere, and mental and emotional climate, are affected by what people hear, see, or take in by osmosis from the art world.

Hans Haacke's art work incorporates the traditional media of painting and sculpture with language, photographs, found objects, invented objects and any other media necessary to communicate his ideas, which are steeped in history and politics and which reflect on social systems. In 1968, when the American economy had seemingly peaked, Haacke's reputation as an artist was also high. That year his work could be viewed in museums across the United States: the Museum of Modern Art in New York; the Milwaukee Art Center; the Museum of Modern Art, Chicago; San Francisco Museum of Modern Art; Albright–Knox Art Gallery, Buffalo. Hans Haacke was invited for a one-person exhibition at the Guggenheim Museum in New York, the exhibition to take place in 1971. A few weeks before its planned opening, the exhibition was canceled because of the extremely controversial issues raised by the work. Chief among those art works was Haacke's now famous *Manhattan Project: Shapolsky* et al. *Manhattan Real Estate Holdings, A Real-Time Social System, as of May 1, 1971* (Collection of the artist, New York City). The proposed piece consisted of a wall-size chart itemizing the buildings controlled by one major Manhattan landlord. Haacke charted the holdings through the use of maps, architectural photographs and typed data sheets. The 142 buildings included a generous number of slums and social conditions with which the Guggenheim did not wish to be associated because the piece might not only precipitate an inspection of Shapolsky's real estate maneuvers, but also call to mind the museum's physical space, social position, and ideological tenets. Haacke believed, as he communicated in the interview, that the museum feared it would emerge as a place occupying a position of material privilege in relation to other terrains.

As Haacke clarified in his notes accompanying the presentation, the Shapolsky group were the largest real estate holders in Harlem and the Lower East Side, investing in housing in impoverished neighborhoods and gaining huge profits through frequent sales and exchanges. Shapolsky emerged, as Haacke researched public records, to be the key figure in a group of about 70 different corporations. Haacke recorded not only the information on the property, but also information on the corporations holding titles. Charting the business transactions, Haacke listed the corporations in columns and traced the exchange of mortgages and properties. What is revealed is a system of family ties and dummy corporations, a myriad of financial exchanges and the mechanics of investment by which profits are made by slumlords. The system is an open one and radiates out to include rental agencies, city agencies, religious, and church groups.

Following the cancellation of the show, newspapers, art journals, television, and radio programs discussed the event in the light of censorship. Thomas Messer, then director of the Guggenheim Museum, acknowledged that Haacke's work "posed a direct threat to the museum's functioning within its stated and accepted premises" (Messer, 1971: 4). Those accepted premises then came to be questioned. What of the role of the museum as sanctuary, as separate, protected place? When the curator of the exhibition, Edward F. Fry, defended the works publicly, he was fired by the museum. Demonstrations protesting the cancellation of the show and the dismissal of the curator followed, and commentaries included speculations on linkage between museum trustees and the Shapolsky real estate group.

No such linkage was ever proven, but the event spotlighted the museum board and its corporate connections and marked the beginning of Haacke's portrayals of the corporate–museum relationship. "There is a direct link between the museum board and the corporate world," asserts Haacke, "Invariably, more and more corporate representatives come on to the boards, not necessarily because their corporations have been putting in more money, but because they can easily grease the wheels of their peers." (From a Nancy Einreinhofer interview with Hans Haacke, February 11, 1991. All quotations of Haacke are from this interview unless otherwise noted.)

In 1974, Haacke created a work of art entitled *Solomon R. Guggenheim Museum Board of Trustees* in which he traced the interconnections among members of the Guggenheim family, other museum trustees, and various corporations frequently sharing the same addresses and offices. For example, a Guggenheim family member and two trustees were listed on the board of directors of the Kennecott Copper Corporation. The Guggenheim family was represented on the board by Peter O. Lawson-Johnston (president of the board), the son of Barbara Guggenheim; his daughter, Wendy L. J. McNeil (vice-president of the board); Michael F. Wettach, another son of Barbara Guggenheim; and the Earl Castle Stewart, son of Elenor Guggenheim. Barbara and Elenor Guggenheim, daughters of the founder, also served on the board at the time.

What the Haacke *Guggenheim Board* piece reinforces is the fact that the Guggenheim Museum and many other American museums are what Haacke calls "family museums" and they are funded primarily by family money and corporate money.

> Key positions in those museums are held by members of the family of the founders. They are not accountable to anybody. The regents may have to OK the charter of the museum, but only if there are flagrant violations of the public trust is there any interference from public authorities. So in many ways, they can do as they please. The major bulk of finances also comes from private sources. Large corporate contributions started sometime in the 60's. Those corporations very often have representatives on the boards, so there's a direct link to the corporate world.

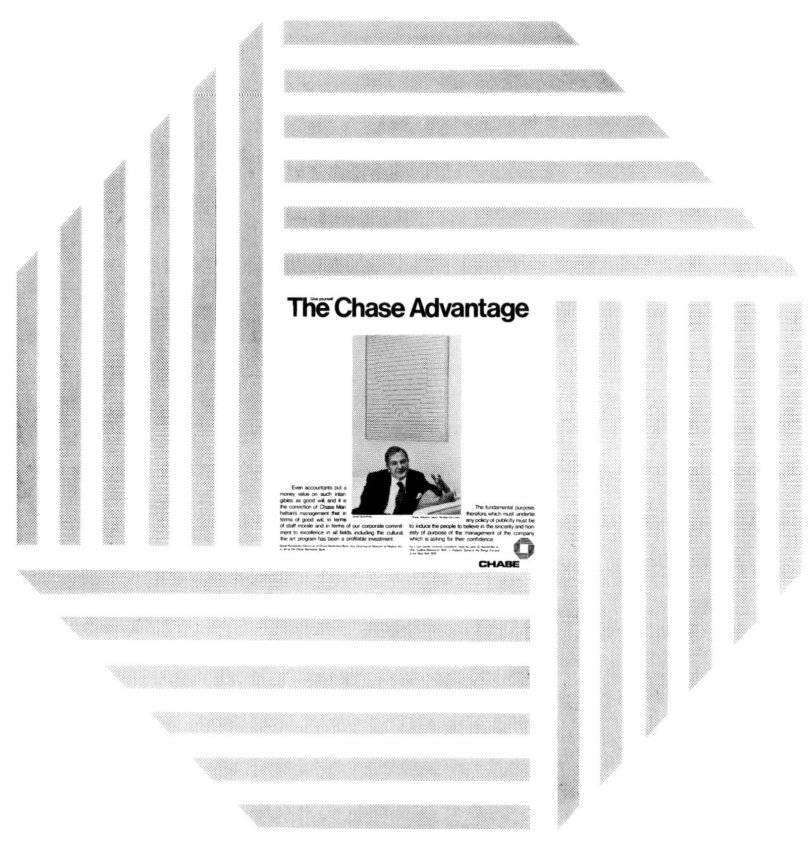

The Chase Advantage, 1976, by Hans Haacke. Silkscreen on acrylic, 48 × 48 in., edition of 6.
Copyright (c) Hans Haacke.

The *Give yourself* Chase Advantage

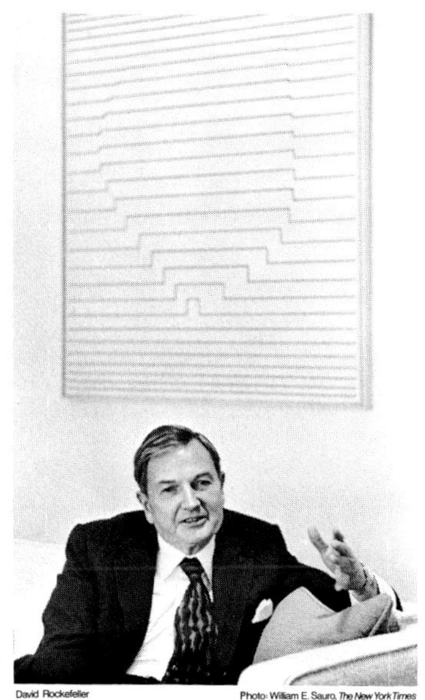

David Rockefeller

Photo: William E. Sauro, *The New York Times*

Even accountants put a money value on such intangibles as good will, and it is the conviction of Chase Manhattan's management that in terms of good will, in terms of staff morale and in terms of our corporate commitment to excellence in all fields, including the cultural, the art program has been a profitable investment.

David Rockefeller (Chairman of Chase Manhattan Bank, Vice Chairman of Museum of Modern Art) in *Art at the Chase Manhattan Bank*

The fundamental purpose, therefore, which must underlie any policy of publicity must be to induce the people to believe in the sincerity and honesty of purpose of the management of the company which is asking for their confidence.

Ivy L. Lee (public relations consultant, hired by John D. Rockefeller Jr., after »Ludlow Massacre«, 1914) in *Publicity: Some of the Things It is and is not*, New York, 1926

CHASE

(Detail)

In 1975, Hans Haacke's examination of the museum board's relationship with the corporation culminated in an installation titled *On Social Grease*, exhibited at the John Weber Gallery in New York City. The installation consisted of large magnesium plaques engraved with public quotes by prominent museum trustees and others regarding the relationship of the museum to business. David Rockefeller, for example, was serving at the time both as chairman of Chase Manhattan Bank Corporation and as the vice-president of the Museum of Modern Art. Rockefeller's quote, excerpted by Haacke from the *New York Times*, reads as follows:

> From an economic standpoint, such involvement in the arts can mean direct and tangible benefits:
>
> It can provide a company with extensive publicity and advertising, a brighter public reputation, and an improved corporate image.
>
> It can build better customer relations, a readier acceptance of company products, and a superior appraisal of their quality.
>
> Promotion of the arts can improve the morale of employees and help attract qualified personnel.

The then president of the Metropolitan Museum, C. Douglas Dillon, was quoted from an article in the *Columbia Journal of World Business*:

> Perhaps the most important single reason for the increased interest of international corporations in the arts is the almost limitless diversity of projects which are possible.
>
> These projects can be tailored to a company's specific business goals and can return dividends far out of proportion to the actual investment required.

What *On Social Grease* illustrates is that those corporate people serving on museum boards can and do articulate the benefits of sponsorship to their colleagues in the corporate world. There is a shared language and cultural context the multinational corporations understand and are teaching to museums through the museum's board members.

This situation is aptly described in the remarkably candid text of the brochure distributed to corporations by the Metropolitan Museum:

> Many public relations opportunities are available through sponsorship of programs, special exhibitions and services. These can often provide a creative and cost effective answer to a specific marketing objective, particularly where international, governmental or consumer relations may be a fundamental concern.

The flyer contained a page of quotes from business executives telling their colleagues why they are sponsors of the Metropolitan. It is apparent that the Metropolitan Museum is presenting itself to the corporation as a stage on which the corporation's interests can be promoted. According to Hans Haacke the museum is presenting itself also as an "agent to influence public policy." Haacke asserts that the museum is telling the corporation that it can be used for a political campaign, to influence legislation. "These tax exempt institutions become lobbying enterprises. The art they show is instrumentalized to push a corporate interest."

In the case of the oil companies, for example, Haacke believes that both Mobil and Exxon, the two giants of the oil industry, are interested in easing environmental legislation. This can be achieved, in part, by what Mobil calls "a good will umbrella." Even the fact that museum visitor profiles reveal the majority of art museum-goers to consider themselves politically liberal, fits into the corporate strategy. "It is the liberals in particular who need to be greased," says Haacke, "because they are the most likely and sophisticated critics of corporations and they are often in positions of influence" (Haacke, quoted in Wallis, 1986: 70). Corporations now understand, says Haacke, that the association with the high prestige of art can function as a subtle but effective means for lobbying in the corridors of government. "It can open doors, facilitate passage of favorable legislation, and serve as a shield against scrutinizing and criticism of corporate conduct" (p. 69).

Haacke details this corporate strategy and titles the piece *The Good Will Umbrella* (Collection of the artist, New York City). First exhibited at the Max Protetch Gallery, Washington, D.C., in May of 1976, the work consists of six large panels on which the familiar red and blue Mobil logo has been silkscreened. Under each logo are facsimiles of pages from a speech delivered by Herb Schmertz, Mobil's vice president for public affairs, to the Eastern Annual Conference of the American Association of Advertising Agencies. The rationale for Mobil's sponsorship of cultural programs is explained in phrases such as: "cultural excellence suggests corporate excellence." These programs project the company's executives as "corporate statesmen" who are therefore entitled to be "listened to on vital public policy issues." They also "provide the opportunity to form useful alliances and valuable contacts" with government leaders.

The importance of good relations with those who control legislation was underlined in a 1988 *Museum News* roundtable on "The Museum and the Corporation." Sandra Ruch, the manager of Mobil's division of Cultural Programs and Promotion stated bluntly:

> I need to rethink everything I present to my management in a completely different way, with a different vocabulary, because there is a new form of management. At Mobil, we have people who want to justify corporate support in two areas, and they are very specific: What can it do for the company in marketing terms, and what can it do for the company in terms of political or governmental relations? ... My job, as a person trying to mediate between the corporate world and the museum world, is to justify that reliance in very specific business terms. Everything we do is specifically oriented to the fact that we are a multinational company. We do things which are totally related to our operations.

It should be noted that Sandra Ruch was addressing the museum community, telling potential applicants what is expected from them and their proposals. Haacke believes the corporate sponsors "set the tone" for exhibitions. "The museum director and the curator can anticipate what would fit into the corporate picture, they know what would attract corporate funding. Accordingly, the show is styled or the topic chosen."

Corporate public relations officers know that the greatest publicity benefits can be derived from a high-visibility event, those art exhibits that draw large crowds and are covered extensively by the media: the blockbuster exhibition. As charitable agendas go, museum underwriting of special exhibitions has been a sure bet for corporations because of the visibility factor. "When we sponsor an exhibit that runs eight or ten weeks, our corporate name is advertised longer than with most other philanthropic causes," says a spokesman for United Technologies (Glennon, 1988: 39).

The special exhibition, in other words, gives the corporation more bang for the buck, a situation smiled on by shareholders. "It's their money," says the CEO of Philip Morris Corporation, "and we're trying to use it in a way that helps our business. We can't be totally altruistic without being irresponsible with somebody else's money" (Glennon, 1988: 41).

Chase Manhattan Bank, the third largest bank in the United States, at the time had its headquarters in the art capital, New York City, and had as its chief executive, until his retirement in 1981, David Rockefeller. We have seen briefly Rockefeller's ties to art and his sympathies regarding corporate sponsorship of museum programs, sympathies which continued at Chase after his departure. We will now look at the Chase involvement with one special exhibition and the "visibility" it provided.

The special exhibition held at the Guggenheim Museum in 1988 featured works of art drawn from the Solomon R. Guggenheim Foundation collections in the Guggenheim Museum in New York and the Peggy Guggenheim Collection in Venice, Italy. "Fifty Years of Collecting" celebrated the anniversary of the Guggenheim Foundation and was sponsored by Chase. In the sponsor's statement at the front of the exhibition catalog, Chairman of the Board, Willard C. Butcher writes: "Sponsoring this presentation is just one way we are continuing Chase's partnership with the arts, which has been going strong for thirty years through our philanthropic contributions and our corporate art collection, which contains many works by the artists represented here" (Butcher, 1987: 7). The bank devised a promotional campaign that included the usual vehicles of exhibition catalogs, posters, newspaper and magazine advertisements, and radio spots, but some new and inventive tactics as well. For example, the bank's automatic teller machines were programmed to display and then print an announcement of the exhibition. In addition, news of the exhibition was slipped into customers' bank statements and credit card statements, and Chase cardholders were offered free admission to the exhibition. The benefits of the campaign were clear to the museum since the exhibition generated the highest attendance in the Guggenheim's history for a comparable time span (Guggenheim *Annual Report*, 1987: 9). As Haacke says, "The corporate blanket is so warm."

What has evolved from the museum–corporate partnership, Haacke describes as a form of addiction.

> The museums have taught the lay public to look for excitement. They have dressed up the notion of art and now the public at large expects something sexy. So the museum has to create extravaganzas, which are expensive. They're under pressure to deliver in order to attract the people. It's like an addiction. You start small then you need more, you need bigger doses. In order to attract the crowds and also to attract the corporate support, blockbusters have become necessary.

No museum has ever accused a corporate sponsor of censorship, but indeed, censorship is the prime concern among those who consider the museum–corporate partnership. The risk involved in museum dependence on corporate donations is that the museum will, in trying to please the corporation and guarantee future funding, propose only attractive, popular shows. This form of self-censorship could threaten the very heart of museum scholarship as esoteric projects are set aside in favor of those with wide appeal. This risk is well understood by museum directors.

J. Carter Brown, as Director of the National Gallery of Art in Washington, considered his museum to be "very lucky" in receiving corporate funding and moved to "enlarge the circle." "Museums have to understand how to make their approach and have to realize they have to put it in terms that will help their people sell that concept further up the line. Just sitting around expecting everyone to realize how significant their project is in cultural terms may not do it." Brown also saw clearly that the selection of projects which could be easily "sold" might eliminate projects which prove more difficult.

> Even if the corporations are not involved in any kind of interference in curatorial decisions, like which objects to put in a show they are sponsoring, there is always the threat of the subtle kind of censorship that follows the decision the museum makes as to what to do. If financial backing to do a project is needed, and if from the beginning the museum people realize that it is the kind of project that nobody is going to want to back, this lack of any interference with a curatorial decision is subtly, by default, interfering with a curatorial decision. (Brown, 1988: 48)

In a more adamant analysis of the situation, Philippe de Montebello, Director of the Metropolitan Museum, described corporate funding as "an inherent, insidious, hidden form of censorship" (quoted in Glennon, 1988: 42).

Perhaps not always hidden. In 1984, Mobil Corporation succeeded in pressuring the Tate Gallery to suspend the distribution of the catalog of

Hans Haacke's one-person show at that museum. The corporation took issue with Haacke's art work and an interview with the artist which appeared in the publication. Mobil charged that their property rights had been violated by the use of their logo in the art works and threatened that the Tate Gallery "will make further distribution of the offending material at their risk and peril." Mobil had sponsored an exhibition at the Tate which closed the day before the Haacke exhibit opened. After almost one year, the Tate Gallery released the Haacke catalog. The Mobil/Tate incident was documented by Haacke in a collage containing the letter, $47\frac{1}{4}$" × $72\frac{1}{2}$", first exhibited at the John Weber Gallery, New York, May, 1985.

Richard Berglund, as head of cultural affairs at IBM Corporation, stated that his company wants to know exactly what will be in an exhibition before they agree to sponsor it.

> We want to see a checklist ... If there is the possibility that something is going to go off in areas that the company could not live with, then we stay away from it" (Morfogan, 1988: 48)

Case study I: the Whitney Museum

Perhaps no other art museum had so completely cast its lot with the corporation as had the Whitney Museum of American Art. Over a five-year period from 1981 to 1986, the Whitney established branch museums on the premises of four corporations: the Whitney at Fairfield opened in 1981, funded by and located in the headquarters of Champion International; the Whitney at Philip Morris opened in 1983 and was funded by Philip Morris Corporation; the Whitney Downtown at Federal Reserve Plaza, relocated in 1986, was funded by IBM and Park Tower Realty (it was originally funded by the Lower Manhatten business community); the Whitney at Equitable Center, established in 1986, was funded by Equitable Insurance Company. The arrangement provided a total of 19,000 square feet of additional exhibition space for the museum, all operating expenses paid by the host corporation, a tremendous amount of publicity for the museum plus exposure of the museum's collections, and generous donations annually from the corporations to the "mother" museum. The arrangement appeared on the surface to be a good thing for the Whitney Museum, but a deeper examination is warranted. Two serious threats to museums posed by corporate involvement have thus far been identified: the self-censorship of curators proposing exhibitions for corporate underwriting in an attempt to please the sponsoring corporation; and the danger of cost-effective procedures interfering with quality curatorial time and undermining scholarship. The Whitney Museum's programs can be viewed in light of these threats.

Tom Armstrong served as the director of the Whitney Museum for sixteen years (1974–90) and during that period of time took the museum to a highly influential position in the art world. Originally dedicated to American art of all periods and media, the Whitney, under Armstrong, changed its mandate to focus on the presentation of contemporary American art and built a collection of the American avant-garde. Under Armstrong's direction also, the museum worked agreements with four corporations to establish the branch museums. Contemporary art and the corporation were related in the eyes of Tom Armstrong. "The Whitney Museum has a product that most museums don't have," he said in a 1986 interview published in *Museum News*. "We represent contemporary art" (Keens, 1986: 28).

In explaining how the Whitney marketed its product to and through corporations, Armstrong's language echoed that of the sponsors.

> If Philip Morris went to McCann Erickson and said, "We want our name in the newspaper for ten times each month", McCann Erickson might say, "That will cost you $150,000 a month". Well, we do that, we put that corporation in a context that their product can't, in the editorial content of the press. We're also allying them with a situation that is noncommercial, beneficial, all of the things that a product-oriented company can't really achieve. The prestige that we bring to them is significant, and we want to be compensated for that. (Keens, 1986: 26)

The most ambitious of the branch projects was the deal struck with the Equitable Life Assurance Society of the United States. The director of Equitable's real estate, Ben Holloway, initiated the Whitney Branch project because "we think it will attract and hold tenants, and that they'll pay us the rents we are looking for" (Glennon, 1988: 40). In other words, contemporary art serves to make this Seventh Avenue business address even more fashionable.

"We were courted by Equitable" brags Armstrong.

> We're being courted all over the country. We've got a winner here. If someone calls me and says, "Mr. Armstrong, I'm developing a building and I want a branch," then I say "Have you got $400,000 a year to spend, plus start-up costs?" Either you play the game or it doesn't work."
> (Keens, 1986: 26)

The Whitney would not release figures in regard to its corporate branches, and the branches were not a part of the museum's annual financial report, but it is confirmed that the arrangement included direct expenses, reimbursement of overhead, and a generous contribution to the museum, above and beyond branch-related expenses. For an additional fee, the museum's curators would advise the corporation on the purchase of art for its collection. Whitney curators, for example, arranged for the purchase of $8 million worth of art in public spaces at the Equitable Center.

In an era of heightened consciousness regarding public relations, image-building has become the incentive for patronage, and the Whitney's director understands this. "We represent decision-making about quality and creativity in our culture" (Keens, 1986: 28). The actual image of quality and creativity conjured up by the exhibits mounted, and subsequently transferred to the sponsoring corporation, was definitely in the eye of the beholder. An informal survey conducted in the lobby of the Equitable Center revealed that passers-by were generally enthusiastic about the Roy Lichtenstein giant *Mural With Blue Brushstroke* which hangs there. Comments included approval of the "upbeat, with-it image" it lent to the building and the fact that it identified the building. (No need to give visitors the formal address.) However, of the 30 pedestrians randomly surveyed, none were able to identify the mural's maker by name, and only three had ever ventured into the adjacent gallery to see the shows provided by the Whitney Museum.

A second informal survey, conducted among people who regularly visit museums and galleries, revealed that, of the 30 people questioned, only four had ever been to a Whitney branch museum. Those four had visited the Equitable Center both to see the Lichtenstein mural and to satisfy a curiosity regarding the corporate–museum relationship. None of the 30 considered the exhibits mounted at the branch museums to be of much interest. The consensus reached after reading the title of the exhibit and the list of participating artists was that neither the objects nor their context was new. Stimulating ideas are offered in shows all over New York City, creating a highly competitive market for art exhibits.

An objective accounting of the activities at the branch museums for the 1988–89 season revealed that each branch presented five exhibitions that year except for Philip Morris, which presented four shows. (The following statistics were compiled from the Whitney Museum's *Annual Reports*.) The Whitney Museum Downtown at Federal Reserve Plaza was unique among the branches in that exhibits presented there were curated by Helena Rubinstein Fellows participating in the Whitney Museum Independent Study Program. (The program was supported by the Helena Rubinstein Foundation.) Under the supervision of Whitney Museum staff, ten Fellows, undergraduate and graduate students from universities throughout the world, developed and implemented exhibition proposals. Working in teams of four, the Fellows selected the work to be exhibited, designed the installation, wrote the essay for the accompanying brochure, and coordinated publicity. Four of the five exhibits presented at the Federal Reserve Plaza branch were organized by Rubinstein Fellows. All were thematic exhibits, exploring some aspect of American art in a broader art-historical context. "Convulsive Beauty: The Impact of Surrealism on American Art," for example, explored the influence of European Surrealism through the ideas of automatism, biomorphism, dream imagery, and the unconscious. Thirty-eight artists were represented by 67 paintings, sculptures, drawings, and photographs. Both the theme and the works presented indicate an in-depth research project.

Exhibitions at the other three branches were curated by the directors of those branches or were traveling exhibits. At Equitable Center, the

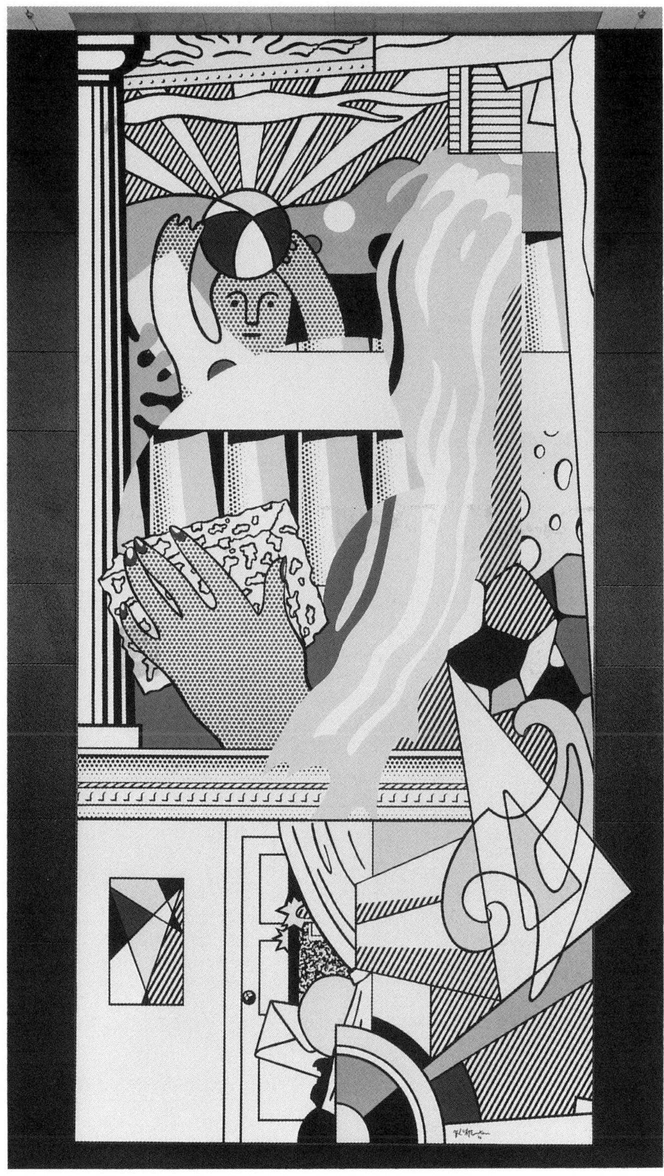

Mural with Blue Brush Stroke 1984–85 by Roy Lichtenstein. Acrylic on canvas, 68 ft. $\frac{3}{4}$ in. × 32 ft. $5\frac{1}{2}$ in.
Collection, The Equitable Life Assurance Society of the U.S.

director curated two exhibitions and borrowed three. At Fairfield, the director curated one exhibition and borrowed four. At Philip Morris, three shows were curated by the director and the fourth show was borrowed.

An overview of the exhibitions at these three branches indicates that the total of fourteen shows were composed of five painting exhibitions, three photography exhibitions, two drawing exhibitions, and one exhibition containing a mix of media. This was a good representation of artists' media.

Thematically, the fourteen shows provided a look at social history (six) and formal art issues (two). Four exhibitions covered portraiture and/or the human figure, and one took nocturne as its theme. Only one of the fourteen shows is based in art history and involves serious research, and that one was developed at the Federal Reserve Plaza branch by Rubinstein Fellows and subsequently traveled to Fairfield.

Nine of the fourteen shows were composed of works of art with representational imagery, and the remaining five contained a mix of realism and abstraction. The issue of abstraction, the dominant theme in twentieth-century art, clearly was not being addressed in any of the three branch museum programs in any coherent way. With the exception of the work of the Rubinstein Fellows at Federal Reserve Plaza, the programs were not concerned with scholarship but rather served as outreach for the museum. The nature of the exhibits may very well indicate self-censorship. The shows were nonconfrontational, not controversial, easily digested along with lunch, easily accessible for the average person, and presented a contemporary, upbeat image for the corporate sponsor.

A comparison of these branch programs and the program of exhibitions at the main site on Madison Avenue should provide further insight. Eleven shows were presented at the Whitney Museum during the 1988–89 season. Of the eleven, eight were originated by Whitney curators, one by Whitney Fellows, and two were borrowed from other institutions. According to media, the shows divided into: three painting, three sculpture, one photography, two architecture, an exhibit of folk art paintings and assorted objects, and the "Biennial," which includes all fine art media. Eight of the eleven exhibitions were one-person shows. Of the nine exhibitions of fine art, four were of abstract work, three dealt with figuration, and two were a mix of recognizable and abstract imagery, predominantly abstract.

The Whitney Museum program consisted of major exhibitions, which occupied a full floor of the museum and were accompanied by a publication, and small undocumented exhibitions held in the Lobby Gallery. The mix from this perspective was seven major shows, four shows in the Lobby Gallery. Of the seven major shows, four were organized by the four Whitney curators (one each), two were borrowed, and the seventh, the "Biennial," was a joint effort of four curators. So the main museum program was a good mix of media, a solid representation of the more difficult art, and an even distribution of curatorial responsibility. One glaring hole in the program is the absence of art-historical themes, both in comparative surveys and one-person retrospectives, a situation which would call into question the scholarship of Whitney curators.

Writing for the *New York Times*, Michael Brenson zeroed in on the problem that year as he found fault with the fact that the museum had built its staff around five young curators with little art-historical experience, representing only one generation. Brenson profiled the curators—the youngest was 33 years old, the oldest was 42—and discovered that only one of them held an advanced degree in art history. No wonder then that, as Brenson wrote, "In so many of the Whitney's catalogs and installations, independent critical and scholarly perspective is absent" (Brenson, 1989: 27).

Commenting on exhibitions at the Whitney, Brenson continued:

> The Whitney should present contemporary art in a way that is unmistakably independent of dealer and collector interference. It should present contemporary art in a way that is measured and searching, offering a perspective that galleries, auction houses and corporations cannot provide. But how is perspective possible in a museum that is so uneasy with history?
>
> No New York museum seems more trendy and hip, and none is more at sea. Who can remember the last Whitney exhibition that seemed finished—in other words, thoroughly conceived, considered and installed? Who can remember a Whitney exhibition that generated confidence in the museum's capacity to deal with either the achievements of the old or the challenges of the new? (1989: 1)

In reviewing some of the shows under discussion (1988–89 season), Brenson criticized the Richard Armstrong catalog of the David Park exhibition, for example, as "hurried." He also called into question the totally American perspective: "This point of view cannot do justice to the achievement of an artist for whom European art remained a lantern and European subject matter a guide" (1989: 27).

Of the Donald Judd exhibition curated by Barbara Haskell, Brenson wrote: "the catalogue provides little insight into the artist's formative years, and the show does not include the figurative works from the 1950's that could have shed light on the absoluteness of Judd's abstract style." He noted that the exhibition "lacks the clarity and conviction that are so much a part of Mr. Judd's achievement" and that the design of the show allowed "no sense of chronology and development" (Brenson, 1988: 32).

Returning to the survey of 30 people who regularly visit museums and galleries, we find that all had been to the Whitney Museum at least once during the 1988–89 season and that 26 of them had seen the "Biennial," the Whitney's famous blockbuster exhibition that fills the entire museum with paintings, sculpture, photographs, films, and videotapes produced within the previous two years. Described by Tom Armstrong as "an overview of what we think is interesting at the present moment, what we think stands out, what makes you think and makes you look," the "Biennial" was the product of the four Whitney curators and was the museum's flagship exhibition.

Some typical comments coming from the people surveyed included "It's about who's cool, who's in;" "The prestige of being chosen for the 'Biennial' is enormous and it impacts on the artist's prices;" "For the artist it means you're alive and well. People want to buy your work;" and "It's who's hot and who's not."

Brenson called the "Biennial" the "foundation" of the museum's program and noted how, "with relish," it was allowed to overrun the entire museum. And yet, he wrote, this is where "judgements are ambiguous" and further, "it is unclear from the catalogue essay just what Mr. Armstrong, Mr. Marshall and Ms. Phillips think. There was talk that this Biennial catalogue would include a real essay. But the painting, sculpture and photography text, although graduating from 'preface' to 'introduction', is still far short of what is needed. Its style is curt, suggesting the essay was written out of obligation. Key ideas remain unclear" (Brenson, 1989: 27).

It seems the "Biennial" was more about fashion and money than about a critical, thoughtful presentation of art. The lack of scholarship, even in this, the museum's single most important exhibition, caused savage criticism by respected art historians in the *Times* and elsewhere.

Is there a corporate connection? Some think so. Hans Haacke's perception of the problem alludes to the fact that the museum curators are charged with fundraising, spending time with corporate executives, to insure funding for the museum.

> They're told to fund-raise instead of doing their curatorial work. But the curators need to rethink their job, and should be allowed and given time to think. Financial constraints could force museums to rely on their own collections. This would be good because it could lead, if we're lucky, to genuine scholarship. It could lead curators to learn more about the collections. (Interview with Nancy Einreinhofer)

Philippe de Montebello sees how the courting of corporate support, specifically for the funding of special exhibits, might undermine scholarship. "Traditional values are upset," he writes, "Basic museum work—conservation, research, cataloging, scholarly publications—gives way to the effort that goes into realizing special events with their quantifiable results." And these quantifiable results tend to obscure the depth of quality of programs, and quality is soon perceived as a "burden on the bottom line," rather than a necessity.

> Aren't museums in danger of creating in this project-oriented world, a whole generation of curators who, because these other duties have denied them sufficient unstructured time for studying and looking, will not have their seniors' knowledge or experience so they can later perform with intelligence and discrimination in more important positions?
> (de Montebello, 1984: 48)

The criticism of Whitney Museum programs was, in part, what spurred the dismissal of the director. Tom Armstrong was forced out in March, 1990 after several months of art world rumors that the board president, William S. Woodside, had asked for his resignation. "Several trustees have complained privately about the quality of some Whitney shows," wrote Grace Glueck in the *New York Times*, "They attribute that in part to Mr. Armstrong's unwillingness to hire a strong chief curator to run the museum's collecting and exhibition programs" (Glueck, 1989b: 21).

The museum and the corporation, a relationship developed in earnest by Thomas Hoving, further evolved with Tom Armstrong. While both of these directors departed their posts with mixed reviews, they also broadened the corporate–museum relationship in irreversible ways.

It is what Philippe de Montebello calls the business administration mentality, and he sees this mentality as dominating museums even at the policy-making level. "This means—I'm simplifying greatly, drawing a straight line to my point—that all museum activities, all projects, all work will soon be cost-accounted and that the right questions may no longer be asked" (de Montebello, 1984: 48).

The "right" questions concern the quality and importance of a project, the "wrong" questions concern the revenues a project might generate. "A museum's exhibition program now tends to be viewed by the administration as being in the service of the museum's budget—instead of the other way around. Exhibitions are exploited by a formidable business machine ... the whole critical mass of staff and services employed to generate, shape and execute exhibitions" is exploited "to the detriment of the staff's custodial as well as creative functions" (de Montebello, 1984: 47).

Warnings from within the profession cite the potential dangers to museums which operate like corporations and to directors who operate like C.E.O.s, but the benefits of the business-administration mentality present a strong draw.

Case study II: the Guggenheim Museum

The Guggenheim Museum Board of Trustees decided on the corporate approach for its museum when, in 1988, it hired Thomas Krens as its director. With an undergraduate degree in political economics (Williams College, 1969) and a master's degree in studio art (State University of New York at Albany, 1971), Krens returned to Williams College as an assistant professor to teach print-making. In 1980 he became the director of the Williams College Museum of Art and in 1984 received a master's degree in public and private management from the Yale School of Management. Obviously, Krens' knowledge of art history was largely self-taught. His appointment as director of the Guggenheim was based on his skills in management and development. Those skills would be employed to oversee the somewhat controversial addition to the Frank Lloyd Wright building in New York as well as the expansion of the Peggy Guggenheim Collection in Venice (Glueck, 1988: 1). He was also at that time managing another major construction project, the Massachusetts Museum of Contemporary Art in North Adams. A complex of abandoned factories was to be converted into the world's largest museum of contemporary art and the support facilities it would require, including a hotel, restaurants, shops, and condominiums. The factories, spread over 20 acres, contain 720,000 square feet of space, 500,000 of which would be dedicated to the exhibition of art.

The idea for the Massachusetts Museum of Contemporary Art began when Krens was director of the museum at Williams College, basically as an economic redevelopment project. Krens negotiated with the state to set up a commission, with Krens as chairman. They passed a $35 million bond issue to finance half the project and enable the commission to acquire the mill complex. According to reports in the *New York Times*, if the museum is not built, the mills would remain empty and the State of Massachusetts would take the loss. Key to the success of the project are the "assets" of the Guggenheim Museum, that is, its collection, which Krens planned to use as a financial base from which to launch the Massachusetts museum.

Thomas Krens was viewed by the art and museum communities as a businessman/entrepreneur who talked about art as a commodity and museums as an industry. He proposed to transform the "industry," to change how museums operate, how they acquire art, how they show it, how they think about it. Museums, he said, are in a crisis, they need to explore "mergers and acquisitions" and understand "asset management." According to Krens, a museum's assets are its collections. Its exhibitions and programs are its "product" (Weisgall, 1989: 58).

Under the Krens directorship, the Guggenheim sold off some of its "assets" to purchase a huge collection of contemporary art. Art world watchdogs were outraged at the deaccessioning of several major paintings by modern masters including Chagall and Kandinsky. How does the Krens decision to deaccession objects from the Guggenheim collection reflect the influence of the corporation? A look at museum deaccessioning policy will begin to answer this question.

At the height of Hovingism, the Metropolitan Museum secretly sold important paintings from its collection and was subsequently investigated by the New York State attorney general. The Hoving scandal did bring some museums to develop more rigorous deaccession policies, and the American Association of Museums Committee for Professional Practices in Art Museums revised and strengthened its deaccession guidelines, but deaccessions have continued to increase in volume and value. For example, the *New York Times* reported that the number of museums which put works of art up for sale at Christie's increased from 28 in 1984–85 to 88 in 1988–89 and that the dollars generated went up from $3.5 million in 1984–85 to $29.6 million in 1988–89 (Kimmelman, 1990a: 1).

Christie's has now established a department to deal specifically with museums.

The Metropolitan's policy since the 1970s has been in keeping with the American Association of Museums and is simply to keep deaccession decisions completely independent of purchasing decisions. This is not to say that the income from the sale of art should not be used for new acquisitions, but rather that the decision to sell a work be based on a policy decision that the museum no longer projects any need for that object. The A.A.M. also recommends that all funds from the sale of art work from the collections be used to replenish the collection. These two policies are generally accepted by American art museums, but, in the case of the Guggenheim, there are some doubts.

First is the question of the importance of the paintings to the collection. Several art historians acknowledged the importance of the paintings, especially the Kandinsky, and the magnitude of the loss to the museum's collection. Gert Schiff, Avalon Foundation Professor of Fine Arts at New York University, specializes in the modern period and believes the Kandinsky *Fugue* to be "one of the most beautiful pictures of his whole expressionist period" (Glueck, 1990: 31). "It really was a centerpiece of the collection" (Weiss, 1990: 130).

Within the museum world there also was criticism. Kirk Varnedoe, director of painting and sculpture at the Museum of Modern Art, said: "The general rule is we won't sell dead artists to buy living artists" (Weiss, 1990: 130). "It is one thing to sell middling Impressionist paintings to buy better Impressionist paintings," wrote *New York Times* critic Michael Kimmelman, "It is another thing entirely to sell works by early 20th century masters to buy Minimalist sculpture from the 1960s and '70s" (Kimmelman, 1990a: 1).

The modern master's paintings were sold precisely for that reason. The paintings were sold in order to finance the acquisition of Count Giuseppe Panza di Biumo's collection of over 200 works of Minimal and Conceptual art. In the process, the Guggenheim set auction records for Chagall ($14.85 million), Modigliani ($11.55 million) and Kandinsky ($20.9 million) for a total of $47.3 million.

So, in disregard of the A.A.M. recommendations, the deaccessioning of these paintings took place not because the museum no longer needed them, but for the purpose of generating money. The revenues from the sale of the paintings would be used to purchase the Panza Collection.

Another strategy in which the museum's collection is used to generate income is that of the franchised Guggenheim. Krens proposed the establishment of Guggenheim museums in Tokyo, Japan; Salzburg, Austria; Venice, Italy; and Bilbao, Spain, in addition to the Soho district of New York City and, as we have seen, the huge complex in North Adams, Massachusetts. The cost of these franchised Guggenheims, according to Krens, would be absorbed by the local governments. They would be staffed by Guggenheim curators, and the art on view would be from the Guggenheim collection and would be rotated between the franchises. Critics of the plan believe the rotation of holdings will put those objects at risk (Kimmelman, 1990b: 1). Part of the plan also calls for computer-generated research which would, again according to Krens, enable curators to turn out six or seven major exhibitions and catalogs each year (Weisgall, 1989: 60). The deaccession of some of the Guggenheim's prize paintings equated art with money. In a similar vein, this attitude toward exhibitions and publications equates them with a commercial product to be manufactured, packaged, and marketed, threatening the imposition of cost-effective procedures on curatorial time and scholarship.

Effective management of any sort requires an understanding of the nature and purpose of the thing to be managed. Art museum management requires a clear sense of aesthetic standards and sound artistic judgement. As the museum director and art scholar Sherman Lee wrote:

> An art museum is not the same kind of institution as a corporation. I don't think many business assumptions are valid for the art museum. We must not think in terms of a balance sheet. I think many museums have been put in financial jeopardy and have been mismanaged by the misapplication of business principles. (Lee, 1983: 78)

Thomas Krens expressed his vision for the museum at the occasion of the opening of the renovated Wright building and the Guggenheim Soho. The Guggenheim

> has aggressively enlarged its permanent collection in scope and depth; it has increased the number of special exhibits under research and development through the agency of a highly regarded international curatorial staff; and it has entered into collaborations with foreign government to establish permanent museums abroad that would be operated by, and in conjunction with, the Guggenheim Museum in New York.
>
> The complexity of these enterprises notwithstanding, the basic rationale for each of these developments can be found in two fairly simple but complimentary objectives, both essential to the continued vitality of the institution. The lesser objective is the practical need to insure the financial survival and prosperity of the Guggenheim as a cultural institution in an uncertain and rapidly changing world. To do this the museum must position itself to attract the largest possible audience and to secure revenue streams consistently higher than ongoing operating costs.
>
> More important, the primary objective goes beyond institutional survival to the museum's continuing development and even redefinition as a paradigmatic form. The new Guggenheim seeks not only to fulfill its original mission, and contribute to the continuing evolution of the cultural enterprise in its broadest sense, but the mission of the institution must be progressively pursued into the 21st century even if it means that the forms must change.
>
> To remain a great institution, the Guggenheim must accommodate the future. That it must honor the conservative tendencies of scholarship and stewardship that have been the traditional hallmarks of the modern

> museum goes without saying. But to realize the promise of its original vision and the statement of utopian optimism that is embodied in the very architecture of the building that houses and symbolizes the museum, and to confront the current perception of crisis that pervades the cultural world, the Guggenheim must redefine itself as a new and challenging institution, one with the capacity and energy to shape the discussion of what museums can aspire to be. (Krens, 1992)

The course of the first objective, the financial survival and prosperity of the Guggenheim, is difficult to assess since the museum has not issued an annual report or made public any financial records since 1989. The attainment of the second objective, "the museum's continuing development and even redefinition" apparently awaits the twenty-first century.

Conclusion

Art and the art museum are considered beneficial to the society. A visit to an art museum may provide an aesthetic experience or an educational opportunity. It may be spiritually, intellectually, or morally uplifting. Art and the art museum are considered to exist outside the realm of commerce yet have the potential for high popular appeal. All of these elements and conditions make the sponsorship of the art museum very appealing to American corporations. A corporation can improve its public image by association with the art museum. Through sponsorship of special exhibitions, a corporation may gain wide public awareness of its product or service and better customer relations. It may even be able to influence government legislation in favor of the corporation.

The benefits to the museum in this relationship are obviously monetary, but what are the dangers? This study indicates, through the analysis of the corporate presence at the Metropolitan Museum, the Guggenheim Museum, and the Whitney Museum, that the museum and its staff may be compromised. The corporation, when underwriting an exhibition, will apply its usual cost-accounting procedures and will expect some predetermined return for each dollar expended. This raises questions about how curatorial decisions might be influenced and how administrative policy might be determined. What may be at risk is nothing less than the very heart of museum scholarship.

8

The scholar and the capitalist: the common goals of Alfred H. Barr and Nelson Rockefeller in building the Museum of Modern Art

Introduction

The Museum of Modern Art in New York began as "an experiment to determine whether sufficient public interest exists to justify the establishment of a permanent institution devoted to collecting, exhibiting, and studying modern art." It was the first American museum devoted to modern art and it expanded quickly to include in its definition of art, modern architecture, design, film, and photography. It was, from its beginnings, the premier American authority of things modern, including the concept of the modern museum. The Museum of Modern Art instituted museum practices previously unheard of, adopting marketing methods, for example, from the American corporation. The fact that it was new, was modern, was considered experimental, allowed the Museum of Modern Art great latitude in developing policies and programs. It was modern, established by capitalists, for the purpose of educating the populace. Thus the three influences on the American art museum being examined here (modernism, capitalism, democracy) are present in full force in the Museum of Modern Art, and their implications may be clarified through a closer look at this one museum.

The Museum of Modern Art has, as an advocate of modernism, influenced museum architecture, supplanting the palace in the park with a modern, climate-controlled structure designed to move large crowds through exhibitions and into a restaurant or retail shop. Attitudes toward exhibition design and the presentation of individual works of art have been altered as a result of the practices of the Museum of Modern Art.

In its mission to collect, exhibit, and study modern art, the Museum has shown a strong democratic tendency. The collection includes not only the rather difficult paintings of the high modernists but also the well-designed yet mundane objects of everyday life. Exhibits at the Museum of

Modern Art have, of course, come from every department and have ranged from, for example, the scholarly exhibitions of Cubist painting to the exhibition of "Useful Objects of American Design Under $10" (1940). In its mission to provide for the study of modern art, this museum has shed light on alternative educational methods which, while distinctly connected to the Museum of Modern Art, have nonetheless provided insights for other museums. Even the refinement of wall labels for the purpose of instruction for all is considered by many to be part of the legacy of Alfred Barr.

The Museum of Modern Art has also had, from its inception and throughout its history, close ties to capitalism. A member of the Rockefeller family, America's foremost capitalists, was present at the birth of the Museum, and the family has continuously been represented on the Museum's Board of Trustees and has instituted, as we shall see, corporate tactics into the Museum's operations.

The three influences of modernism, democracy, and capitalism were intertwined from the beginning and have grown together through the years. The protagonists in this development were the founding director, Alfred Barr, and the founding family, the Rockefellers, in particular, Nelson Rockefeller. Alfred Barr, in his position of founding director, proved to be not only a modernist, but a populist, and in time, a capitalist. The Rockefeller legacy brought forth the Museum and set it on a self-supporting course with the help of what Nelson Rockefeller called "enlightened capitalism." The roles of these key people were critical in the development of the Museum, and the results have influenced the museum world up to the present day. The common goals of the scholar and the capitalist came together to build a democratic, consumer-oriented museum without sacrificing excellence. The beginnings of that collaboration will be examined in this chapter.

Alfred H. Barr, founding director

Alfred H. Barr, Jr. was born in Detroit in 1902, son of a Presbyterian minister, and raised in Baltimore from the age of nine (Marquis, 1989: 3–6). In 1918, he entered Princeton University and soon after enrolled in Charles Rufus Morey's course in medieval art, a course which would forever influence Barr's thinking. Taught as a record of that civilization, combining painting and sculpture with architecture, murals, illuminated manuscripts, and crafts, the medieval art course became Alfred Barr's education model.

Following graduation from Princeton in 1922, Barr was awarded a Master of Arts degree (1923) in art and archaeology and assumed a teaching assistantship at Harvard University's department of fine arts. Barr completed his course work toward the Ph.D. and in the Fall of 1926 was appointed to the position of Associate Professor of Art History, Wellesley College. At this time he also enrolled in Paul Sachs' museum

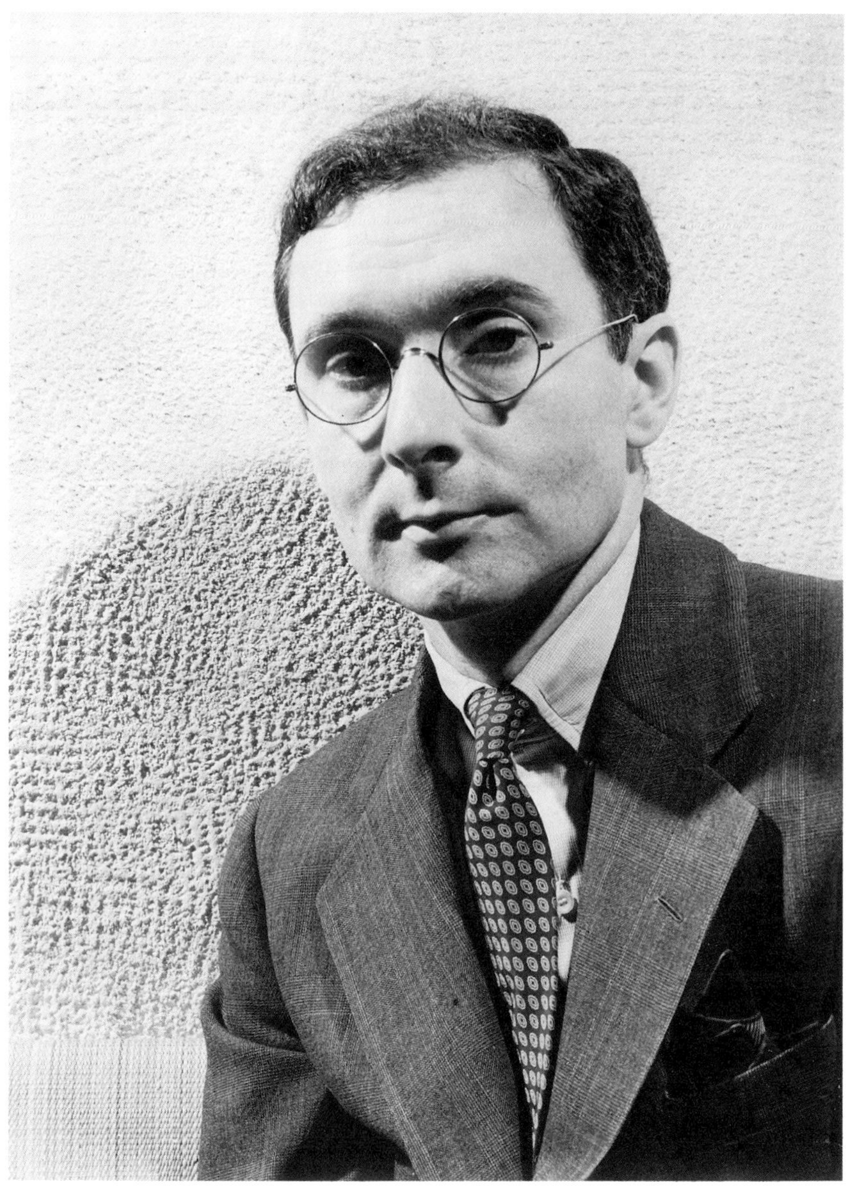

Alfred H. Barr, Jr. c. 1929–30.
The Museum of Modern Art, New York.

course at the Fogg Museum, Harvard University. Sachs arranged for a twelve-month traveling scholarship for Barr, which enabled the young scholar extended time in England, Holland, Germany, Russia, and France. Most significant among these travels was a visit to the Bauhaus at Dessau, where he met the architect Walter Gropius, and artists Paul Klee, Herbert Bayer, Oscar Schlemmer, Josef Albers, Lyonel Feininger, and Lazslo Maholy-Nagy (Lynes, 1973: 28; Marquis, 1989: 48–9). The influence of this school, where all the arts (painting, sculpture, textile design, graphic design, photography, industrial design) were taught under the umbrella of architecture, reinforced and expanded on Morey's educational methods. Barr called the Bauhaus building designed by Gropius "the most important structure of its decade." He wrote that the Bauhaus was "the one school in the world where modern problems of design were approached realistically in a modern atmosphere" (Bayer and Gropius, 1938: 7).

This firsthand exposure to a modern art school where all the modern arts, crafts, materials, techniques, and ideas were taught in concert seemed a variation of Morey's medieval art course at Princeton. Barr developed a course at Wellesley, the first of its scope at any college in America, which covered modern painting, sculpture, architecture, music, film, photography, and design. He also developed a course of lectures on modern art which included "*The Bauhaus at Dessau* ... Walter Gropius the visionary; the executive; the architect ... The painters Kandinsky, Feininger and Klee ... The curriculum: Material, Technique and Form, (Albers); architecture, (Gropius, Hannes Meyer); furniture and decorative arts; photography, (Moholy-Nagy); theater and ballet, (Schlemmer); typography and posters, (Bayer). The Bauhaus as a national and international influence" (Barr, 1929a).

When the founders of the Museum of Modern Art, upon the recommendation of Paul Sachs, offered the position of director to the then 26-year-old Alfred Barr, the young scholar proposed the organization of the new museum be based on his course at Wellesley. The Museum, he proposed, could begin with exhibitions of painting and sculpture and then expand to the other areas of modern art, including drawing, prints, photography, and design.

Barr succeeded, in time, in introducing photography, film, design and decorative arts, and architecture. The practical, commercial, and popular arts would be exhibited along with the traditional fine art media. In 1932, he established a Department of Architecture and a Department of Circulating Exhibitions and a reference library of 2,000 volumes. In 1934, he initiated the Design Collection, and in 1935, the Museum of Modern Art Film Library (now called the Department of Film) was established, the first department in any museum in the world devoted to this twentieth-century art form. The Department of Photography was founded in 1940, the first curatorial department dedicated to photography.

In retrospect, it seems extraordinary that this man of 26 years, at a time when few Americans knew anything of modern art, was able to thoroughly grasp the concept of modernism in its variety of forms and idiosyncratic manifestations. He viewed them in the context of the whole of art history, amassed this storehouse of ideas and images, organized them in some thematic way, and made them available to the general populace.

Barr as populist

When he issued essays regarding the opening of the Museum, Alfred Barr referred to the history of the public's relationship to advanced art and the cultural necessity of the Museum of Modern Art.

> New York has been extraordinarily negligent in providing a public institution where such loan exhibitions might be seen with some consistent regularity. More serious still is the absence of any permanent public collection of modern art in New York. (Barr, 1930a: 13)

Barr recognized from the beginning the importance of educational efforts in order to reach the uninitiated public and went on to say:

> Although the Museum has no definite educational program in addition to its exhibitions it is eager to cooperate with other educational institutions. During the first exhibition the galleries were specially opened to classes from Barnard, Colombia and New York University, as well as to various private lecturers and groups of artists.

Barr did view the exhibition itself as the primary educational tool.

The first exhibition opened November 7 on the twelfth floor of the Heckscher Building at Fifth Avenue and 57th Street and included paintings and drawings by the European masters of modern art—Cézanne, Gauguin, Seurat, and Van Gogh. The catalog, with an essay by Barr, marks the beginning of the Museum's publication program and lists 35 paintings by Cézanne, seven of which were watercolor; 25 paintings by Gauguin and one drawing; seventeen works by Seurat including four oil studies and six pencil drawings; and 25 oil paintings by Van Gogh plus three works on paper (Barr, 1929b). This bringing-together of more than one hundred works by these modern masters lent credibility to the museum and excited the public.

According to the *Herald Tribune*, November 10, 1929, "several thousand" people attended the exhibition on the first day it was open to the public. An article in the *New York Times* two weeks after the opening noted that "attendance at the museum has increased steadily" and reported almost 3,000 people in attendance on a Saturday afternoon. Final tallies show a total attendance of 47,000 people, indicating a clear interest in modern art (Barr, 1930a: 13).

The choice of Cézanne, Gauguin, Seurat and Van Gogh to introduce modernist ideas to New York was a success as indicated by attendance but also because it constituted an intelligent art-historical lesson. Barr described the artists as "especially honored pioneers who founded new traditions and ... rediscovered old ones." "Gauguin whose burning color and exotic sentiment conceal somber power; Van Gogh the master—and the victim—of spontaneous artistic combustion; Cézanne arriving by infinitely patient trial and error at conclusions which have changed the direction of the history of art; Seurat who proved that great art can proceed from cool exquisite calculation; here are four painters!" "Yet so revolutionary are certain aspects of their work that it is still subject to misunderstanding and, for a recalcitrant few, a battle ground of controversy" (Barr, 1929b: 11, 27).

The second exhibition of "Nineteen Living Americans" (1929–30), was organized at the insistence of the Board in an effort to demonstrate that the Museum would champion American artists as well as Europeans. "Ballots containing over a hundred names were distributed among the trustees who were asked to check the fifteen painters who each thought should be shown in the Museum's first exhibition of American painting. The results were tabulated and carefully studied by a committee who drew up the list of nineteen." Unfortunately, it lacked real focus, so diverse were the artists. Burchfield, Demuth, Hopper, Marin, O'Keeffe, and Sloan were represented (Barr, 1929–30: 9).

The third exhibition, called "Painting in Paris," contained works by Braque, Chagall, de Chirico, Matisse, Miró and Picasso among others. An instructional catalog crafted by Barr to enlighten visitors regarding modern painting seems to have been well received, since attendance was recorded at 58,575. Clearly, there was an enthusiastic audience for European modern art, the art Alfred Barr believed to be central to Modernism. "Surely Paris in the early twentieth century need bow to no other period of painting" Barr proclaimed in the catalog as he placed these European modernists amidst the whole history of art (Barr, 1930b: 16). Always the educator, Barr produced a catalog essay describing the modernist movements in simple and direct terms. "The 'fauves' painted pictures using crude distorted heavy outlines and harsh 'unnatural' colors which were as much a proclamation of emancipation as the result of 'aesthetic exigency.' They were possessed by two passions—the problem of design and the expression of emotion. To these two ends they sacrificed the contemporary conception of natural appearances" (p. 12). Barr offered a definition of cubism as "a simplification of landscape, figures and other objects into quasi-geometrical blocks and cylinders." A movement which passed through several phases and, by 1917, had evolved from the imitation of nature to the creation of an abstract design" (p. 13). He went on to describe the Surrealists as originating from "a group of literary advance-guardists with political opinions ... For them the dream is the supreme experience; the sub-conscious the exclusive source of artistic values" (p. 15).

While Barr held a vision of a Museum of Modern Art that would be triumphant, he put the challenge of supporting such an institution to the public. "The present galleries are as yet only a challenging experiment. At the end of two years it should be possible to determine whether New York really wants a permanent Museum of Modern Art" (1930a: 13).

The success of these first exhibitions and catalogs insured the continued support of the Board for Barr's vision of the Museum. Exactly ten years later, on May 10, 1939, the Museum of Modern Art's new modern museum building at 11 West 53rd Street would be dedicated by the President of the United States, Franklin D. Roosevelt. The events leading to the construction of the first modern museum building and to the development of the collection it housed, already the most distinguished of its kind in the world, are inextricably tied to the exacting intellectual tenacity of Alfred Barr and to his comprehension of how populist support could produce capital.

Barr as capitalist

The scholarly exhibitions he organized and the informative catalogs he authored combined with lively social events to keep the press reporting and the public coming. Barr aided the public relations endeavor by hiring, in 1930, an expert in the field to develop a strategy for a membership drive and a fundraising drive. (See also "Thomas Hoving and the corporate museum partnership" in Chapter 7.) The Museum of Modern Art was also the first museum to organize, in August of 1933, an in-house Publicity Department. In the course of the next ten years 1.6 million people would view 125 special exhibitions and the Museum's *Bulletin* would report more than 4,000 members. Through the generosity of the Museum Board, a collection of modern art would be built consisting of 271 paintings, 97 sculptures, 308 watercolors, six pastels, 149 prints, and an unrecorded number of drawings (compiled from records in the MOMA *Bulletin*).

The heart of the Museum's collection was the gift of one of the founders, Miss Lillie Bliss. Bequeathed at her death in 1931, the collection was transferred to the Museum in 1934 when the condition of a sufficient endowment had been met. It was recorded in the *Bulletin* that, to fulfill the terms of the Bliss bequest, "the Museum, by a quiet six weeks' campaign among its friends, raised a $600,000 Endowment Fund" (*Bulletin*, April, 1934: 1). The collection contained paintings by Renoir, Degas, Pissarro, Gauguin, Seurat, Toulouse-Lautrec, Matisse, Modigliani, and Picasso and scores of drawings and prints. Perhaps most important of all was the collection of 21 paintings by Cézanne (10 watercolors and 11 oils). "With the Bliss collection," wrote Alfred Barr in the *Bulletin*, "New York can look London, Paris, Berlin, Amsterdam, Chicago in the face so far as public collections of modern art are concerned" (*Bulletin*, April, 1934: 4).

Although Barr was reserved and scholarly, he clearly was not above appealing to potential donors on the basis of financial gain through investment in modern paintings. He acknowledged that private patronage was necessary for the health of the arts and the success of his museum. Barr could describe the difficulty, even hostility, with which modern paintings might be met and then go on to cite the increase in monetary value for the same works of art.

> International exhibitions in Paris (1906–12), Cologne (1912), London (1911), and in New York, the famous Armory exhibition of 1913, precipitated general excitement flavored with rage and laughter. But the paintings by Cézanne, Seurat, Van Gogh and Gauguin, which hung in these exhibitions and seemed then unintelligible and ridiculous, are bought by collectors now for sums ranging from $10,000 to $100,000. A single concrete example is provided by Seurat's *La Grande Jatte* which was sold at the death of the painter in 1891 for $200, sold again somewhat later for $390 and was purchased for the Birch–Bartlett Memorial Collection of the Chicago Art Institute about 1925 for approximately $25,000. In 1930, an offer of over $400,000 was refused. This represents an increase in 'bid' value of about 200,000 percent in forty years. (Barr, 1936a: 2)

Barr's ability in this regard was, in part, the legacy of his teacher Paul J. Sachs, who trained his student-curators to court collectors and present solid arguments for investments and donations. Sachs was responsible, through his museum course at Harvard University, for training the administrators of many of America's largest and most important museums at the time, including the Metropolitan Museum of Art, the National Gallery in Washington, and the Boston Museum of Fine Arts. His influence is worth noting because of its breadth and because it helped shape the Museum of Modern Art.

Paul J. Sachs arrived at the Fogg Museum at Harvard University directly from a family-owned Wall Street brokerage house in 1914 at the age of 36. His background in finance played a critical part in his expansion of the Fogg and influenced the content of his course instruction. Sachs developed a year-long graduate museum course in which he taught his students not only the appreciation of art, but the administrative skills he believed America's curators should have. Sachs provided guest lecturers, some of whom would be the future employers of his students. He also took his students on tours of private collections, collections of potential donors to America's museums. These connections served to lend prestige to the course and success to the students, many of whom went on to responsible positions in American museums (Lynes, 1973: 12; Marquis, 1989: 36).

Some of Sachs' central tenets were: the acknowledgement of European influence on American culture, the role of education in appreciating artistic efforts, and the need for an elite to guide the populace (Sachs, 1939: 6, 7). He viewed his students as this elite. They were expected to return to the populace and instruct it. "It has been well said that 'All government calls for an elite; business calls for an elite;' and I might add that sound museum administration and scholarship must rest upon an elite" (p. 7). Sachs thought of the curator as artistic interpreter. He trained his elite core to determine both the cultural and monetary value of a work of art and to covey the cultural value to the museum visitor while figuring out how to raise the money to acquire the object for the museum's collection. His students were first of all administrators trained in a market economy that favored a distinctly American consumption of art (see Chapter 7).

The Museum of Modern Art under the direction of Sachs' most famous student, Alfred Barr, would be the first testing ground for Sachs' ideas about the museum profession. The Museum of Modern Art, at its inception, operated like no other museum of that time, for Alfred Barr not only served as director, but also curated all the exhibits, wrote the catalogs, and determined what the museum should purchase. As the museum grew and these functions became more complex, the museum operated more and more along the lines of a private American corporation, and Alfred Barr's role changed. But initially, his position was what Sachs prescribed to create a museum operating on the highest level of scholarship and reaching the populace as well.

The structure of the museum, educational by its nature, was in place. This structure, combined with catalogs, wall labels and lectures, provided the means of instructing the masses brought into the museum through the prodding of the popular press. The pragmatic stance of viewing art as investment was also taken and, although Alfred Barr may not have realized it at the time, his constantly changing exhibitions created for the museum a consumer constituency.

Barr as modernist

It seems a most appropriate notion that a modern museum would be in constant flux, reflecting, in its tempo, modern society. It is said that our modern culture, and the economy on which it is based, annihilates everything that it creates—physical environments, social institutions, metaphysical ideas, artistic visions, moral values—in order to create more, to endlessly create the world anew. This disposable, consumer culture forces us to grapple with the question of what is essential, what is important, what is meaningful. That is the question most often addressed by modern artists (see Chapter 5).

Historians trace the beginnings of modernism to discoveries in the physical sciences which changed our ideas about the universe and caused a reinterpretation of religious doctrine. Scientific discoveries also transformed production, and industrialization was born. Modernization created new human environments and destroyed old ones, the tempo of life speeded up, and immense demographic upheavals resulted in rapid urban growth. Mass communication and new forms of corporate power created an ever-expanding capitalist world market. Modernism nourished an amazing variety of visions and ideas which found form in the art and architecture of the twentieth century. The Museum of Modern Art was created to embody the ideas and visions and forms of modern culture and would do so, in large part, through its architecture.

The sleek new building that opened in 1939 to house the world's greatest collection of modern art in all its manifestations was the result of architectural ideas discovered and promoted by Alfred Barr years earlier. Barr visited the Bauhaus in Dessau, Germany in 1927 and was inspired by its comprehensive approach to the visual arts. Just as the Bauhaus mix of fine arts, commercial arts, and industrial arts constituted the basis of Barr's departmental structure of the Museum of Modern Art, so would its architecture influence the design of the Museum's building.

Shortly after the Museum of Modern Art was founded, Barr invited two like-minded scholars to organize an exhibition of Bauhaus-style architecture. Henry-Russell Hitchcock and Philip Johnson curated "Modern Architecture: International Exhibition," which was accompanied by a catalog detailing the new architecture Barr himself labeled the "International Style" (Hitchcock *et al.* 1932).

> A number of progressive architects have converged to form a genuinely new style which is rapidly spreading throughout the world [Barr wrote in the catalog essay]. Both in appearance and structure this style is peculiar to the twentieth century and is as fundamentally original as the Greek or Byzantine or Gothic ... The aesthetic principles of the International Style are based primarily upon the nature of modern materials and structure and upon modern requirements in planning. Slender steel posts and beams, and concrete reinforced by steel have made possible structures of skeleton-like strength and lightness. The external surfacing materials are of painted stucco or tile, or, in more expensive buildings, of aluminum or thin slabs of marble or granite and of glass both opaque and transparent. Planning, liberated from the necessity for symmetry so frequently required by tradition is, in the new style, flexibly dependent upon convenience.
>
> These technical and utilitarian factors in the hands of designers who understand inherent aesthetic possibilities have resulted in an architecture comparable in integrity and even in beauty to the styles of the past.
>
> (Hitchcock *et al.* 1932: 12)

Barr, always the educator, edges the reader toward an understanding of the architects' plight:

> just as the modern architect has had to adjust himself to modern problems of design and structure so the modern public, in order to appreciate his achievements, must make parallel adjustments to what seems new and strange. (Hitchcock *et al.* 1932: 12)

He then goes on to instruct the reader/museum visitor in a definition of International Style architecture, a definition that holds true to this day.

Barr sets down four principles of architectural design he calls the principles (1) of volume; (2) of regularity; (3) of flexibility; and (4) the "comprehensive principle of positive and negative."

The principle of volume is clear:

> The modern architect ... conceives of his building not as a structure of brick or masonry with thick columns and supporting walls resting heavily upon the earth but rather as a skeleton enclosed by a thin light shell. He thinks in terms of volume—of space enclosed by planes or surfaces—as opposed to mass and solidarity. (p. 14)

The principles of regularity and flexibility are related in Barr's definition. He refers to the historic use of bilateral symmetry, that is, balanced masses on either side of a central axis, and to the horizontal division of the facade. This is compared to the modern building which reveals its structure through both horizontal and verticle division which may very well be asymmetrical, depending on the function of the building, ergo: flexibility.

Barr also makes reference to the lack of decoration when he writes: "He [the architect] permits the horizontal floors of his skyscraper and the rows of windows in his school to repeat themselves boldly without artificial accents or terminations" (p. 15). The structure revealing itself and its function constitutes the aesthetics of the building.

The fourth "comprehensive principle of positive and negative" refers to the positive use of materials, technically appropriate, applied in delicate proportions, and the elimination (therefore negative) of any kind of ornament or artificial pattern. In his essay, Barr acknowledges that the "lack of ornament is one of the most difficult elements of the style for the layman to accept" and goes on to explain that "Intrinsically there is no reason why ornament should not be used, but modern ornament, usually crass in design and machine-manufactured, would seem to mar rather than adorn the clean perfection of surface and proportion" (p. 15).

The exhibition accompanied by its 200-page catalog toured the United States, in different versions, for over seven years spreading the new architectural message. By praising the architecture's modernity, originality, and, most important, its aesthetic qualities, Barr focused on architecture as art. By using the Bauhaus building at Dessau, designed by Walter Gropius, as the best illustration of the principles of modern design, Barr demonstrated how a modern institution might propagate the faith. And when, in 1936, the Museum of Modern Art initiated plans to build a new building, it would, of course, be in what had come to be known as the International Style. Alfred Barr had great hopes that the new museum building might be designed by one of the architects that had been associated with the Bauhaus, perhaps Walter Gropius or Mies von der Rohe. But alas, this was not to be (Lynes, 1973: 190; Marquis, 1989: 168, 169).

Philip Goodwin was an architect and a trustee of the Museum and was selected by his fellow trustees to be architect for the new Museum of Modern Art. He appointed a young American, Edward Durell Stone, as his associate for the project. Edward Durrell Stone had been the codesigner of the Rockefeller's Radio City Music Hall and had the backing of Nelson Rockefeller.

Barr was terribly disappointed, and resigned from the Building Committee in defeat, an act which might be viewed as the symbolic end of one period and beginning of another. Alfred Barr no longer held the directorship prescribed by Paul Sachs. Alfred Barr's scholarship and expertise, as evidenced in exhibitions and catalogs, had established the Museum's credibility, and his efforts in spreading the modernist message had taken the form of modern marketing techniques. The groundwork was complete for the Museum to move toward a truly capitalistic structure, one that would be initiated by Nelson Rockefeller.

The new Museum of Modern Art building designed by trustee Philip Goodwin and associate Edward Durrell Stone received a warm welcome when it opened just three years later in 1939. It was in fact the first International Style building in America and was praised in *Architectural Forum* for its "efficient and flexible plan, superlative use of materials, color, furnishings ... a thoroughly distinguished addition to the best modern architecture has produced" (August, 1939: 116).

Nelson Rockefeller presided at the opening of the new building, presiding in his new post of President of the Board of Trustees. Alfred Barr, while respected as a scholar, was no longer idealized as the all-knowing cultural administrator. The power had begun to shift, and the future and the character of the Museum of Modern Art would now begin to be defined to a large extent by the Board.

The Rockefeller charitable legacy

Nelson Rockefeller, son of John D. Rockefeller, Jr. and Abby Aldrich Rockefeller, was first appointed to the Museum Board in 1932. The importance of Nelson Rockefeller's role in the development of the Museum of Modern Art is the result, in part, of his presence during the Museum's formative years. (In contrast, by the time his younger brother David came of age, the character of the Museum and the direction in which it would move were well established.) Nelson played an important part in establishing the physical plant, the collections, and the financial operation of the Museum. He had a sincere interest in modern art, an interest stimulated no doubt by his mother. This combined with his unfaltering faith in capitalism, inherited perhaps from his father and grandfather.

The Rockefeller legacy began with Nelson's grandfather, John D., a Cleveland, Ohio bookkeeper who at the age of 23 went into business with Samuel Andrews, the inventor of an inexpensive process for the refinement of crude petroleum. At the age of 30, John D. formed the Standard Oil Company and within six years had gained control of 90 percent of the oil refineries in the United States, with a virtual monopoly on their marketing facilities as well.

Rockefeller's business dealings were questioned by individual Americans, newspapers and popular journals, and the United States Supreme Court which, by an antitrust decision in 1911, broke Standard Oil into smaller companies. Although his philanthropic tendencies were present even prior to his financial success and grew as his earnings grew, Rockefeller's generosity was regarded with suspicion (Collier, 1976: 3–4). Not until John D. Rockefeller had earned almost $1 billion and given away $500 million (the largest sum ever donated by an individual) did the public become satisfied that the scale of his good works matched that of his wealth.

John D. Rockefeller established large philanthropic institutions with the guidance of Frederick T. Gates, a Baptist minister and fundraiser. Gates established guidelines for various Rockefeller philanthropies. In 1913, the Rockefeller Foundation was chartered, and $100 million was set aside "to promote the well-being of mankind throughout the world" (Collier, 1976: 65). Rockefeller would invest $500 million over the next twelve years to promote higher education in the United States; medical research throughout the world; scientific agriculture; the fine arts and the refinement of taste; and Christian ethics and Christian civic virtue. These funds would be administered by the Rockefeller Foundation, the Rockefeller Institute for Medical Research, the General Education Board, and the Laura Spelman Rockefeller Memorial Fund (Collier, 1976: 100).

By the time John D. Rockefeller, Jr., came of age, presiding over the family's philanthropic institutions was a full-time job. Junior, as he was called, was president of the Foundation and on the board of the Institute for Medical Research while Gates held the chairmanships of both foundations. In 1917, Gates stepped down and Junior assumed full control of both chairs. With his wife, Abby Aldrich, Junior extended the family's interests beyond the initial activities of the Rockefeller–Gates philanthropic institution. Rockefeller Junior contributed to the establishment and maintenance of National Parks from Maine to California. In 1925, he supplied the Metropolitan Museum of Art with a collection of medieval art objects and later constructed the Cloisters Museum as a branch of the Metropolitan Museum to house the collection. In 1927, he began the restoration of Colonial Williamsburg, one of several restorations he financed in the United States and Europe. In 1928, he began construction of his most ambitious project, Rockefeller Center.

Abby Aldrich Rockefeller, like her husband, was interested in art. She had been educated in the prominent European art movements as was the custom of her class in that time, and upon her marriage to John D., Jr., she began to collect the art a wealthy family was expected to own: Old Masters.

Abby Aldrich Rockefeller was also a woman with an adventurous spirit. She maintained a gallery of modern art housed on the top floor of the family's New York City mansion. Much to the chagrin of her rather conservative husband, Abby studied the new art, invited the art intellectuals of the day to her gallery (including Alfred Barr), and instilled in her children an appreciation for modern art (Chase, 1950).

Her love of modern art was so strong that in 1929 Abby Rockefeller, along with two other wealthy socialites, Mrs. Cornelius Sullivan and Miss Lillie P. Bliss, founded the Museum of Modern Art. These women, and a handful of recruited founding fathers, had access to the intellectual and material wealth necessary to successfully launch the new endeavor during a period of national catastrophe, the stockmarket crash of 1929 and the Great Depression. In retrospect, it seems an unlikely time to begin such a daring adventure, but, as Mrs. Rockefeller wrote to her sister the same year the museum idea was formed:

> To me art is one of the great resources of my life. I believe that it not only enriches the spiritual life, but that it makes one more sane and sympathetic, more observant and understanding, regardless of whatever age it springs from, whatever subjects it represents. (Rockefeller, 1929)

Surely this period in American history had need of an enriched spirituality.

The Rockefeller influence on the Museum of Modern Art not only was present at the museum's inception but has stretched across the years directing its growth and defining its mission. A Rockefeller, as we have seen, participated in the conception of the idea of the museum; a Rockefeller gave the land for the museum; the building resulted from Rockefeller donations, and the collection was built in large part with Rockefeller support. There has always been a Rockefeller on the Museum of Modern Art board, and the Rockefeller philosophy of expansionism has prevailed.

At the time of her death in 1948, the Museum of Modern Art *Bulletin* stated Abby Rockefeller's enthusiasm for the Museum. "She served as a Trustee continuously since November 1929, was its first Treasurer, has held the offices of 1st Vice-President and 1st Vice-Chairman, and has worked unfailingly on countless committees" (*Bulletin* 1948: 23). "It was to modern art that she gave her heart," wrote the *New York Herald-Tribune*, "and the city should long be grateful to her for her discerning eye and her generous, modest leadership. To say that she was a leading spirit in the foundation of the Museum of Modern Art is to understate the case" (*Bulletin*, 1948: 23).

Her love of modern art and dedication to the Museum would have a profound influence on the lives of two of her sons, Nelson and David, and on her daughter-in-law, Mrs. John D. Rockefeller III (Blanchette). All three would serve Abby Rockefeller's Museum of Modern Art in many capacities, giving generously of their time and money.

Nelson Rockefeller would be the first. During his Freshman year at Dartmouth College, Abby took Nelson on a Christmas vacation excursion to the studios of some modern artists, including Arthur B. Davies, one of the initiators of the Armory Show of 1913. When Nelson wrote to his

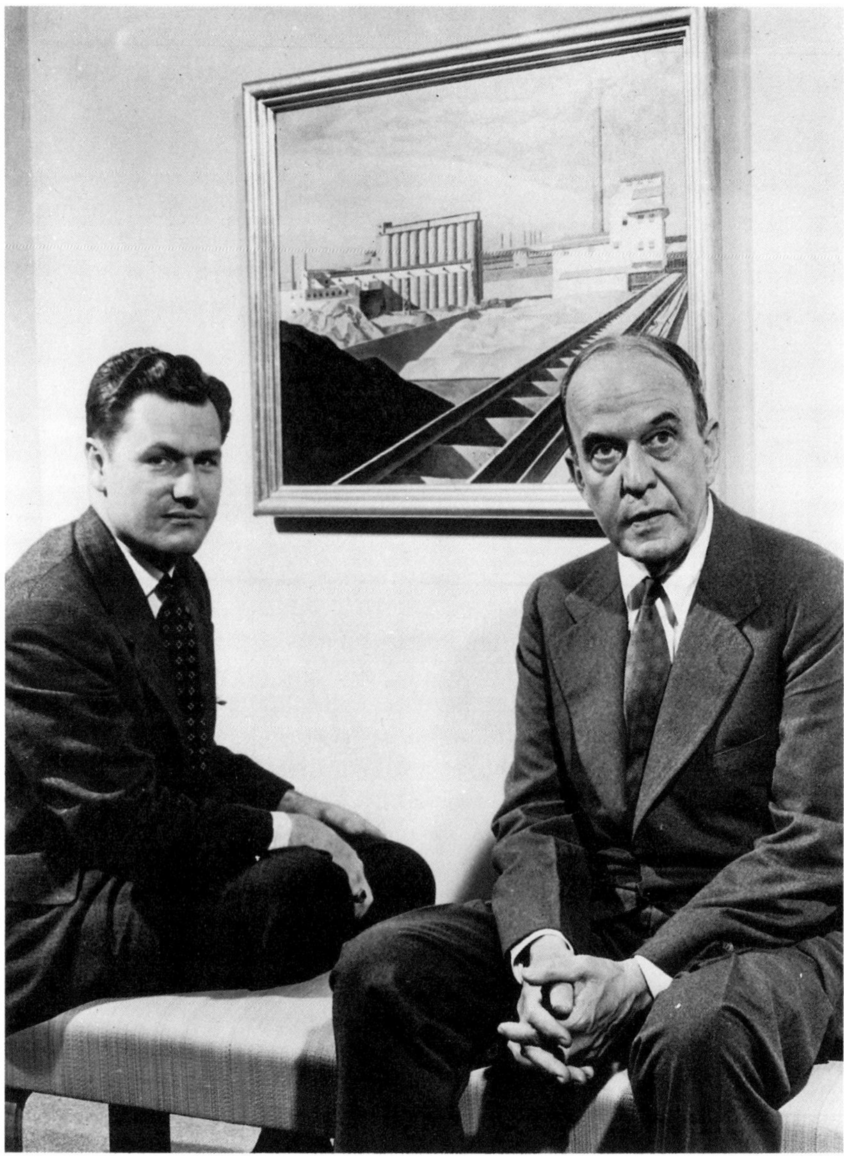

Nelson A. Rockefeller and Stephen C. Clark, 1939.
The Museum of Modern Art, New York.

mother regarding the experience, she answered: "If you start to cultivate your taste and eye so young, you ought to be very good at it by the time you can afford to collect" (Rockefeller, 1929).

Nelson Rockefeller, enlightened capitalist

Nelson Rockefeller edited a journal called *Fine Arts* while a student at Dartmouth and practiced on his own the art of photography. Upon graduation from college his mother arranged for him to serve with her on the Museum's Board of Trustees. Nelson was 23 years old. Within two years he was made chairman of the Finance Committee, and five years later he was elected President of the Museum (information compiled from records in the Museum of Modern Art *Bulletin*).

In a 1941 CBS radio interview, Nelson, then President of the Museum, spoke.

> How did my interest in art begin? Well, my family has always been interested in art, and I more or less grew up with it. We have always had discussions and plans about art at home.
>
> I am interested in art that relates to the life of our own day, expresses the spirit of our time; that isn't cloistered and set apart; that includes the house and the motor car and the rest of the things we live with, as well as painting and sculpture. To my mind, that is the way art can be made to mean something to the individual: to be part of the materials of living.
>
> The true enjoyment of art is more than a vague and dutiful respect paid to the traditions of the past. At home, when we put a picture on the wall, I am not so much interested in its historical value, as in the pleasure it gives; the contribution it makes to the room and to the house. But what attracts me most to the art of our time is its vitality—the way it explores new possibilities and makes use of new materials.
>
> That is what I like best about the Museum. It is trying to make the art of today useful and enjoyable to the public of today. Our contemporary arts need not wait fifty or a hundred years before they are widely appreciated.
>
> (Rockefeller, 1941)

Mrs. John D. Jr. certainly was interested in having her son assume a position of influence in the Museum, but she was not only ambitious for Nelson, she was ambitious for her museum and recognized that he would serve it well.

When Nelson assumed the presidency of the Museum in 1939 he was 30 years old and the Museum of Modern Art was just ten. It was the beginning of a new era, because the Museum was moving into its new home, a modern building designed to be a modern museum. It was an era of new ideas in museum administration, including the application of the methods of what Nelson referred to as "enlightened capitalism."

Nelson Rockefeller knew the Museum well, for he had served as its Treasurer, Chairman of the Advisory Committee, and as a member of the Executive Committee and of the Building Committee. (Unless otherwise noted, all information was gleaned from the *Bulletin*, and the MOMA *Financial Reports*.) Although he was only 30 years old, he was already the President of Rockefeller Center and a director of Creole Petroleum Corporation, a subsidiary of Standard Oil. Nelson Rockefeller understood corporate management and was quick to apply capitalist principles to the operation of the Museum. His plan was to cut expenses by operating more efficiently and increase income by marketing the product, modern art, in a variety of forms, including books and posters. He also looked to the continued expansion of the Museum and its programs.

It is said the desire to always enlarge, making things more visible, more monumental, was a part of the Rockefeller character. Evidence of this can be seen throughout the City and the State of New York. Some of the trustees believed the Museum should strive to live within its means, and one trustee, Henry Allen Moe, wrote a memo to this effect and presented it to Nelson. Rockefeller responded to Moe: "I'm not used to this down operation, I'm used to expanding operations, and if this report is adopted by the board I would have to resign the presidency." The memorandum was withdrawn and Nelson proceeded with his plans (Lynes, 1973: 392).

The Museum of Modern Art had, almost from its inception, a method and a means for publicity. It issued its first *Bulletin* in 1933, and this became the means of communication between the Museum and its members. When Alfred Barr established a Publicity Department, it was a first for an American museum.

For the opening of the new museum building, however, Nelson Rockefeller hired an expert public relations person to coordinate publicity (Lynes, 1973: 198). Julian Street, Jr. engaged CBS for a radio broadcast covering the formal opening. He arranged for Lowell Thomas to host the radio show, and guests included Edsel Ford and John Hay Whitney in New York; Walt Disney talking about the importance of film from Hollywood; Robert Hutchins, President of the University of Chicago, asserting that "Perception is understanding," and direct from the White House in Washington, D.C., Franklin Delano Roosevelt stated that

> The standards of American taste will inevitably be raised by this bringing into far-flung communities results of the latest and finest achievements in all the arts. In encouraging the creation and enjoyment of beautiful things we are furthering democracy itself. That is why this museum is a citadel of civilization ... Because it has been conceived as a national institution ... The opportunity before the Museum of Modern Art is as broad as the whole United States" (Roosevelt, 1939)

The broad reach and influence of the Museum was both illustrated and acknowledged.

Publicity would bring to the museum an increase in attendance (the increase from 119,803 in 1939 to 585,303 in 1940 includes 145,000 visitors to the Italian Masters Exhibit), in membership dollars (from April, 1939 to April, 1940, Museum membership doubled, growing from 3,110 to 6,846), and in financial support through increased sales of printed matter (107,814 books and catalogs were distributed, 9,145 color reproductions and 123,542 postcards sold). All this was intended to help keep the annual deficit from getting out of hand and to eventually put the Museum on a self-supporting basis.

That year, for example, income from admissions, memberships, and so on, furnished about one-third of the Museum's budget. The other two-thirds were income from the endowment fund, from foundations, and donated, principally from trustees. Abby Aldrich Rockefeller donated substantial amounts to the general budget as well as for designated purposes. She also worked to build the Museum's collections, donating four collections that year: a collection of American folk art containing 35 paintings and eighteen sculptures; a collection of 22 modern paintings with six additional works to be added later; 1,311 prints; 22 watercolors plus 68 purchased separately for the Museum; a collection of 40 modern sculptures; and one photograph and 62 posters (MOMA *Annual Report*, 1940: 33, 34).

America's entry into the war would impact greatly on the Museum, on its budget, its policies, its exhibitions. Nelson Rockefeller temporarily resigned from an active role in the museum as the war took him away from New York City. As soon as the war ended, however, he again played a key role in the Museum's progress as he assumed, in 1945, the office of First Vice President and the Chairmanship of the Fund Raising Committee which was charged with balancing the Museum's budget (the $758,000 budget for 1945 included a deficit of $71,250, or 9.3 percent) and broadening its base of financial support by enlarging the Endowment Fund. In 1946, as Stephen C. Clark resigned as Chairman of the Board (a position he had held since 1939) to be replaced by John Hay Whitney, who had served as President, Nelson Rockefeller again accepted that position.

Rockefeller had selected Monroe Wheeler, a publisher and a publicist, to assume the position of Director of Publications. With this change, the operation became more professional. The quality of the content and design of museum publications, always outstanding, was maintained or improved, and the Museum of Modern Art's books won many awards. Simon and Schuster were retained to handle the distribution of museum catalogs to book stores, libraries, and so forth, and foreign language editions were introduced and distributed internationally. The market was therefore broadened, and the publications department began to turn a profit. The 1945 *Annual Report* indicates that the Museum sold 50,000 books, 22,000 color reproductions, and 70,000 postcards. Nelson Rockefeller wanted the entire operation to run as efficiently as the publications department and hired efficiency experts to examine the problem and recommend where staff might be cut or at least used more effectively.

Rockefeller's reputation for prudent financial management was established prior to assuming the position of President the first time. In 1939, *Time* magazine reported on the opening of the new building.

> The Rockefeller-sited Museum also acquired, for its tenth anniversary, a Rockefeller president: brisk, hefty, sunny Nelson Aldrich Rockefeller, 30-year-old second son of John D. Jr. As Treasurer of the Museum since 1937, Nelson raised the funds for the new building, on which only $200,000 of $2,000,000 remained last week unpaid. (*Time* 1939: 84)

Nelson Rockefeller believed in Darwin's concept of the survival of the fittest and applied this to American corporate capitalism. Survivors are those who can "adapt to their environment... if we are as smart and intelligent as I think we are ... and if we can get rid of the emotional things ... I'm very optimistic about the future" (Scheer, 1975: 185). In Rockefeller's view, the Museum was too dependent on donations from trustees, and he was determined to correct that. In the 1939–40 *Annual Report* the Museum's "operating disbursements" were $529,464.89, and $234,593.93 of that was supplied through contributions, which still left a deficit of $39,060.83. By 1948 donations from trustees appeared relatively constant at $320,296; however, the Museum budget had more than doubled to $1,131,413. Therefore, the Museum's dependency on the generosity of the trustees was adjusted from 44 percent down to 28 percent. Income came from memberships ($163,397), admissions ($91,811), publications ($124,929), traveling exhibitions ($69,643), and assorted other moneymakers such as the restaurant ($37,087), film showings and art instruction ($29,640). Income from investments totaled almost $50,000 (MOMA *Annual Report*, 1948).

Five years later, under the guidance of Rockefeller, the Museum's expenses totaled $1,280,027, a full 65 percent of which was earned income ($832,787). Special grants amounted to $117,932; income from the Endowment Fund was $81,927, and gifts from trustees totaled $297,828. That year the Museum recorded in the *Financial Report* a surplus of $50,447.

The fact that a museum budget could be in excess of $1 million and two-thirds of that be earned through services was an astonishing accomplishment for a privately endowed institution. The Museum of Modern Art, born on the edge of the Great Depression, grew rapidly in spite of hard economic times through the generosity of the trustees. In the postwar years, with the application of corporate management techniques, the Museum could count on earned income, thus insuring its survival.

The Museum of Modern Art's exhibitions, catalogs, and collections reflected the scholarship of Alfred Barr, while the management of those "assets" reflected Nelson Rockefeller's application of the principles of "enlightened capitalism." Without sacrificing quality, The Museum of Modern Art launched a program geared to instruct the masses, as was its mission.

Conclusion

Alfred Barr tried to define the work of modern art for the man on the street. In *What Is Modern Painting?* (1943), he wrote

> When you look at these pictures, you may become upset because you can't understand them all at first glance. These paintings are not intended to sell you anything or tell you yesterday's news, though they may help you to understand our modern world. Some of them may take a good deal of study, for although we have seen a million pictures in our lives we may

> never have learned to look at painting as an art. For the art of painting, though it has little to do with words, is like a language which you have to learn to read. Some pictures are easy, like a primer and some are hard with long words and complex ideas; and some are prose, others are poetry, and others still are like algebra or geometry. (p. 3)

This democratic commitment to assisting in the appreciation of art by non-scholars was to a great extent what allowed the Rockefeller marketing plan to function successfully.

Alfred Barr broadened the terms "research" and "publish" to include in the audience not only scholars but all interested laymen. He wanted publication to mean not only the scholarly work but any outreach to the public, including printed materials, lectures, the gallery label, and every kind of reproduction. Knowing the audience you wish to reach is certainly the first step in planning how to market a product. Barr recognized the museum visitor as a consumer from every age group, from every occupation, profession, and educational level, and with varying degrees of comprehension of the new art.

This, combined with his belief in the relevance of these art forms, made him an impressive proponent.

> My belief in the cogent importance of twentieth century art lies not so much in the greatness of its achievement as in this one simple, obvious, and overwhelming fact—the twentieth century happens to be the period in which we are living. It is our century: we have made it and we've got to study it, understand it, get some joy out of it, *master* it! (Barr, 1941: 3)

The early educational democratic nature of the museum propelled it toward a consumer-oriented role. Because the early emphasis was not so much on collecting as on changing exhibits it lent itself to a consumer mind-set. Even as the collection was built, so too was constructed a myriad of activities around it, and all those materials which would serve to educate (books, posters, etc.) could be sold in the museum store.

The presence of Nelson Rockefeller's philosophy of enlightened capitalism formed the financial and operational policies of the museum. The Museum of Modern Art's Board of Trustees included like-minded capitalists, (Ford, Goodyear, Guggenheim, Whitney, Clark, Paley) who were also art lovers who built the Museum's collection and the building to house it. The Museum of Modern Art's trustees always had an important role in the affairs of the Museum and are no doubt responsible for the notion, strange in the museum world, that the collections were capital on which the management had to earn a dividend.

The Museum of Modern Art developed as a center for design, film, photography, all the modern arts, and arranged for its collections to tell the story of modern life. The Museum was now on a wide and fast track of building what would soon be the largest and most important collection of modern art in the world as well as a program to market it for a profit thus sustaining its operations. This early success brought with it new questions and new problems.

9

Transformations: a developmental examination of the Museum of Modern Art

Introduction

"To be modern," wrote Marshall Berman,

> is to experience personal and social life as a maelstrom, to find one's world and oneself in perpetual disintegration and renewal, trouble and anguish, ambiguity and contradiction: to be part of a universe in which all that is solid melts into air. To be a modernist is to make oneself somehow at home in the maelstrom, to make its rhythms one's own, to move within its currents in search of the forms of reality, of beauty, of freedom, of justice, that its fervid and perilous flow allows. (Berman, 1982: 345–6)

The Museum of Modern Art possesses the power in its collections and exhibits and programs and publications to convert its constituency into modernists, making them at home in the maelstrom. That constituency numbers about 1.5 million visitors per year to the Museum plus the untold millions who read the publications and view the traveling exhibitions. In the sixty-something years of its existence, the Museum of Modern Art has institutionalized what was a radical art idea. Modernism as a revolutionary art movement lies frozen in the art objects which document its history and explain its tradition.

The success of modernism in our culture is a historical fact. We have defined it as a period and assigned it approximate dates. We have absorbed its vocabulary and are fluent in its ideology. When we consider the buildings we occupy—the house, the office—when we look around these spaces at the furniture and utensils, we see the evidence that our world, the world beyond the museum, was formed by the hand of modernism. Though we speak of our postmodern period, modernism as ideological foundation still wields power and influence through the institution of the Museum of Modern Art. No other institution has played a greater part in the historic transformation of our culture, our cultural institutions, and, so importantly, the art they hold.

The Museum of Modern Art, the first and greatest of America's museums to be devoted exclusively to this field, has changed with the frequency and in ways befitting a modernist institution and continues to do so. In February, 1996, the Museum announced that it had purchased neighboring real estate that will provide about 250,000 square feet of new space to the Museum's existing 350,000 square feet. The addition, which will take up to ten years to develop, from plan through construction, will almost double the size of the museum and allow for different kinds of spaces, such as loft-like galleries for the exhibition of contemporary art, and rooms for video art and digital technology (Vogel, 1996: 1).

This chapter will review the two other major transformations of the Museum of Modern Art. The capital campaign of 1959 which resulted in the museum expansion completed in 1964, and the capital campaign of 1980, which resulted in the addition completed in 1984. Both campaigns were driven by the desire to serve a wider constituency, exhibit more of the Museum's collections, and generate more income. Both resulted in building expansion and program and policy changes that reverberated throughout the museum world. To set the stage, let us first look to the early days of the enlightened capitalists who drove the transformation and to the war years that presented an early threat to the Museum.

Background of the first Museum of Modern Art building

When the first modern museum building opened on the tenth anniversary of the founding of the Museum of Modern Art, it was the Museum's first permanent home; the land and much of the building were gifts from the Rockefeller family.*Time* magazine described the new site:

> Just off Fifth Avenue on 54th Street, touched by the midday shadow of Rockefeller Center's enormous slab, stood the old four-story and nine-story mansions of the Rockefeller family. Town dwellings of the elder and younger John D. Rockefeller for, respectively, 40 and 25 years, the houses were abandoned two years ago to wreckers. Last week the site became part of a long garden. In the garden were evergreens, arbors, trees, wattle screens, and sculpture by Lachaise, Despian, Zorach, Lipchitz. One fair spring night it was filled with hundreds of men with starched white bosoms and hundreds of rustling ladies. Back of them stood a new, long, spacious building faced with marble and glass; inside it other crowds could be seen, swishing past its plate-glass panels like frilly fish in a bright aquarium.
> (*Time*, 1939: 84)

It was a million-dollar property and a million-dollar building. Virtually all the donations to the building fund came through the solicitation of Nelson Rockefeller, according to then president, A. Conger Goodyear.

> As a member of the Building Committee, Treasurer of the Museum, Chairman of the Finance Committee, Member of the Executive Committee, First Chairman of the Advisory Committee, his finger has been usefully employed in practically every one of our pies. (Goodyear, 1939: 10)

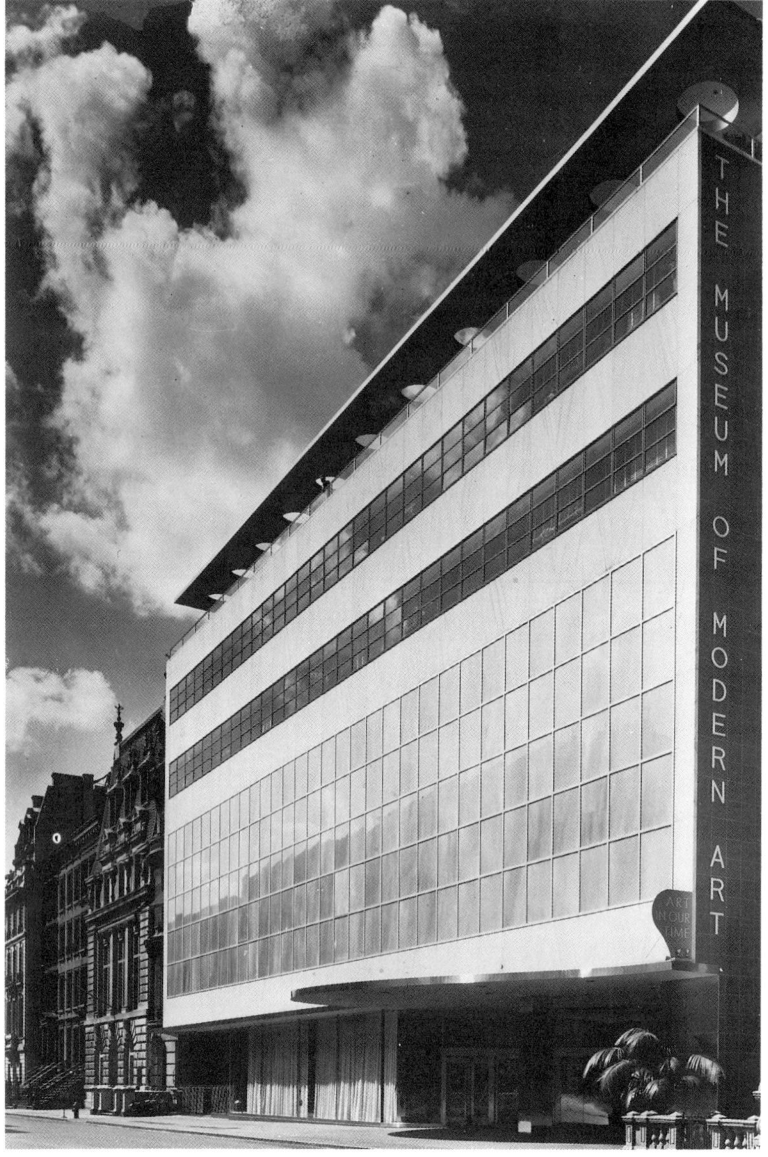

The Museum of Modern Art, New York, 1939. Philip L. Goodwin and Edward D. Stone, architects.
The Museum of Modern Art, New York.

It was at this time that Nelson Rockefeller assumed the position of President of the Museum of Modern Art. He served in that position until called to public service because of World War II. In 1946, Rockefeller returned to New York and to the presidency of the Museum and continued in that post until 1953.

In his years away from the Museum he assured Rockefeller support through special funding from both the Rockefeller Foundation and the Rockefeller Brothers Fund (information compiled from *Annual Reports* of the Museum of Modern Art). He also, along with his brother David, encouraged Blanchette Rockefeller (Mrs. John D. Rockefeller, 3rd) to assume what was by then considered a Rockefeller responsibility, an active and supportive role in the Museum. Blanchette served the Museum of Modern Art in many capacities, including that of President of the Museum. The Rockefeller brothers viewed her as perpetuating their mother's enthusiasm for modern art and the establishment that housed it.

At Nelson's request Blanchette Rockefeller established in 1954 the Museum's Junior Council, a group of early-middle-aged men and women of wealth who would support the museum through work and monetary donations and from whose ranks the Museum trustees would rise. Blanchette also served on the Executive Committee, the Collections Committee, the Exhibitions Committee and the International Council. In 1959 she was named President of the Museum, served through 1964 and assumed that responsibility again in 1972. Blanchette Rockefeller was therefore President through the two major transformations. (Information is compiled from the *Bulletin*, unless otherwise noted.) David Rockefeller also assumed positions of responsibility. But Nelson was the first to champion his mother's dream.

The first edition of the *Bulletin* to be published following Nelson Rockefeller's ascendancy to President in many ways reveals the conflicts the new Museum of Modern Art would face. On the cover is pictured the sleek new modernist building, first of its kind in America, and immediately inside is this announcement to members: "For the first time the Museum is now able to provide commodious club rooms for the exclusive use of its members. The penthouse of the new building is entirely devoted to their uses, and tea is served daily" (*Bulletin*, July, 1939). In light of this sort of promotion it's not surprising that, according to long-time employee Zara Cohan, the Museum of Modern Art came to be known affectionately as "The Museum of Modern Lunch."

Within the same edition of the *Bulletin* was printed the speech delivered by Professor Paul J. Sachs of Harvard University to the trustees of the Museum on the occasion of the opening of the new building. The talk, divided into two parts, addressed in a serious tone the problems facing American museums and the specific problems of the Museum of Modern Art. This speech emphasized the possible dangers awaiting an art museum so broadly marketing its products and services. While focused on the need for scholarship, severe discipline, and higher standards, Paul Sachs warned against the

> pressure to vulgarize and cheapen our work through the mistaken idea that in such a fashion a broad public may be reached effectively. That is an

especially tempting error because of the intense competition for public attention in American life. In the end a lowering of tone and of standards must lead to mediocrity. (Sachs, 1939: 11)

The war years

One of the greatest threats to the integrity of the Museum came with America's entry into World War II. It is easy to imagine that the war would make loan exhibits from Europe impossible, but surprising to realize that the exhibits mounted during this period were very much concerned, not with modern art, but with reaching a wide audience and supporting the war effort.

A review of the Museum's programs during the early 1940s reveals that the Museum mounted a number of war-related exhibitions such as "Army Illustrators," a collection of drawings by soldier-artists depicting army life. "Image of Freedom" was a photography show meant to interpret the abstract ideal America was fighting for in concrete photographic terms. "Wartime Housing" was cosponsored by the National Committee on the Housing Emergency and won praise from the President of the United States. "Such an exhibition will, I am sure, serve to bring forcibly to public attention some of the problems involved in providing adequate housing for war workers and their families" (Roosevelt, 1942: 2).

"The Road to Victory" was a massive undertaking curated by the Museum's Director of Photography, Edward Steichen, and given a large play in the *Bulletin*. The show, which occupied the entire second floor, was lauded by the press as "poignantly memorable," "a genuine contribution to the war effort," "a declaration of power and an affirmation of our will to win the war." Steichen is referred to in all notes on the exhibition as "Lieutenant Commander Edward Steichen, U.S.N.R." and 90 percent of the photographs were supplied by departments and agencies of the United States government (*Bulletin*, June, 1942).

The October–November, 1942 Museum *Bulletin* was dedicated to "The Museum and the War." It listed the government agencies the Museum had served by preparing and circulating exhibits and films or acting in an advisory capacity. The Museum itself was used as a social club for enlisted men, providing refreshments in the garden, dancing in the galleries. The Museum established an Armed Services Program which contributed to a rehabilitation program for veterans through art therapy, physical therapy, occupational therapy, educational therapy, creative therapy, and psychotherapy.

Through the war years, the Museum addressed what was on the minds of Americans, and which, as we have seen, was not the modern arts. During this period of national crisis, the Museum's role in advancing modern art had been diminished, and because of this the influence and importance of Alfred Barr was also lessened. On October 15, 1943,

Stephen Clark, President of the Board of Trustees, asked for the resignation of Alfred Barr. The man who just four years earlier had been called by A. Conger Goodyear, "the pituitary gland" of the Museum because of his "profound influence" on its growth was being forced out. "The skeleton cannot prosper without it" Goodyear had warned, "and when its activity is diminished, this leads to obesity and mental defects" (Goodyear, 1939: 6).

The firing of Alfred Barr is a legend in the art world, but a legend with numerous, speculative variations. One version of the story has Barr relegated to a corner of the museum library to conduct his research and writing. Another version has Barr holding out in the library, refusing to abandon his beloved museum. The reason for his dismissal usually casts Stephen Clark as the villain, jealous of Barr's understanding of modern art and angry at Barr's less than expert managerial skills.

What Stephen Clark offered as explanation for the "retirement" was Barr's failure to produce a book on modern art. Now he would be able to "devote his full time to writing the works on modern art which he has had in preparation and which his heavy directorial duties have made impossible for him to undertake" (*Bulletin*, February–March, 1944). The previous July, however, the Museum of Modern Art had published Alfred Barr's 84-page catalog of the collection: *Painting and Sculpture in the Museum of Modern Art*. This summary of the Museum's acquisition history, policy, and accomplishment contained over 700 works by more than 300 artists and was designed as another educational tool, defining schools and movements. This fact serves to cast doubt on Clark's explanation for the dismissal. It is not unreasonable to consider Alfred Barr a victim of the war. The war had after all taken its toll on the Museum. Even though attendance was up (the Museum of Modern Art was voted the fourth favorite place to visit in New York City, usually by sailors and soldiers, ranked after the Statue of Liberty, the Empire State Building, and the Rockefeller Center), income was down because military personnel were not charged admission. The Museum was operating at a deficit (MOMA *Annual Report*, 1943). Since the Museum's operations were mainly in the service of a government at war, producing documentary films and various propaganda, there was at this moment no need for a modern art scholar. This is important to note, because it demonstrates what can happen when a museum loses site of its essential purpose—in this case, the curatorship of modern art.

Nelson Rockefeller was in Washington, D.C., fully withdrawn from any managerial role in the museum. Neither Blanchette nor David Rockefeller had yet come of age. Mrs. John D. Jr. alone represented the Rockefellers. Barr's mentor Paul Sachs and other founding trustees such as Frank Crowninshield and Duncan Phillips now served only in honorary positions. Other Barr supporters such as Philip Johnson and Eddie Warburg were in the armed services.

By November, 1944, however, Alfred Barr had been appointed Chair of Modern Painting and Sculpture, a position created for him in May, 1944.

> Mr. Barr's duties will be to carry on research and publication in modern painting and sculpture with particular reference to the Museum's collection. He will have no curatorial responsibilities such as acquisition and care but beginning with the summer of 1945 he will be in charge of exhibiting the collection of Painting and Sculpture. He will be available also for consultation and advice. (*Bulletin*, November, 1944: 12)

The ending of World War II saved Alfred Barr's connection with the Museum.

In January, 1945, yet another reorganization was announced as James Johnson Sweeney replaced James Thrall Soby as Director of the Museum's Department of Painting and Sculpture. "In a reorganization of the Department of Painting and Sculpture there has been a considerable revision of duties, making the Department head in the future fully responsible for the activities of the Department." Mr. Soby reportedly resigned to devote his entire time to writing (*Bulletin*, January, 1945: 20).

Now the war was over, Nelson Rockefeller was back on the Board as the First Vice President and Chairman of a special Fund Raising Committee. In the financial report for that year, it was resolved by the Board that the Museum, operating at a $70,000 deficit, should balance the budget as soon as possible and broaden the base of financial support. Nelson Rockefeller was charged with designing a plan of action. Through the remaining 1940s the museum struggled to recover from the war years, continued to expand its educational programs with special offerings for veterans, and published several major books including Alfred Barr's *Picasso: Fifty Years of His Art*.

The first expansion

In 1953, the Museum of Modern Art established a permanent collection. Up until this point the Museum collected works of art with the understanding that they would be transferred to other institutions, mainly the Metropolitan Museum of Art. On February 15, 1953, the Museum of Modern Art terminated its agreement with the Metropolitan and issued the following statement:

> The Museum has come to believe that its former policy ... did not work out to the benefit of its public. It now believes it essential for the understanding and enjoyment of its entire collection to have permanently on public view masterpieces of the modern movement, beginning with the latter half of the nineteenth century ... The creation of a permanent core within the collection constitutes a radically important departure from the Museum's past policy. It must be stressed that this permanent nucleus will be composed only of great masterworks. (*Bulletin*, 1953: 3)

With this change in policy the Museum stepped up its acquisitions and filled in the gaps of what was already the world's most representative collection of modern art. Implicit in the commitment to a permanent collection was the understanding that the Museum's facility would require expansion. Over the next few years the collections grew rapidly until, by 1959, they included 18,510 objects.

In 1959, with Blanchette Rockefeller as President and Nelson Rockefeller as strong a force as ever as the Chairman of the Board of Trustees, the Museum launched a major fundraising campaign to again expand its building and its programs. This was the year of the Museum's 30th anniversary, and the annual budget at this time was $2 million. It was twenty years since Nelson was president for the first time and the original building opened. In those twenty years the annual attendance at the Museum had more than quadrupled, as had the membership, and the collection had increased from 2,685 objects to 18,510 (Figure 9.1). (All figures are compiled from MOMA *Annual Reports* unless otherwise noted).

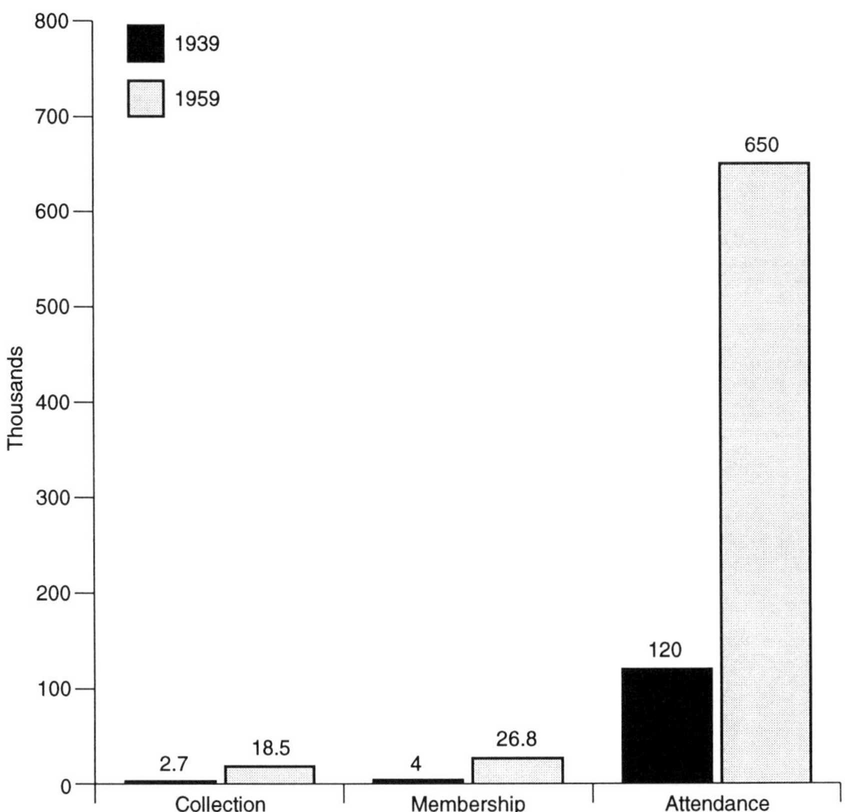

Figure 9.1 *Museum of Modern Art, New York: General Growth, 1939–59.*

Nelson Rockefeller, who had been in charge of raising the money to build the 1939 building, again assumed a leadership role to meet the $25 million goal of the Thirtieth Anniversary Campaign, as the new building fund was called. He officially launched the drive with a dinner at the Four Seasons Restaurant in New York City, where he introduced James Hopkins Smith, Jr. as chairman of the drive and announced that almost $10 million of the $25 million was already in hand, thanks to the Rockefellers and other trustees. In addition to this, the Rockefeller Foundation gave a grant of $1.5 million; the Rockefeller Brothers Fund promised to match all gifts up to $6 million, and John D. Rockefeller, Jr. gave another $2.5 million. David Rockefeller was named Honorary Chairman of the Thirtieth Anniversary Committee.

David Rockefeller, youngest of the five sons of John D. Jr., made his career in banking. Educated at Harvard University and the University of Chicago, David joined Chase Manhattan Bank in 1946 and moved through the ranks to become chairman of the board and chief executive officer. He shared his mother's enthusiasm for modern art and at the time of her death assumed her place on the Board of Trustees of the Museum of Modern Art (information compiled from the MOMA *Bulletin*). In his own right, as president of Chase Manhattan Bank, and with guidance from the Museum of Modern Art, David Rockefeller established what is considered today to be the grandfather of corporate art collections. Begun in 1959, the Chase Manhattan art collection now contains 13,000 objects, 80 percent of which are modern, mostly contemporary (after 1945) (Severinghaus *et al.* 1984). Under David Rockefeller's direction the bank established a professional curatorial staff and an art committee, the first members of which included Alfred Barr and Dorothy Miller plus curators from the Guggenheim Museum, the Metropolitan Museum, and the Museum of Fine Arts in Boston. Reminiscing in the "Foreword" of the 1984 publication on the collection, David Rockefeller explained how controversial were the first commissioned works and how the museum could influence opinion. "Many of the more conservatively minded members of our board and senior management were shocked and displeased by what was acquired ... Nevertheless, it was recognized that we had world-renowned experts on our Art Committee who had made the selection and the bank went forward with the project" (Severinghaus *et al.* 1984: 11–12).

The Museum of Modern Art's financial situation was dependent on the consumption of art by a relatively wide public. Clearly, the more visitors the museum could accommodate the more income could be generated through admissions, membership dues, sales of publications, and other services. These accounted for more than half of the total income in 1959 as the Museum announced its Thirtieth Anniversary Campaign to raise $25 million (*Annual Report*, 1959). The Museum's public and the demand for its services had spurred the development of the fund which would provide for the expansion of the Museum's facilities, activities, and finances.

That year 650,000 people had visited the Museum, an institution of international influence. Known for its collections and exhibitions of modern art forms, it was, however, a much simpler institution than we know today, still finding its way in the world of commerce. Today, the Museum houses an 8,000 square foot retail shop with a multi-million-dollar inventory. In addition, the Museum runs another store situated across the street. By contrast in 1959 there was a simple counter in the lobby which served as the book store, and across from that was located the membership desk. Zara Cohan, a member of the Museum staff from 1956 until 1965 sat at that membership desk and remembers the intimacy and human atmosphere of the place.

> I always wanted to work at the Museum of Modern Art because I loved going there and I loved being a member. The whole idea of modern art, that wonderful building, New York City, it was very exciting. This was really before television. People read the *New Yorker* magazine and it always carried stuff about the Museum. New York had been dubbed the art capital of the world and The Museum of Modern Art was located in mid-town. The arts were no longer just for the rich and you weren't a sissy if you liked the arts. The Museum was a human and civilized place to visit.

Zara Cohan describes the Museum as an often quiet place of manageable size:

> You saw one, possibly two paintings of each artist and of course lots of Picassos. There was *Guernica* and the sculpture garden. The sculpture garden was marvelous. It was very small but it was an oasis and in the summer they had a modern jazz quartet perform.

The Museum's predicament, as perceived by the Board of Trustees, was its physical restriction. The collections and activities, and the demands for services had grown phenomenally, and the museum building could no longer contain the Museum. In 1959 only about 150 paintings were on exhibit, just 10 percent of the painting collection. The Museum that boasted the world's finest collection of twentieth-century prints could exhibit only about a dozen (less than one quarter of 1 percent). Of the collection of almost 4,000 architecture and design objects, none were on display except in an occasional temporary show.

As a privately supported and administered institution, the Museum of Modern Art received no subsidy from municipal, state, or federal government. The public it served contributed substantially to its support through admissions and payment for various services yielding the largest gross earned revenue of any museum in the world. The indicators pointed to the need for an expansion of the physical plant which would result in the expansion of earned income. This became the objective of the Thirtieth Anniversary Campaign along with the goal of enlarging the Museum's endowment to ensure a base income. Earned income and annual contributions alone could not furnish the Museum with sufficient funds to give its program flexibility and enable it to meet the growing need for the research, experimentation, and educational work essential to the fulfillment of its purposes but producing no direct financial return.

The plan included the construction of the new East Wing to be erected on the unoccupied corner along 54th Street. The Museum was also deeded two brownstones adjacent to the main building which would be incorporated into the Museum. The plan for the new Museum would double the gallery space and expand the Sculpture Garden by 40 percent. It would allow for a more complete showing of the holdings in painting and sculpture and special galleries for changing exhibitions. New galleries would allow for the exhibition of prints and drawings (the Paul J. Sachs Galleries) with special facilities for the study of photography and prints. For the first time the Museum would have space in which to show outstanding examples from its collection of mass-produced utensils, furniture, textiles, posters, and architectural drawings and models.

One floor of the new building was designated office space; the Conservation Program would have an enlarged laboratory; committee rooms would provide conference space for outside groups. The main lobby, opening onto the Sculpture Garden, would provide space for the Museum's first bookstore and membership offices. The architect of the new building, Philip Johnson, allowed unhampered circulation between the original building and the new building at both gallery and office levels.

Upon the completion of this plan, the Museum of Modern Art became the first and only institution in the world able to show continuously the visual arts of the recent past as manifested in painting, sculpture, drawings, prints, photography, films, architecture and design. "Centuries of collecting have made the great European museums preeminent in the arts of earlier epochs" reads the Thirtieth Anniversary Campaign promotion,

> But in contemporary art, our Museum will outrank all others. The new Museum will in fact become the only American art museum which, in its own field, is foremost in the world. Inevitably it will be a magnet attracting to New York from every quarter of the globe all those interested in the visual arts of our time.

In June of 1964, the new Museum of Modern Art opened to the cheers of its members and the widespread publicity it has always generated.

> In the museum's new, enlarged quarters, designed by Philip Johnson, there are modern muses all over the place: in the 32,000 square foot sculpture garden that ramps up onto the roof of a new two-story building (beneath which is the monstrous new gallery and an underground art school); in the new six-story glass and steel tower that carries right through onto every floor of the old museum building, from which five gigantic abstract banners will whip on gala occasions. (*Newsweek*, 1964: 49)

Pictured on the cover of this issue are Alfred Barr and René d'Harnoncourt with a Picasso painting as backdrop. Alfred Barr, here 62 years old, is referred to as a scholar and a showman. He is called "the museum's director of collections but he is really its spirit made flesh." Inside is a photograph of a young Nelson Rockefeller and the museum model *circa* 1938. "It is a unique museum, it is a people's museum," he is quoted as saying, and proud of the fact that the museum, with no tax subsidy, is so largely self-supporting. "I went to Jones Beach with Robert Moses when it first opened," Rockefeller tells the reporter.

> There was a 25-cent admission, 25 cents for parking, and things like that. "How do you get away with this?" I asked him. He told me his theory of appreciation—that people appreciate things for which they have to pay a small amount. I went back to the trustees of the museum and told them I thought that something like that might be a good idea. They put it into effect, and it worked. (*Newsweek*, 1964: 52)

Amidst the success and all the congratulatory verbiage there lingered a feeling of uneasiness, perhaps fear, that this tremendous expansion involved dangers of vulgarization and impersonalization. "I think the trouble might have come with the fact that they realized how important they had become," reflects Zara Cohan.

> The Museum would sneeze and it would be reported in the papers. It made them [Barr and d'Harnoncourt] very cautious because they were extremely ethical. They were interested in the objects as art, not in monetary terms but they realized that the price of the art went up when they did something. I think they became frightened of that power.

Paul Sachs had warned against the dangers the Museum would face as it expanded and against the dangers of timidity:

> The Museum must not stop taking risks:—for the reputation of the Museum of Modern Art will rest upon its successes more than upon its mistakes. In the field of modern art chances must be taken. The Museum should continue to be a pioneer:—bold and uncompromising.
> (Sachs, 1939: 11)

John Canaday, the art critic for the *New York Times*, published a series of articles in 1967, just three years after the expansion, in which, while acknowledging the Museum as a powerful and beneficial force in American cultural life, he also accused it of "coasting." "... it could coast for a long time before anybody realizes that it is approaching a standstill." Much of the problem, Canaday asserted, was the result of the Museum's popularity. That, he reasoned, was indicative of a cultural backfire.

> This may be true in all museums, but it is most distressingly true in a museum where people pass blind before a kind of art that they were never meant to understand and would offer them very little reward if they did. Perhaps we should think only of the one person in a hundred or several hundred who finds the museum something more than an expensively decorated place of entertainment with an impressive cachet. Yet it is difficult to look at these hordes of people of all ages, all economic brackets and all degrees of intelligence above those that require institutional care,

> and believe that the museum has really taught many of them to make any distinction between the great sculpture in the museum garden and the Alice in Wonderland sculpture in Central Park. (Canaday 1967a)

Standing in the busy temple of art, it is difficult to remember the tranquility the art museum once possessed. That loss, the loss of the quiet, contemplative, perhaps spiritual place where a work of art could reveal itself slowly, where the visitor could, in silence and privacy, approach an understanding of the content and meaning of the art, that is the great tragedy of the democratization of the art museum.

> The atmosphere is not that of a place where art is offered for contemplation with the privilege of personal response. There is a goading to accept the offered product as the only acceptable one ... the whole place, now grown to great size, is one enormous boutique. (Canaday, 1967b)

"I remember when the Museum put on the exhibition 'The Responsive Eye'," says Zara Cohan. "Well, everything, including garbage cans, had optical art on it. Clothes, handbags, you name it. The mass culture took over and made a popular thing out of it ... It's hard to believe but the Museum had become a jazzy focal point."

This was the challenge facing the Museum, to find the correct balance, to measure the quality of the art against its popular appeal, to be brave in presenting new ideas but not fooled by the sparkle of newness; to fight the danger of timidity warned against by Paul Sachs while fighting also the inclination to slide into the consumer culture by providing one new and improved and even more exciting exhibition after another. It was a delicate balance to be sure.

The Thirtieth Anniversary Campaign provided the expanded building and the financial security of a substantial endowment which would supplement the Museum's earned income. What it also provided for the Museum was a position of centrality in the American culture. The museum of 1956 described by then employee Zara Cohan as an intimate and delicate and quiet place for art ("And it was true that sometimes you could fall asleep because nobody would come to the membership desk.") became a memory of the 1964 bustling, expansive, triumphant corporation.

The second expansion

Over the next ten years smaller additions were made to the new museum complex, but the second major expansion, plans for which were made public in 1976, was of such scope that it stunned the most jaded patrons. The publicity department referred to it as a "combined-use project," which translates as an enormous expansion of the existing museum building and the construction of a 44-story private residential tower above the new building. The Museum expansion, projected to cost $55 million, would be subsidized by the sale of the Museum's air rights to the developer of the apartment tower. The Museum of Modern Art had entered the real estate business.

The expansion proposal, which would link the Museum to the sometimes unpredictable real-estate market, caught the attention of art world watchdogs and set them barking. Critics were concerned about the impact this involvement would have on the Museum's nobler priorities, concerned about the special privileges of tax breaks secured in Albany through special legislation, and concerned about the demolition of adjacent buildings considered to be of historic significance. But this powerful museum and its powerful board marshaled the forces to overcome all objections and moved the project forward. Three years after the initial announcement, architectural plans were in place, the funding was arranged and demolition on the site had begun.

After considerable deliberation, the Museum had selected an architect: Cesar Pelli, newly appointed dean of the Yale School of Architecture. The design he proposed involved substantial changes to the existing museum building and major new construction.

The new construction, known as the West Wing, would provide 46,500 square feet of new gallery space, more than doubling the present space, as well as a new auditorium, service and support areas. The six floors of the new wing were planned as part of the combined-use structure which would rise to 580 feet above 54th Street and contain 263 private residences. A new, four-story, steel and glass *Garden Hall* (18,000 square feet) on the north side of the Museum overlooking the Sculpture Garden and housing a new system of escalators and circulation areas would connect the Museum's public facilities. An expanded, two-story *Garden Wing* at the east end of the Sculpture Garden would provide a public Garden Café on the ground floor and a Members Dining Room on the floor above. The North Wing, containing the education center, galleries, and conservation and storage facilities, would be renovated. Finally, the galleries and service areas in the original 1939 building and the 1964 East Wing would be renovated and the Abby Aldrich Rockefeller Sculpture Garden would be refurbished. Summed up, the project called for 170,000 square feet of new space and 200,000 square feet of completely renovated space, providing a total of 370,000 square feet for the expanded museum (statistics gleaned from the Museum of Modern Art 1984 Expansion and Renovation Project Fact Sheet).

The Museum's participation in the project came under the auspices of the Trust for Cultural Resources of the City of New York, a corporation established by legislation designed specifically for the Museum of Modern Art's needs and passed by New York State in 1976. The legislation provided for the creation of specific trusts in individual cities throughout the State. These trusts are empowered to act on behalf of cultural institutions owning property rights, to participate with private developers in the construction of combined-use facilities, providing separately for commercial development and for expansion and improvement of a cultural institution's facilities.

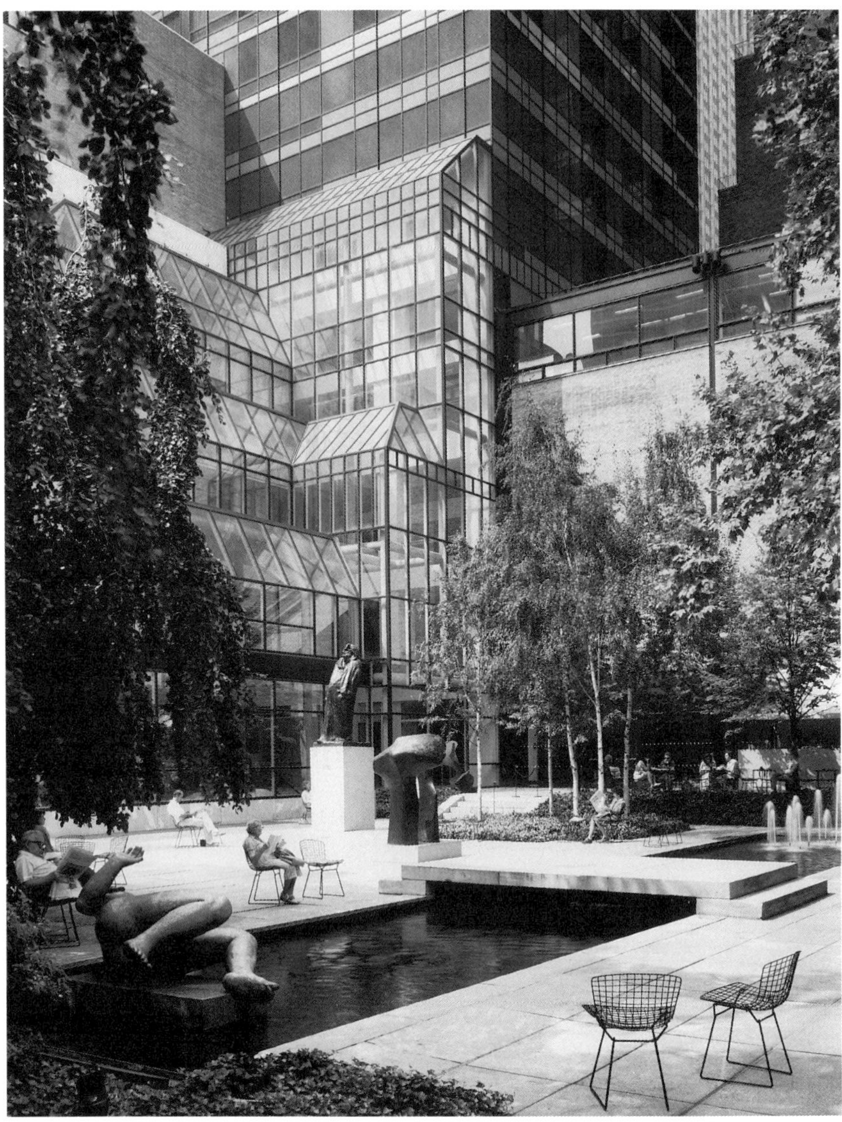

The Abby Aldrich Rockefeller Sculpture Garden, The Museum of Modern Art, New York, 1964, designed by Philip Johnson. View of the Garden Hall of the Museum, designed by Cesar Pelli & Associates, 1984. Photographed Summer 1987.
The Museum of Modern Art, New York.

The Museum of Modern Art sold its air rights to a private developer through this newly established trust. "If the Museum were to have negotiated this arrangement directly with the developer, it would have had to pay taxes on 'unrelated business income' represented by the income from this development" (Curtis, 1983: 68).

The development—the condominium tower—produced tax-equivalency payments used by the Trust to repay the cost of the Museum's expansion program over a long period of time. In the meantime, the Trust issued $40 million in tax-exempt collateralized bonds in January, 1980, and an additional $20 million in March, 1984. The Museum provided $49 million of its endowment as collateral to support these bonds. The $17 million it received from the air rights sale were held in escrow. So, the property owned by the Museum and therefore not subject to taxation was used to generate a source of income for the Museum's expansion costs. This second major expansion of the Museum of Modern Art was, like the 1959 expansion, demanded by the growth of the permanent collection (now numbering over 100,000 works of art) and the necessity to accommodate the ever-increasing number of visitors, estimated at more than one million a year (see Figures 9.2a and 9.2b).

As the Museum began the construction project, which would span four years, it also opened a major retrospective exhibition of one thousand works by Pablo Picasso. This exhibition was the first to employ the use of advanced sale admission tickets which designated not only the day but the hour the holder could enter the Museum. In this way, the Museum was able to move more than 7,000 visitors through the galleries each day. The Picasso show signaled the coming of the new Museum of Modern Art with a furthering of the consumer management techniques and new traffic patterns designed to handle the crowds. The new building would contain escalators to move visitors swiftly from floor to floor, and such public areas as a 12,200 square foot main lobby and education center and an 18,000 square foot Garden Hall. There would be 20,700 square feet dedicated to restaurants and 8,000 square feet for the Museum Store (MOMA 1984 Fact Sheet).

In discussing the design of the Garden Hall, the central public space of the new Museum, the architect, Cesar Pelli, explained that he had to try to understand the Museum's new, expanded functions and, in doing this, provoke a topological change.

> You see, the Museum was originally designed as a house. You moved from floor to floor and, on each floor, there was a tight-knit group of rooms. The path led from room to room and back to the stairway and elevators. The 1964 addition of the East Wing added to the number of rooms but did not change the type. The new West Wing is of such magnitude, however, that the circulation type had to be changed. Now, after strolling from gallery to gallery, the visitor will have a more pronounced pause when moving to another floor or another Museum wing via the glass-enclosed Garden Hall.
>
> The Hall has been designed like a glove, a minimum enclosure, to gather the east–west, horizontal circulation between wings using connecting halls, and the vertical circulation between floors using escalators.
>
> The gallery type has not been changed much in the expanded Museum. The rooms remain basically apartment size ... Designing the galleries agreed well with my attitude toward architecture. You see, I don't believe

> the architect has any business imposing his preferences, biases, or prejudices about every possible function on earth on people who know well how these functions take place. The Museum of Modern Art has incredibly well developed theories and attitudes about how modern art should be exhibited, and we took advantage of them. (Pelli, 1984: 3–5)

In fact, the curators of each department were consulted and exercised much control over the design of their galleries. This policy resulted in the new museum retaining the feeling of intimacy for which the old museum was known. The galleries on average retained the scale determined to be proper for the exhibition of modern art. "Through and including the work of Pollock and Rothko," reported Bill Rubin, Director of Painting and Sculpture, "the work should be seen in apartment-sized spaces rather than palazzo- or church-like spaces. Rothko once remarked 'I paint big to be intimate'. He envisioned his pictures in a sense displacing walls, not, as would be the case in a very large space, looking like objects hanging on a wall ... The history of modern art up through abstract expressionism

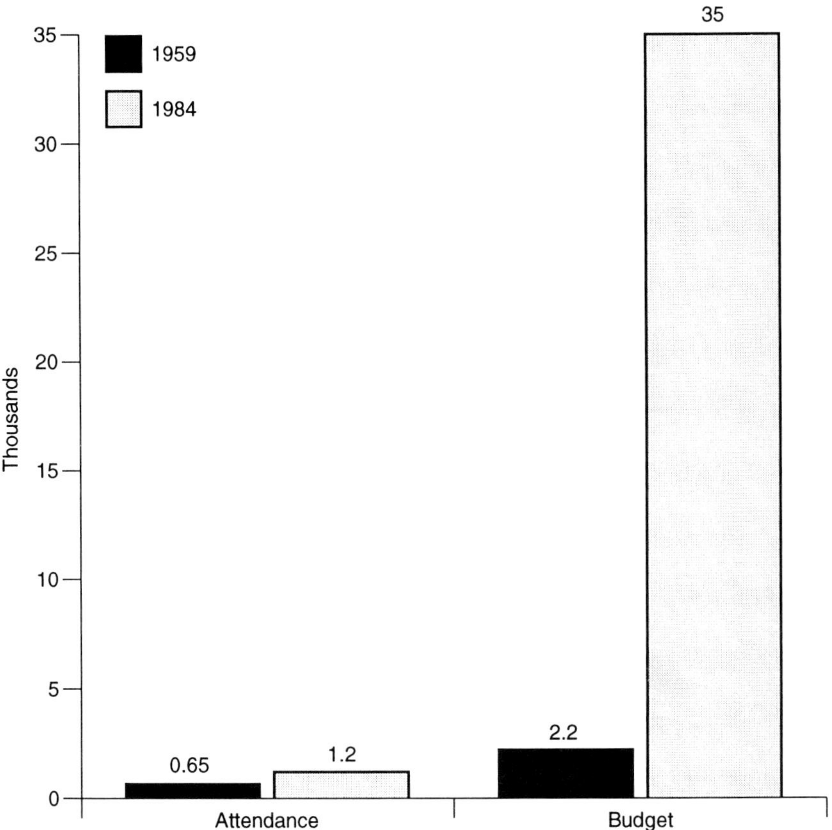

Figure 9.2a *Museum of Modern Art, New York: General Growth, 1959–84.*

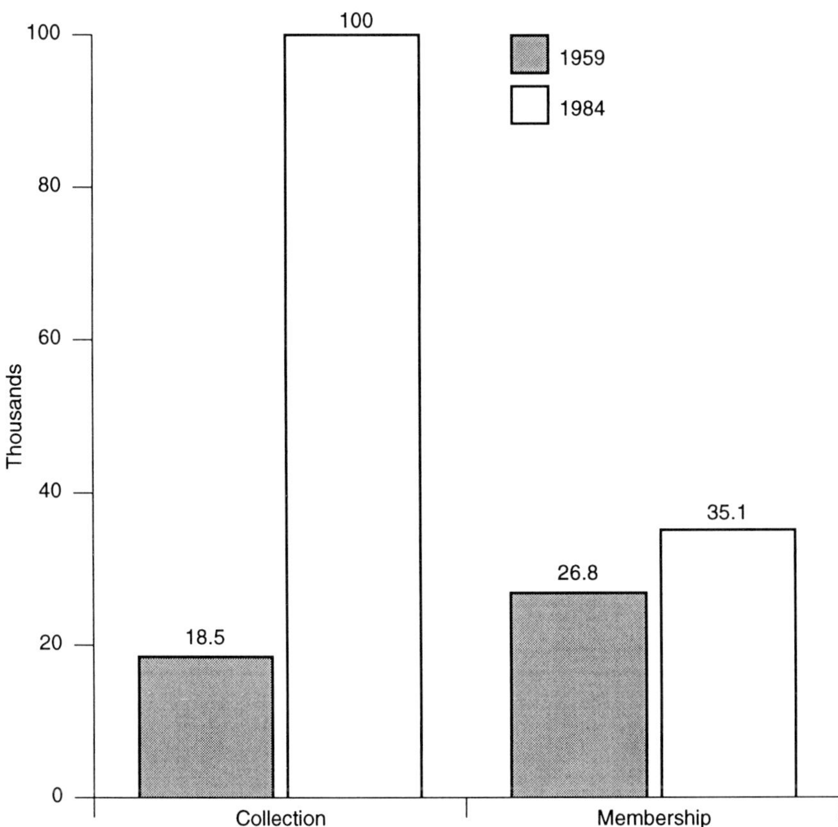

Figure 9.2b *Museum of Modern Art, New York: General Growth, 1959–1984*

needs spaces which are essentially like those we have always had." Rubin also insisted that the floors of these galleries be carpeted to make them quieter and more comfortable and also to enhance the private character of the space. "A museum is a museum, and you can't pretend it's an apartment, but the carpet does tend to minimize the viewer's sense of being in a big public area" (Rubin, 1984: 2). The doubling of the exhibition space (Figure 9.3) allowed for more of the collection to be shown but also allowed for more space between the paintings. The general layout remained chronological, as it had been, with all the national schools represented. "We have tried to keep a kind of ecumenical, art-historical view of the entire modern movement" said Rubin. "That was Alfred Barr's idea from the beginning, and we've maintained it throughout" (p. 4).

The Painting and Sculpture installation is located at the top of the escalator on the second floor of the Garden Hall in the original museum building. A descriptive press release takes us through the new galleries.

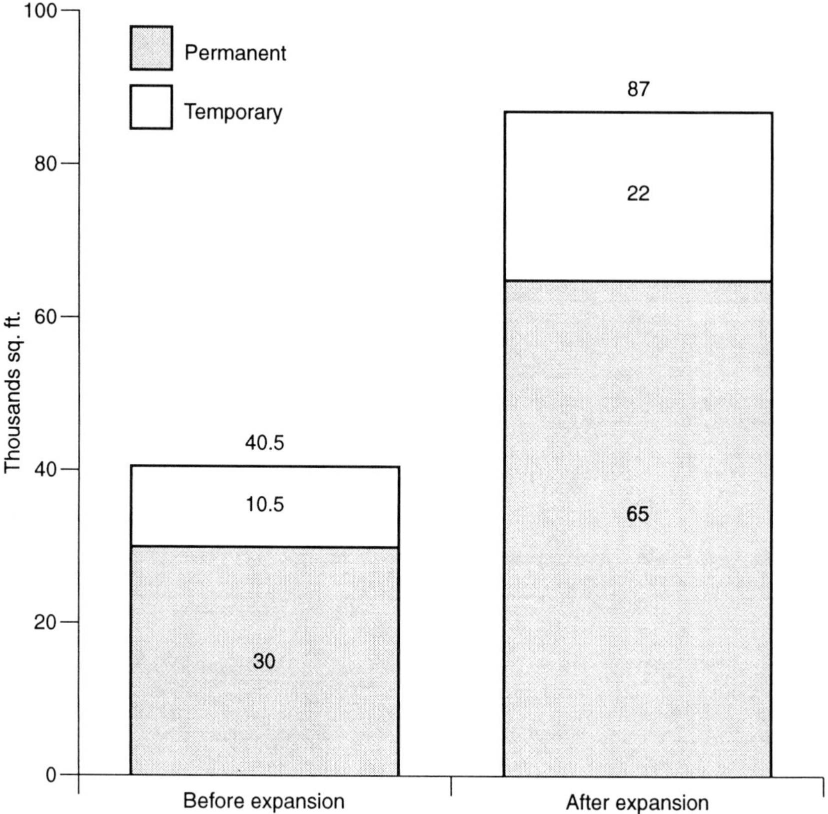

Figure 9.3 *Museum of Modern Art, New York: Comparison of Exhibition Space, 1984 Expansion.*

Moving east through Post-Impressionism, Fauvism, Cubism (particularly works by Picasso), Futurism, Constructivism and through the stairway lobby into the West Wing, the visitor enters a major Matisse gallery, followed by special galleries for the School of Paris, including more Picasso, Dada and Surrealism, de Chirico and Miró. In the second floor stairwell hang works from the Russian School by artists such as Malevich, and Lissitzky. On the third floor the visitor moves west through the American art of the 1920s—Hopper, Wyeth, O'Keeffe, Stuart Davis—to early American Surrealism, then Dubuffet, Pollock, and into the late 1940s and early 1950s.

The Matisse cutouts and a special gallery for *The Swimming Pool* (acquired several years ago by the Museum, and shown only twice) serve as an introduction to a gallery for major works of the New York School, including Pollock and the Abstract Expressionists—Motherwell, Rothko, Gottlieb, de Kooning and, farther on, works from the later School of Paris. The area beyond is uncarpeted and has movable walls. This flexible area contains works from the 1960s to the 1980s, beginning with Robert Rauschenberg, Jasper Johns, Pop Art, and the Colorfield artists, Ellsworth Kelly to Kenneth Noland, and on to the Minimalists and the Conceptualists.

In a *New York Times* article, Michael Brenson reviewed the new galleries now hung with the permanent collection.

> Make no mistake about it, the painting and sculpture that is the glory of the museum has been charted by a very particular hand. William Rubin, director of the department of painting and sculpture, has approached his task of installing the foremost collection of modern art in the world with complete responsibility and all the courage of his formidable conviction. Knowing that the present installation of two floors and 40-odd galleries of painting and sculpture may be his legacy to generations of artists, Mr. Rubin has left nothing to chance. He has emmeshed every work in a complex network of correspondences and cross-references. His installation has a density and control that almost oblige the visitor to consider it as a work of art itself. (Brenson, 1984: 1)

All reports indicate that the weeks leading up to the opening of the new Museum were hectic and breathless and consisted of fourteen-hour days and seven-day weeks, but at last the Museum was ready. Robert Hughes described the 55-year-old "refurbished dame" as "more or less pulled together: slip awry, flushed under the powder, panting somewhat, but ready for the preopening openings, the dinners, the disputes and the final arrival of the general public" (Hughes, 1984: 78). The fact that the Museum could be anthropomorphized in this way is an indication of the genuine affection, a personal fondness held for this institution. The *New York Times* voiced it similarly: "If people all over the country were nervous about the five-year surgery at MOMA, it was because the patient on the operating table was a dear friend" (1984).

At the opening the guests heard a congratulatory message from President Ronald Reagan ("With its innovative plan for public and private cooperation, the Museum once again has pioneered in bringing the arts to so many more people.") and remarks by Mayor Ed Koch. Governor Mario Cuomo said the Museum represented the embodiment of New York's "restless genius."

> Its presence here in the heart of the city has been reshaped, expanded, made new—a transformation that adds to its magnificence without detracting from its soul. In the very structure of these changes—in the brick and glass of its new home—the Museum makes us all take a fresh look. A fresh look at the art and architecture that form the basis of modern culture, at the special blend of change and continuity which is at the heart of this institution and this city. (Bennetts, 1984:4)

Art and architecture at the base of modern culture, an idea easily accepted in 1984, an idea connecting the new museum with the museum of 1929. "The museum in its new and greatly enlarged premises remains loyal to the beliefs of those who began it," wrote critic John Russell. "It is, that is to say, a museum in which the maps of early modern art were charted once and for all by Alfred Barr, the first director, and his colleagues. It is also a museum that, now as 50 years ago, is intensely personal" (Russell, 1984: 1).

That personal, intimate feeling, always the strength of this museum, was maintained in the size of the new gallery rooms. The human scale of the galleries had always been a demand of modernist painting, painting that itself was personal and intimate.

The trustees and staff had done everything possible to retain the aesthetic character of the Museum and had succeeded in this regard, but of course the new Museum, promoted in the popular press as never before, attracted hordes of people who disturbed whatever intimacy the gallery architecture might have provided. So, on the one hand, the Museum celebrated the success of the new galleries in continuing the spirit of the old Museum of Modern Art, and on the other hand, revealed its new self by announcing its principal purpose through its principal architectural image—the Garden Hall. This dazzling light-filled space holds a lively display of structural detail and banks of escalators which provide dramatic views of the garden and beyond. It serves as both the main traffic artery and also the Museum's new identifying image. The image is one in the modernist tradition but with a high-tech look, it is also a high-powered corporate look, and of course, it reveals its important function—moving large numbers of people.

Alfred Barr had set out to create a new kind of museum in America—a museum that would bring together all the many disparate activities of the modern movement and make them available for the education and edification of the people. The Museum of Modern Art is still that institution and is central to our understanding of the culture of this century. But with expanded facilities comes an ever-expanding audience whose presence may create too great a gap between the original ideal and the museum as fact.

10

Conclusion

According to the American Association of Museums' definition, an art museum is "a permanent, non-profit institution; essentially educational and aesthetic in purpose, with professional staff, which acquires or owns works of art, cares for them, interprets them, and exhibits them to the public on some regular schedule." The basic function of the art museum is therefore, threefold: acquisition, preservation, and presentation of works of art. The basic purpose of the art museum is educational and aesthetic. As a means of summarizing the various investigations thus far, and examining the influences of modernism, capitalism, and democracy in some cohesive manner, our focus will first be on the function of the art museum as defined by the American Association of Museums, and then on the fulfillment of its basic purpose (educational and aesthetic) in the light of these findings.

The third aspect of the museum's function, that of presentation, involves its own collection plus borrowed objects, constitutes the public side of the museum's function, and demonstrates most profoundly the three influences of modernism, democracy, and capitalism. The first two aspects, that is, acquisition and preservation, are closely linked, being concerned with the museum's own collection, and so will be considered first, and in concert.

The museum's function: acquisition and preservation

The Director of the museum and the curatorial staff are responsible for identifying objects to be acquired. The Director must submit all recommendations to the Board of Trustees for approval, and the final decision rests legally with the Board. The Association of Art Museum Directors states in *Professional Practices in Art Museums* (1992) that, since purchases represent the expenditure of moneys committed to public trust for which the Board is responsible, no acquisition should be approved without full knowledge of the Director's opinion. This procedure applies to gifts to the collection as well. The Association of Art Museum Directors also advises that "gifts and bequests should be unrestricted whenever possible" and that "No work should be accepted with a guarantee as to attribution" (AAMD, 1992: 7).

The deaccession of a work of art from the collection is governed by equally strict guidelines from the Association of Art Museum Directors.

Full justification of the deaccession should be presented to the Board by the Director. Decisions should be related to the museum's "written policy rather than to exigencies of the moment," and funds obtained through such sales must be used to replenish the collection. "Disposal of collections," states the American Association of Museums' *Code of Ethics*, "through sale, trade, or research activities is solely for the advancement of the museum's mission." Further, the Association of Art Museum Directors requires "particularly rigorous examination" of the proposed disposal which "should be pursued with great caution."

The preservation of the museum's collection is the responsibility of the Director in consultation with the appropriate curator and conservator. Preservation includes the accurate cataloging of works as well as the care and conservation of their physical condition. The highest professional standards must be applied to handling, storing, and exhibiting. The exhibition and lending for exhibition of works of art are also factors in preservation. In exhibition, according to the American Association of Art Museum Directors, the Director "has the paramount responsibility of ensuring the safety of each object." In lending works of art, the safety of the object during transit as well as the conditions of its temporary domicile must be considered. Also to be considered is whether the work will be exposed to undue risk by reason of "inherent vice" if loaned. As recorded in the American Association of Museums' 1994 *Code of Ethics*, the museum must ensure that "collections in its custody are protected, secure, unencumbered, cared for, and preserved."

With these guidelines in mind, the practices of art museum directors in this study will be examined to determine how capitalism and American corporate practices might influence the museum's functions of acquisition and preservation.

Since American art museums were founded and built primarily by the wealth and will of Morgan, Rockefeller, Whitney, Guggenheim, Getty, Carnegie and other likeminded industrialists, merchants, and bankers, it is quite likely that their capitalist ideology mixed easily into the makeup of the museum to settle deeply and to surface later when need demanded. The basic structure of the museum was modeled after the corporation, with a Board, Officers and a Chief Executive Officer. This structure has been, for the most part, a blessing in that it has provided a system of policy and procedural checks, and balanced budgets, while leaving the expertise in the museum's specialty to the professional staff.

In New York's Museum of Modern Art the mix of the scholar in the person of Alfred Barr and the capitalist in Nelson Rockefeller produced a museum so successful that it would serve as a model for America. Barr was left to build a collection, curate exhibitions, publish catalogs, and educate the masses, while Rockefeller and the other trustees insured the financial stability of the institution. And while Barr introduced into the museum operation certain practices learned from the worldly corporation (the implementation of a publicity plan is one prime example of this), he was nevertheless tenacious in his pursuit of excellence in aesthetic matters. Never did he allow the capitalist influence to distort museum policy.

In today's museum world, however, instances of capitalism as the dominant ideology abound. One proof of the presence of capitalistic thinking is seen in the language. The museum's collection may be termed "assets," its exhibitions and programs are called its "product." The museum visitor is viewed as the "consumer" of this product, and marketing techniques are employed to attract large numbers of consumers while special exhibitions and programs insure return visits.

The capitalistic influence on the art museum had its genesis with the founding of the Metropolitan (Chapter 3) and realized a happy coexistence with the development of the Museum of Modern Art (Chapter 9), but did not attract the worried eyes of the art world until 1967. Thomas Hoving, as director of the Metropolitan Museum of Art, revolutionized museum operations and the public's perception of the museum as he introduced the ways of the corporate world into museum operations in an effort to sell his product for the purpose of generating revenue (Chapter 7). Under Hoving, the Metropolitan developed a master plan which included building five new wings, enlarging exhibition areas by one third, and planning a program of special exhibitions on a scale never before witnessed. The pace of the exhibition schedule and the "frantic loans" placed the museum's permanent collection at risk, according to Anthony M. Clark, head of the department of European paintings. Clark resigned his position at the Metropolitan in 1975 and charged Hoving's regime with "hucksterism," saying it was lacking in honesty, simplicity, professional grace and skill.

At the height of "Hovingism," the Metropolitan Museum secretly sold important paintings from its collection and was subsequently investigated by the New York State Attorney General. The Attorney General's office and the museum worked out "Procedures for Deaccessioning and Disposal of Works of Art," a somewhat complicated arrangement the main point of which consists of notifying the Attorney General in advance of the sale. The time line for notification is determined by the value of the work of art and by the exhibition record. Works must be either exchanged with other museums or sold at public auction. The Hoving scandal resulted in more rigorous deaccession policies being developed in museums across the country, but questions concerning deaccession still arise. In 1990, the Guggenheim sold off three important paintings for the purpose of generating money, not because they were no longer meaningful to the museum's collection. The museum received $47.3 million for these "assets" at auction. This was in blatant disregard of the Association of Art Museum Directors' recommendations and was condemned by some museum professionals as well as art critics and art historians.

Thomas Krens, Director of the Guggenheim Museum, arranged for the sale of the paintings to gain the money needed to purchase a collection of contemporary art. Many viewed this deaccession as revealing an attitude that equates art with money, the exhibition of art with product, and that product as something to market. Krens envisions huge exhibitions organized to travel to satellite museums around the world. This talk of art in quantitative, economic, and strategic terms drew criticism in light of the director's responsibility for the care and conservation of the collection.

The museum's function: presentation

The presentation of works of art, the third function of the art museum, is carried out by the professional staff although the general program policy is established by the Board of Trustees and the Director. Program goals should be established by the Board and Director, according to the Association of Art Museum Directors, while the content and implementation of the programs are the responsibilities of the Director and staff. "Special exhibitions attract larger and diverse audiences and stimulate participation in other aspects of a museum's program ... The significance of an exhibition's contribution to knowledge is a major factor in justifying its selection and presentation" (AAMD, 1992: 9). Obviously, exhibition is the primary means of presenting works of art, but included also in the definition might be programs such as slide lectures, gallery talks, film and video programs, and art classes. Publications, including exhibition catalogs, instructional and historical books and pamphlets, study guides and aids, and other supplementary materials, are essential.

The Association of Art Museum Directors recommends both scholarly and popular publications in conjunction with the collection and special exhibitions. It is the responsibility of the Director to establish and maintain standards of quality for all forms of presentation.

> Sound scholarship and creative effort must be the basis for information communicated. In particular, every effort should be made to avoid incorrect attributions, errors of fact, cultural bias, or distortion. However innovative or unconventional the program, freedom of artistic expression and the integrity of the work of art must be respected. (AAMD, 1992: 10)

It should also be noted that the various means of promoting the museum's programs to the public can influence attitudes toward the museum and its holdings and should therefore be governed by professional standards. Public relations activities, advertising and promotional campaigns, membership programs, sales of printed matter and reproductions, fundraising endeavors, can all play important parts in the development of the public's perception and should be closely monitored.

It is in the area of presentation that we see the influence of modernism, democracy, and capitalism quite clearly. The impact of modernism on both the design of the museum and of the exhibition coupled with the influence of democracy and capitalism on museum practices will be explored.

The impact of modernism on presentation

The first American museums were modeled in the ancient architectural styles and the various revivals of those styles (Chapter 3). This, in the minds of American museum-goers, was the proper repository for art, since it represented not only European high architecture but the palaces where culture, wealth, and power resided. Americans moored in the elitist/democratic paradox, would build the European palace on Main Street, fill it with master works, and open it to the people.

The Museum of Modern Art in New York City was the first modern museum building in America (see Chapter 5). Constructed in 1939, the museum building was designed by Philip Goodwin and Edward Durell Stone to embody the ideas and forms of modernism, as it would house the world's greatest collection of modern art. It represented modernism with an architecture known as the International Style, formulated in Germany during the 1920s, but packaged and disseminated by two influential Americans, Alfred Barr and Philip Johnson, in their 1932 exhibition "Modern Architecture: International Exhibition."

As Barr wrote in the catalog essay,

> A number of progressive architects have converged to form a genuinely new style which is rapidly spreading throughout the world. Both in appearance and structure this style is peculiar to the twentieth century and is as fundamentally original as the Greek or Byzantine or Gothic ... The aesthetic principles of the International Style are based primarily upon the nature of modern materials and structure and upon modern requirements in planning. Slender steel posts and beams, and concrete reinforced by steel have made possible structures of skeleton-like strength and lightness. The external surfacing materials are of painted stucco or tile, or, in more expensive buildings, of aluminum or thin slabs of marble or granite and of glass both opaque and transparent. Planning, liberated from the necessity for symmetry so frequently required by tradition is, in the new style, flexibly dependent upon convenience. (Hitchcock, *et al.* 1932: 7)

The Museum of Modern Art was the first International Style building in America and was designed to be flexible and efficient. It was planned to function as a place to show art and to accommodate the comparatively large following the Museum had attracted. There was a lounge and a film theater, but most important, the galleries were spacious, white-walled apartments perfect for viewing the European modernist paintings that were the centerpiece of the Museum's collection. It was not until World War II caused the migration of European artists to New York that modernist ideas began to dominate American artistic thought and American modernist art began to develop in its own right, making the American conversion to modernism complete (Chapter 5).

Surrealism was recognized as the most widely influential aesthetic movement between World Wars I and II, and it was the Surrealist artists who moved from Paris to New York in the early 1940s. Surrealism looked to the subconscious, dream world as a means to discover and express truth. It depended on intuition and instinct rather than rational, logical thought processes. André Breton, the poet and Father of Surrealism, defined it as the "belief in the higher reality of specific forms of associations, previously neglected, in the omnipotence of dreams, and in the disinterested play of thinking." The impact of the Surrealists on the New York art world resulted in what is generally considered the first truly American modern art movement, Abstract Expressionism.

Abstract Expressionism inherited from Surrealism an intense interest in psychology and psychoanalysis, especially an interest in the role of the unconscious in the making of art. Seeking a means to express in their art certain universal truths, the Abstract Expressionists employed signs and symbols and myths in a method learned from the Surrealists. Jackson Pollock, as an example, connected with the Surrealists in both the use of symbolic imagery and in the methods of automatism. The automatic painting method was believed to reveal the universal symbols inhabiting the inner mind, but also placed a new emphasis on the process of painting. The process interested all of the Abstract Expressionists who used it to register the energy, drama, and passion of the moment. It was Pollock, however, who took the automatic techniques to the extreme to produce his "drip" paintings. The unstretched, often unsized canvas was placed directly on the studio floor and Pollock, paint in hand, would move around and across the canvas, applying the paint in whole body gestures, producing not works of the easel size, but rather great murals. The Abstract Expressionists, fully cognizant of their moment in time, produced paintings reflecting the age that produced the airplane, the television, and the atomic bomb; large paintings that could compete with the advertising billboards that had begun to dot the nation's highways. Paintings that would catch the attention of a people on the run and provide, in the hectic atmosphere of postwar New York, a slow, introspective, meditative art with spiritual overtones. These paintings required exhibition spaces with white walls and high ceilings, free from worldly distractions.

In 1959, the Museum of Modern Art launched the Thirtieth Anniversary Campaign, which would provide for the construction of a new East Wing (Chapter 9). Designed by Philip Johnson, the six-storey glass and steel tower would almost double the Museum's exhibition space and would further expand the modernist architectural ideas developed at the Bauhaus.

The Bauhaus artists, like the Surrealists, immigrated to the United States during the war and, in due course, exerted their influence, first on American architecture and design and then on American art (Chapter 5). This influence produced work that was functional, rational, and austere. The modern museum would be designed according to its purpose: a building in which to exhibit modern art and through which would pass large numbers of people. The high priest of Bauhaus philosophy, Walter Gropius, believed that architecture was "the ultimate art form in which beauty and utility, design and structure could be combined. Buildings were conceived not merely as functional necessities but as experimental answers serving psychologically based needs" (Kuhn 1971: 14). The modern museum, therefore, would be designed, not just to guide people, and offer refreshments and educational aids, but also to serve as a kind of asylum, a place away from the secular, where the sacred icons of modernity might be contemplated. The Bauhaus-influenced architecture produced a museum perfectly suited for the needs of the new art known as the New York School, the "psychologically based" needs of both the exhibitor and the visitor, and the requirements of the enlightened capitalists who would begin the commercialization of the museum.

The Bauhaus artists also influenced fine art philosophy, although this was a delayed impact. Taking positions in some of America's most influential art schools, they taught the principles of modernism to students who would be the next generation of artists. The standards of simplicity of line and geometric form, and truth in materials; and the rational, functional, intellectual approach to the creation of art, resulted, in the end, in a minimalist aesthetic. The art movements of this period—geometric painting, minimalist sculpture, and even Pop Art—reveal this objective approach to creating art (Chapter 5).

Donald Judd, a prominent sculptor within the Minimalist movement, wrote an essay called "Specific Objects," in which he expressed his preference for a literal use of materials, space, and concepts. Judd's sculptures were composed of materials of industrial steel and aluminum machined to perfection, creating geometric forms placed in a literal space in an ordered, rational configuration. They were clearly descendants of the Bauhaus philosophy of truth and pragmatism.

What Minimalism required to be fully realized was an exhibition space equally stark and fully removed from the outside world.

> The ideal gallery, subtracts from the art work all cues that interfere with the fact that it is "art". The work is isolated from everything that would detract from its own evaluation of itself. This gives the space a presence possessed by other spaces where conventions are preserved through the repetition of a closed system of values. Some of the sanctity of the church, the formality of the courtroom, the mystique of the experimental laboratory joins with chic design to produce a unique chamber of aesthetics. So powerful are the perceptual fields of force within this chamber that, once outside it, art can lapse into secular status. (O'Doherty, 1986: 14)

Donald Judd's aluminum cubes were actual aluminum cubes, containing no illusion or metaphor. Removed from the pristine white-walled gallery, these sculptures could easily be absorbed by the secular environment.

The designing of works of art specifically for the modern gallery space became a common practice throughout the 1970s. The art propagated by

Bauhaus philosophy required a gallery influenced by Bauhaus design in order to be seen. The Bauhaus dictum of "form follows function" became routine thought for designers of exhibition spaces. Edward Larrabee Barnes, architect of numerous American art museums, believes museum design should not be about creating an architectural monument, but should be focused on the art and on the way people move through the museum.

> I am dedicated to the idea of anonymous white spaces ... I feel definitely that the rooms themselves have to represent calm, well-proportioned spaces. The sequence and the sense of flow must work, and the way you move through it must be graceful. I think it's a very difficult thing to explain how you can do architecture with a strong central idea ... and at the same time have that idea opt for this function of bringing out these various shows which go through it. (Diamonstein, 1980: 18)

The architecture to accommodate the site-specific art of the 1960s and 1970s was, in the beginning, "found architecture," that is, the great iron-bound buildings of the Soho district of lower Manhattan. These raw and rough, high-ceilinged lofts were low-rent places to which artists and art dealers flocked. The creation of museum architecture mimicking the Soho studio and gallery quickly followed, and in 1976 the Museum of Modern Art announced a major expansion plan (Chapter 9). The new construction, known as the West Wing, would provide 46,500 square feet of new gallery space. Summed up, the expansion planned for a total of 170,000 square feet of new space and 200,000 square feet of renovated space.

The architect, Cesar Pelli, worked with the curators of the various departments to determine the design which was based on the Museum of Modern Art's "incredibly well developed theories and attitudes about how modern art should be exhibited" (Pelli, 1984). The galleries, for the most part, retained the apartment-like scale approved for the exhibition of modern art and the carpeted floors recommended by then Director of Painting and Sculpture, Bill Rubin. "A museum is a museum, and you can't pretend it's an apartment," he said, "but the carpet does tend to minimize the viewer's sense of being in a big public area" (Rubin, 1984). The galleries for the art produced from the 1960s to the 1980s, however, reflected those Soho lofts. These were designed to be greater expanses with no carpeting and movable walls which allowed flexibility. In February, 1996, the Museum announced another expansion plan which will provide, among other things, additional loft-like spaces for the exhibition of contemporary art.

The impact of democratic concerns on presentation

The central architectural image of the new Museum of Modern Art is the Garden Hall with its escalators and dramatic view of the sculpture garden. It is a symbol of the triumph of architecture in the service of the people.

The modern museum in its function of presentation, exists to present art for the people. The Garden Hall is designed to meet this function. It is designed to welcome the masses, service the masses, and move them out into the galleries. The Garden Hall is the axis where the influence of modernism meets the influence of democracy.

Modern architecture, as it appears in the museum, has served the public well. The same demands of truth and pragmatism that produced art forms difficult for the general populace to appreciate, provided, when applied to architecture and design, democratic solutions. In other words, while modern art was elitist, modern architecture was really democratic. This was reflected in the shift that occurred in the design of the art museum.

The first art museums, those great palaces in American parks, were accessed by way of a staircase, usually marble and often flanked by fountains. The columnated entry was a common theme, leading into a great hall, with the galleries beyond, perhaps at the top of yet another marble staircase.

The first Museum of Modern Art building was entered at street level, a less intimidating and more democratic approach. Today's Museum of Modern Art continues that custom as do most modern museums, including the Whitney and the Guggenheim. In Washington, D.C., the differences can be observed between the West Building of the National Gallery (1941), where the marble stairs lead into a great columnated rotunda, and the East Building (1978), accessed from street level through revolving doors.

Those first art museums were not designed to cater to visitors' creature comforts. There were no restaurants or book stores and few, if any, places to sit and rest. The modern museum has an information center near the entry, where maps are dispensed indicating not only exhibition areas, but rest areas, restaurants, lavatories, lounges, coat rooms, and shops. These buildings consider seriously issues such as traffic flow, lighting, climate control, and wheelchair accessibility.

The first art museums, while considered educational institutions, did not strive to explain the work, its significance, its historical precedents. The modern democratic museum couples the art exhibited with informative signage, gallery talks, publications, video presentations, recorded tours. American democratic ideals demanded education to be every person's right. The museum was soon recognized as a potential center for public education for people of all ages and economic and social levels (Chapter 6). Inherent in the commitment to make art available to a large and diverse public is the danger of a program so democratic in its scope that its content is reduced to the lowest common denominator. Inherent in the opening of the galleries to the masses is the danger that the quiet, contemplative atmosphere required for an aesthetic experience is lost in the commotion. These issues will be addressed further when the educational and aesthetic purpose of the museum are examined.

The impact of capitalism on presentation

The democratic program of presenting exhibitions for the larger population is directly connected to the influence of capitalism which brought with it profit-making procedures dependent on consumers for success (Chapter 7). As director of the Museum of Modern Art, Alfred Barr instituted what were considered then unusual practices for an art museum. Since, in the early years, the museum was not set on a course to establish a permanent collection, it depended on loans for its exhibits. All exhibits were therefore temporary, and with each show change came new announcements, parties, and publicity. Barr established the first public relations office in an American museum. The changing exhibitions and press coverage kept a steady flow of visitors coming. It was Nelson Rockefeller who determined that the Museum should charge admission. The visitors therefore generated income, and the changing shows and press coverage became essential to maintaining the income. Barr produced, in an effort to educate the visitors, exhibition catalogs and brochures which were quickly consumed by the public, and another source of income was realized. Thus the beginnings of income-generating activities were explored at the Museum of Modern Art (Chapter 8).

It was at the Metropolitan Museum, however, under the directorship of Thomas Hoving, that museum operations were thrust in the direction of all-out consumerism, and programs such as a temporary exhibit or the publication of a catalog were viewed not solely as educational endeavors but as sources of income. Special exhibitions were events to be promoted in the press, thus increasing museum attendance and therefore museum income, not only from admission charges but also from parking charges, restaurant charges, museum shop sales, and membership dues. For example, the 1965 pre-Hoving annual report cites two major sources of income: New York City (25 percent) and the Museum's endowment (67 percent). By 1976, only 10 percent was contributed by the City, and 17.7 percent came from the endowment. Although the actual dollar amounts from these two sources had increased, their percentage of the total budget had declined, because Hoving's blockbuster shows were, at this point, generating 59 percent of the operating budget. These exhibitions not only generated huge incomes for the Museum through admission charges and other revenues but were also substantially self-supporting ventures because they attracted corporate support.

During the first four years of his tenure, Hoving tripled the number of exhibitions to a grand total of 62 shows for the 1972–73 season. The crowds and commercialism generated by these shows disturbed many museum professionals and, as we have seen, caused the resignation of the head of the department of European painting, Anthony M. Clark.

"Hovingism," as these commerce-oriented museum practices came to be called, was debated at professional meetings and criticized in professional journals but, in the end, Hovingism, in various degrees, infiltrated the offices and boardrooms of American museums, changing forever their policies and practices.

The Guggenheim Museum under the directorship of Thomas Krens has demonstrated the most visible adoption of the museum-as-commerce philosophy (Chapter 7). We have noted the controversy over the auctioning of certain paintings from the museum's collection and the concern expressed regarding the subsequent purchase of Count Giuseppe Panza di Biumo's collection of contemporary art. Krens' degrees in economics and management and his lack of art scholarship may account for his view of the art museum as an industry in need of reform. He believes museums are in a crisis, they need to explore "mergers and acquisitions" and understand "asset management." Philippe de Montebello, director of the Metropolitan Museum, is worried:

> A museum's exhibition program now tends to be viewed by the administration as being at the service of the museum's budget—instead of the other way around. Exhibitions are exploited by a formidable business machine ... the whole critical mass of staff and services employed to generate, shape and execute exhibitions is exploited to the detriment of the staff's custodial as well as creative functions. (de Montebello, 1984: 47)

Hans Haacke, the artist who has made the museum–corporate relationship the centerpiece of his work, fears for the loss of art scholarship as the hurried exhibition curator relinquishes reflective time (Chapter 7).

The museum director and art scholar Sherman Lee wrote: "An art museum is not the same kind of institution as a corporation. I don't think many business assumptions are valid for the art museum. We must not think in terms of a balance sheet. (Lee, 1983: 78).

A major influence on the development of this view of the exhibition as an income-generating activity has been the underwriting of exhibitions by corporations. With corporate support the exhibition becomes a major source of income for the museum, and therein lies the incentive Haacke described as a form of addiction. The corporate support demands that the museum create and promote extravaganzas in order to attract visitors. The corporation wants the publicity, the museum wants the corporate support, and the crowds want the blockbuster.

Museums, in the process of courting corporate support, have become adept at corporate methods and corporate thinking. This situation is illustrated clearly in the text of a brochure distributed to corporations by the Metropolitan Museum:

> Many public relations opportunities are available through sponsorship of programs, special exhibitions and services. These can often provide a creative and cost effective answer to a specific marketing objective, particularly where international governmental or consumer relations may be a fundamental concern.

This brochure also contained a page of quotes from business executives telling their colleagues why they are sponsors of the Metropolitan.

Corporate officers know that the greatest publicity benefits will be derived from the art exhibitions that generate publicity and draw large crowds. The underwriting of such an exhibition has been a sure bet for the corporation because of the visibility factor. The 1988 show at the Guggenheim Museum called "Fifty Years of Collecting" is a good example of this. The show featured art held by the Solomon R. Guggenheim Foundation from the collections in both the Guggenheim Museum in New York and the Peggy Guggenheim Collection in Venice. Chase Manhattan Bank sponsored the exhibition and mounted a massive advertising campaign, which included newspaper, magazine, and radio advertising, and direct mail marketing. The benefits of the campaign were clear to the museum since the exhibit generated the highest attendance in the Guggenheim's history for a comparable time span (Guggenheim Museum *Annual Report*, 1987: 9).

Corporate sponsorship of exhibitions has raised concerns regarding art scholarship since it is feared, first of all, that in their efforts to secure donations, the museum staff will propose only those exhibitions perceived to be attractive to the corporation and the public, setting aside esoteric projects with a more selective appeal. "If financial backing to do a project is needed," says J. Carter Brown, discussing corporate funding, "and if from the beginning the museum people realize that it is the kind of project that nobody is going to want to back, this interferes with a curatorial decision" (Brown, 1988: 48). In a more blunt analysis, Philippe de Montebello describes corporate funding of exhibitions as "an inherent, insidious, hidden form of censorship" (quoted in Glennon, 1988: 42).

The second area of concern for art scholarship is addressed by Hans Haacke when he points to the time involved for curators doing business with corporate representatives, time away from curatorial duties. For example, Whitney Museum curators, during the heyday of corporate involvement with that museum, arranged for the purchase of $8 million worth of art in public spaces at Equitable Center. Perhaps more than any other art museum the Whitney Museum of American Art, under the directorship of Tom Armstrong, attached itself to corporations and depended on corporate support. And no other art museum has come under fire for lack of art scholarship to the degree of the Whitney Museum. The analysis of the Whitney exhibition program recorded in Chapter 7 reveals the lack of any comparative art-historical themes. Michael Brenson questioned in a 1989 *New York Times* article:

> Who can remember the last Whitney exhibition that seemed finished—in other words, thoroughly conceived, considered and installed? Who can remember a Whitney exhibition that generated confidence in the museum's capacity to deal with either the achievements of the old or the challenges of the new?

To assume a connection between corporate involvement and lack of scholarship is not unreasonable. Philippe de Montebello raises concerns for this entire generation of corporate-influenced curators who, because of the time given to fundraising and donor services, have been denied "sufficient unstructured time for studying and looking" and therefore "will not have sufficient knowledge or experience so they can later perform with intelligence and discrimination in more important positions" (de Montebello, 1984: 48). The traditional values of the museum have been upset, and the basic work of the museum has been set aside. The danger is that instead of research and scholarly publications, the curators' efforts go into special events, according to de Montebello, which are measured by quantity, not quality.

As has been noted, presentation involves also the various means of promoting the museum's program, including sales of printed matter and reproductions, activities which grow as the museum seeks more sources of income. The Association of Art Museum Directors has expressed concern in this regard, in particular with the manufacturing and marketing of reproductions. Nelson Rockefeller came under attack when, in 1978, he announced the establishment of the Nelson Rockefeller Collection Incorporated, a business to produce and market duplicates of objects from his art collection. These reproductions were advertised as being indistinguishable from the originals, a claim that art critic Hilton Kramer called shameless. "At best reproductions are mementoes ... to suggest that they somehow have the power to function as equivalents of the artist's own work is ... a serious corruption of taste." Kramer went on to criticize the art museums he said "cynically led the way into corruptions of this sort" (quoted in Gilmour, 1979: 80).

Guidelines for reproductions of works of art were recommended by the Association of Art Museum Directors in an effort to maintain a climate of artistic integrity.

> Recently, a proliferation of "art-derived" materials, coupled with the marketing of copies of original works, has created such widespread confusion as to require clarification in order to maintain ethical standards.
> (AAMD, 1992: 25)

The Association recommended four steps to insure the public's understanding of reproductions: museums should mark the objects as reproductions; offer them in sizes and materials other than those used by the artist in the original; price them according to standard marketing practices; assure through advertising that the buyer understands the object is not an original and that there is no qualitative comparison.

The area of presentation, as we have seen, is the public side of the museum and encompasses the exhibition programs, their topics, ways and means, their support activities, the publications, reproduction, various printed matter, and all aspects of the museum's public relations. It is in this public area that the influences of modernism, democracy, and capitalism come to play, and it is here that the dangers of those influences can be most clearly recorded and analyzed in order to insure the integrity of the museum's function.

The museum's purpose: educational and aesthetic

The art museum fulfills its function for a purpose. That purpose is educational and aesthetic and, as recommended by the American Association of Museums, should be supported by a joint commitment of the Board of Trustees and the professional staff. The following is a summary of the advantages for and challenges to the fulfillment of the museum's purpose incurred through the influences of modernism, democracy, and capitalism.

The American art museum is at the service of the public, a public who in this democratic society is viewed as entitled to access to the country's art treasures (Chapter 2). The museum stands with its doors open, its treasures gathered for the benefit of all the people. The primary benefit is understood to be knowledge, knowledge gained through observation, instruction, and experience. The museum attempts to guide the visitor by arranging the paintings and other objects of art in some systematic or thematic way that allows for study and comparison. The museum also provides supplemental information through labels, exhibition catalogs, lectures, and so on. The knowledge gained in the art museum has been perceived from the beginning as improving somehow the minds, morals, and taste of the visitor and creating therefore better citizens.

This benefit of knowledge is imparted to the museum visitor in two different ways. The knowledge gained from the aesthetic experience is what Sir Herbert Read describes as the primary humanizing element in the development of human consciousness. "Without the creative arts there would be no advance in myth or ritual, in language or meaning, in morality or metaphysics" (Read, 1960: 92). The knowledge gained by educational experience is verbal; that is, it is conveyed through the printed or spoken word and concerned with the conditions surrounding the work of art, such as historical or biographical information, or perhaps formal or technical information. Together, the aesthetic and educational compose the purpose of the art museum.

Educational programs are at the service of the museum's aesthetic purpose. They are viewed theoretically as the means to the end. For many years art museums employed a hands-off education policy, believing that the art work should stand alone with no verbal explanations. This approach allowed for the aesthetic experience (an emotional, intellectual, spiritual response to a work of art as a work of art) but did not attempt to elicit it. The knowledge that the visitor gains from the aesthetic experience is not necessarily rational or logical. It is non-verbal and not easily communicated from one individual to another. Educational programs therefore cannot directly provoke an aesthetic experience.

Let us consider for a moment the purpose of the museum, aesthetic and educational, and consider the opposing aspects of the purpose. The educational purpose, that is, giving instruction or information, is by definition active. The aesthetic purpose, on the other hand, is passive and private, a very personal experience, difficult, if not impossible to verbalize. The educational programs developed in the art museum depend on words to convey information. They are often interactive, public events.

How have democratic concerns, modernism, and capitalism impacted on the museum's purpose and has this impact put the museum at odds with itself? These are the questions to be addressed, beginning with the impact on the museum's educational programs followed by a consideration of the aesthetic purpose of the museum.

The impact of democratic concerns on the museum's purpose

American art museums began their educational pursuits mainly because of democratic concerns (Chapter 6). Key people in key museums wrote and taught their ideas regarding the educational mission of art museums. John Cotton Dana, director of the Newark Museum from 1909 to 1929, was a firm believer in the museum as a democratic institution of learning, an institution with exhibitions and programs made available to all the people. The influence of his ideas is still being felt. Benjamin Ives Gilman is generally considered to have invented the gallery talk at the Museum of Fine Arts in Boston, a democratic method now standard in art museums. As director of America's first modern art museum, Alfred Barr faced new challenges in the presentation of the new art forms. The often-times unrecognizable images in modern painting required new educational methods, a situation that probably accounts for Barr's innovations. He is credited with placing the first wall label alongside a painting, and he produced instructional catalogs to accompany every exhibition.

> When you look at these pictures, you may become upset because you can't understand them all at first glance. These paintings are not intended to sell you anything or tell you yesterday's news, though they may help you to understand our modern world. Some of them may take a good deal of study, for although we have seen a million pictures in our lives we may never have learned to look at painting as an art. For the art of painting, though it has little to do with words, is like a language which you have to learn to read. Some pictures are easy, like a primer and some are hard with long words and complex ideas; and some are prose, others are poetry, and others still are like algebra or geometry. (Barr, 1943: 3)

Barr had to work at democratizing the Museum of Modern Art since the average citizen found this art especially intimidating. He also taught his new audience the correct pronunciation of artists' names (Ma-tees, Say-zann) while leading them from paintings with familiar, recognizable imagery to abstract compositions.

Because the difficult paintings that modernism produced demanded explanation in order to satisfy democratic concerns, the modern museum professional developed new educational methods. If it were not for the difficulty posed by abstract painting, museum educational practices might not have developed so rapidly.

The impact of capitalism on the museum purpose

With certain educational methods in place (such as the exhibition catalog and the gallery talk), the major expansion of educational programs was spurred by the realization that they generated income for the museum. Nelson Rockefeller at the Museum of Modern Art introduced capitalist practices in promoting exhibitions through the press and then charging admission (Chapter 8). The Metropolitan Museum engaged corporate sponsors for museum exhibitions and programs and adopted their methods for quantitative evaluations of these events (Chapter 7).

From the educational standpoint, modernism, democracy, and capitalism have worked together to produce the world's most efficient and effective museum education programs. When we consider, however, the degree of fulfillment of the museum's aesthetic purpose, the achievement level seems somewhat dubious.

Modernism succeeded, through its impact on architecture, to provide not only a functional, comfortable place to view art, but a separate place, away from the secular world with (as it was designed) no visual distractions. The perfect white cube was the space in which the visitor could commune with the work of art and experience the aesthetic. It might also be argued that modernist painting and sculpture made people more attuned to aesthetics since they were forced to move beyond a response to obvious subject matter alone. Modernism was at the service of aesthetics, a situation not true of democracy and capitalism (Chapter 5).

The influence of capitalism on the museum and the democratic impulse of the museum's educational programs combined to create galleries so packed with people as to negate the possibility of an aesthetic response. The educational programs geared toward the masses may also pose a problem in three ways. Firstly, the lecturing to tour groups in the galleries can be a distraction to other visitors and should therefore be carefully scheduled. Next, the intellectual level of educational programs should be closely monitored to avoid the "common denominator syndrome" in which little or no scholarly material is presented. And thirdly, the natural thrust of the educational program toward those things which surround the work of art (biographical information on the artist, technical information on the process, and historical information on the subject or school) should not override the aesthetic purpose but rather clear a path for it.

Capitalist marketing techniques helped bring in the large numbers of museum visitors, and the danger exists for capitalist thinking to influence them. The quantitative versus qualitative analysis of art can lead people to judge a painting's worth according to its monetary value rather than its aesthetic value. It can propose the judgement of an exhibition be based on attendance rather than scholarly research and quality of content. It can influence curators in this regard, stealing their reflective time while demanding attention to the bottom line, subjugating scholarly exhibitions in favor of the popular.

The duality of the museum's purpose, educational and aesthetic, may very well be at the heart of the elitist/democratic paradox of the American art museum. The educational purpose and the programs born of it serve the museum's democratic needs and have come to dominate the art museum, posing the danger of doing so at the expense of the aesthetic. Since aesthetic knowledge seems to spring from a place that is predominantly nonrational and without verbal requirements, it could be theorized that the nature of the work of art might always elude museum educators. In any case, the educational and aesthetic are at odds: in terms of active/passive, public/private, and verbal/nonverbal. Their peaceful coexistence and, more, their mutual support, constitute the challenge set before us as we move into the next century and on to the maturation of the American art museum.

Bibliography

Adam, T. R. (1939) *The Museum and Popular Culture.* New York: George Grady Press.

Alexander, Edward P. (1982) *Museums in Motion.* Nashville, TN: American Association for State and Local History.

—(1983) *Museum Masters.* Nashville, TN: American Association for State and Local History.

Allen, Frederick Lewis (1965) *The Great Pierpont Morgan.* New York: Harper and Row.

Alsop, Joseph (1982) *The Rare Art Traditions.* New York: Harper and Row.

American Association of Museums, Committee on Ethics and Standards (1981) *Guidelines for Reproductions of Works of Art.* Washington, D.C.: AAM.

—(1984) *Museums for a New Century.* Washington, D.C.: AAM.

—(1989) Position paper. Washington, D.C.: AAM, September.

—(1994) *Code of Ethics for Museums.* Washington, D.C.: AAM.

American Council for the Arts (1989) Position paper. Washington, D.C.: ACA, July.

Andrews, Wayne (1990) *The Surrealist Parade.* New York: New Directions.

Architectural Forum (1939) "Museum of Modern Art," August.

Association of American Painters and Sculptors (1913) *International Exhibition of Modern Art.* New York.

Association of Art Museum Directors (1992) *Professional Practices in Art Museums.* New York: AAMD.

Aubry, Octave (1964) *Napoleon.* New York: Crown.

Baker, Paul R. (1986) *Richard Morris Hunt.* Cambridge, MA: M.I.T. Press.

Barr, Alfred H., Jr. (1929a) "A Course of Five Lectures on Modern Art," Department of Art, Wellesly College, MA, April and May, 1929.

—(1929b) *First Loan Exhibition: Cézanne, Gauguin, Seurat, Van Gogh.* New York: Museum of Modern Art, 1929.

—(1929–30) *Nineteen Living Americans.* New York: Museum of Modern Art.

—(1930a) "The Museum of Modern Art," *Art News*, 28(14), 13, January 4.

—(1930b) *Painting in Paris.* New York: Museum of Modern Art.

—(1932) *A Brief Survey of Modern Painting.* New York: Museum of Modern Art.

—(1936a) *The Museum of Modern Art*. New York, New York: Museum of Modern Art.

—(ed.) (1936b) *Fantastic Art: Dada Surrealism*. New York: Museum of Modern Art.

—(1938) Preface to *Bauhaus 1919–1928* by Herbert Bayer with Walter and Ise Grogius. New York: Museum of Modern Art, 1938 (Boston: Charles T. Branford, 1959).

—(1941) "Modern Art Makes History Too," *College Art Journal*, **6**(1), 3–6, November, Wisconsin College Art Association.

—(1942) *Painting and Sculpture in the Museum of Modern Art*. New York: Museum of Modern Art.

—(1943) *What is Modern Painting*? New York: Museum of Modern Art.

—(1944) "The Future of the Art Museum as an Educational Institution." Paper presented at the Art Institute of Chicago, March 14.

Battcock, Gregory (1966) *The New Art*. New York: Dutton.

—(ed.) (1968) *Minimal Art*. New York: Dutton.

Bayer, Herbert and Gropius, Walter, (eds.) (1938) *Bauhaus 1919–1928*. New York: Museum of Modern Art.

Bazin, Germain (1979a) *The Museum Age*. New York: Universe Books.

—(1979b) *The Louvre*. London: Thames and Hudson.

—(1979c) *The Louvre Museum*. New York: Universe Books.

Bennetts, Leslie (1984) "Modern Art Museum Is On Display," *New York Times*, Section B, p. 1, May 8.

Berenson, Bernard (1930) *The Venetian Painters* (1894), reprinted in *The Italian Painters of the Renaissance*. Oxford: Clarendon Press.

Berman, Marshall (1982) *All that is Solid melts into Air*. New York: Simon and Schuster.

Biddle, Livingston (1988) *Our Government and the Arts: A Perspective from the Inside*. New York: American Council for the Arts.

Bill to establish the National Gallery, (H.J.R. & 217), (P.R. #14, 75K Congress), Washington, D.C., 1937.

Bill to incorporate the National Institution, (S. No.258) Washington, D.C., February 17, 1841.

Blandy, Doug (1987) "Art Social Action, and the Preparation of Democratic Citizens," in *Art in a Democracy*, (ed.) Doug Blandy and Kristin G. Congdon, New York: Teachers College Press.

Blashfield, Edwin Howland (1913) *Mural Painting in America*. New York: Charles Scribner's.

Boston Museum of Fine Arts *Bulletin*. November 1904, Vol. 2, No. 6.

—*Bulletin*. February, 1906, Vol. 4. No. 18.

—*Bulletin*. April, 1906, Vol. 4, No. 19.

—*Bulletin*. June, 1907, Vol. 4, No. 27.

Bourdieu, P and Passeron, J.C. (1977) *Reproduction in Education, Society and Culture*. Beverly Hills, CA: Sage.

Brenson, Michael (1984) "A Critic's Walk through the New Modern Museum," *New York Times*, Section C, p.1, May 18.

—(1988) "An Unwavering Vision: Donald Judd at Whitney," *New York Times*, Section C, p. 32, October 21.

—(1989) "The Whitney Today: Fashionable to a Fault," *New York Times*, Section 2, p.1, 27, January 1.

Breton, André (n.d.) *Manifeste du Surréalisme*. Paris: Aux Editions Du Sagittaire, Simon Kra.

—(1972) *Surrealism and Painting*. New York: Harper and Row.

Brown, J. Carter (1988) "The Business of Creating a Partnership" (Round Table), *Museum News*. January–February.

Brucker, Gene, (ed.) (1971) *The Society of Renaissance Florence: A Documentary Study*. New York: Harper Torchbooks.

Burke, Peter (1986) *The Italian Renaissance: Culture and Society in Italy*. Princeton, NJ: Princeton University Press.

Burt, Nathaniel (1977) *Palaces for the People*. Boston: Little, Brown.

Canaday, John (1967a) "The Agony of the Museum of Modern Art," *New York Times*, Section 2, p. 25, June 4, 1967.

—(1967b) "Art: 39 Steps from Mission House to Boutique," *New York Times*, Section 2, p. 25, June 11, 1967.

Canfield, Cass (1974) *The Incredible Pierpont Morgan*. New York: Harper and Row.

Carnegie, Andrew (1986) *Autobiography*. Boston: Northeastern University Press.

Cashman, Sean Dennis (1984) *America in The Guilded Age*. New York: New York University Press.

Chase, Mary Ellen (1950) *Abby Aldrich Rockefeller*. New York: Macmillan.

Clark, Stephen (1944) Announcement regarding Alfred Barr, *Museum of Modern Art Bulletin*, **11**(4) February–March.

Cleveland Museum of Art *Annual Reports*: 1989, 1994.

—*Bulletin* (1950), Vol. 37, Nos. 1–10.

—*Bulletin* (1951), Vol. 38, Nos. 1–10.

—*Bulletin* (1952), Vol. 39, Nos. 1–10.

—*Bulletin* (July, 1990) Vol. 77, No. 6.

College Art Association (1989) Position paper, New York: CAA, October.

Collier, Peter and Horowitz, David (1976) *The Rockefellers: An American Dynasty*. New York: Holt, Rinehart and Winston.

Curtis, Cathy (1983) "Museums on the Move," *Museum News*, June.

D'Amico, Victor (1951) "Creative Art for Children, Young People, Adults, Schools," *Museum of Modern Art Bulletin*, **19**(1), Fall.

de Montebello, Philippe (1984) "The High Cost of Quality," *Museum News*, August.

Denon, Dominique Vivant (1973) *Voyage dans la Haute et la Basse Eqypte*. New York: Arno Press.

D'Harnoncourt, Anne and McShine, Kynaston (eds.) (1973) *Marcel Duchamp*. New York: Museum of Modern Art.

Diamonstein, Barbaralee (1980) *American Architecture Now*. New York: Rizzoli.

Dow, Jay Wheeler (1979) *American Renaissance: A View of Domestic Architecture* (1904) reprinted in *The American Renaissance*. New York: Brooklyn Museum.

Dowd, David Lloyd (1957) *Napoleon: Was He the Heir of the Revolution?* New York: Reinhart.

—(1969) *Pageant-Master of the Republic: Jacques-Louis David and the French Revolution*. Freeport, NY: Books for Libraries Press.

Duncan, Alastair (1980) *Tiffany Windows*. New York: Simon and Schuster.

Einreinhofer, Nancy, *et al.* (1990) *Public Art in New Jersey During the Period of the American Renaissance*. Wayne, NJ: Museum Council of New Jersey.

Eliot, Alexander (1949) "Handful of Fire," *Time*, December 26.

Ferguson, Wallace (1948) *The Renaissance in Historical Thought*. New York: Houghton Mifflin.

Finley, David Edward (1973) *A Standard of Excellence*. Washington, D.C.: Smithsonian Institution Press.

Furtwangler, Adolf (1904) Letter to *The Evening Transcript* reprinted in the *Boston Museum of Fine Arts Bulletin*, 2(6), November.

Gamarekian, Barbara (1989a) "House Panel Favors Restricting Arts Grants," *New York Times*, Section C, p. 3, June 30.

—(1989b) "House Sends Art Endowment Message on Taxpayer's Taste," *New York Times*, p. 18, July 13.

—(1989c) "Senate Panel Asks Ban on Grants to 2 Arts Groups," *New York Times*, Section 3, p. 19, July 26.

—(1989d) "Committee Opens Hearings on Grants to the Arts," *New York Times*, Section C, p. 26, November 16.

—(1990) "Hundreds in the Arts Rally for Grants Without Strings," *New York Times*, Section C, p. 14, March 21.

Gay, Peter (1984) *Age of Enlightenment*. Amsterdam: Time-Life.

Gilman, Benjamin Ives (1907) "The Museum Past, Present, and Future," *Boston Museum of Fine Arts Bulletin*, 4(27), June.

—(1918) *Museum Ideals of Purpose and Method*. Cambridge, MA: Riverside Press.

Gilmour, Pat (1979) "The Art of Reproduction," *Arts Review*, March 2.

Glennon, Lorraine (1988) "The Museum and the Corporation: New Realities," *Museum News*, January–February.

Glueck, Grace (1988) "Thinking Big at the Guggenheim," *New York Times*, Section 2, p. 1, May 29.

—(1989a) "Art on the Firing Line," *New York Times*, Section 2, July 9.

—(1989b) "Whitney Director Said to be Under Fire," *New York Times*, Section C, p. 21, December 12.

—(1990) "Guggenheim to Sell 3 Works to Help Buy Others," *New York Times*, Section C, p. 31, March 23.

Goode, George Brown (1901) *The Genesis of the United States National Museum*. Washington, D.C.: Government Printing Office.

Goodyear, A. Conger (1939) "Mr. Goodyear's Speech," *Museum of Modern Art Bulletin*, 6(3–4), May–June.

Gould, Cecil (1957) *Italian Renaissance Painting*. New York: Phaidon.

Graham, John (1937) "Primitive Art and Picasso," *Magazine of Art*, 30(4), April.

Gropius, Walter (1984) "Systematic Preparation for Rationalized Housing Construction" and "Address at the Formal Opening of the Bauhaus Building," in *Documents of the Bauhaus*, compiled by Hans Wingler, Cambridge, MA: M.I.T. Press.

Guggenheim, Peggy (1979) *Out of This Century*. New York: Universal Books.

Guggenheim Museum *Annual Reports*: 1987, 1988–89.

Guilbaut, Serge (1984) *How New York Stole the Idea of Modern Art*, Chicago: University of Chicago Press.

Hahn, Peter (1990). In Magdalena Droste *Bauhaus 1919–1933*. Berlin: Bauhaus-Archive Museum Für Gestaltung.

Hale, J. R. (1977) *Florence and the Medici: The Pattern of Control*. London: Thames and Hudson.

Hamblen, Karen A. (1987) "Qualifications and Contradictions of Art Museum Education in a Puralistic Democracy," in *Art in a Democracy*, ed. Doug Blandy and Kristin G. Congdon, New York: Teachers College Press.

Hendon, William S. (1979) *Analyzing the Art Museum*. New York: Praeger.

Hibbert, Christopher (1987) *The Rise and Fall of the House of Medici*, New York: Viking-Penguin.

Hitchcock, Henry-Russell; Johnson, Philip and Mumford, Louis (1932) *Modern Architecture: International Exhibition*. New York: Museum of Modern Art.

Honan, William (1989a) "The Endowment vs. the Arts: Anger and Concern," *New York Times*, Section C, p. 33, November 10.

—(1989b) "Frohnmayer Says He'll Seek End of Art-Grant Law," *New York Times*, Section C, p. 26, November 16.

—(1989c) "National Arts Chief, in a Reversal, Gives Grant to AIDS Show," *New York Times*, Section A, p. 1, November 17.

Hook, Judith (1984) *Lorenzo De Medici: An Historical Biography*. London: Hamish Hamilton.

Hoving, Thomas (1975) *The Chase, The Capture: Collecting at the Metropolitan*. New York: Metropolitan Museum of Art.

—(1984) "Branch Out," *Museum News*, February.

—(1993) *Making the Mummies Dance*. New York: Simon and Schuster.

Howe, Winifred E (1974) *A History of the Metropolitan Museum of Art* (Copyright MMA, 1914) New York: Arno Press.

Hughes, Robert (1984) "Revelation on 53rd Street," *Time*, 123, 78–80, May 14.

Hunt, Lunn (1984) *Politics, Culture and Class in the French Revolution.* Berkeley: University of California Press.

Hunter, Sam (1984) *The Museum of Modern Art.* New York: Harry Abrams and the Museum.

Huyghe, Rene (1967) In *Louvre, Paris.* Arnoldo Mondadori, (ed.), New York: Newsweek.

Jarves, James Jackson (1960) *The Art Idea.* Cambridge, MA: Harvard University Press.

Jean, Marcel (1967) *The History of Surrealist Painting.* New York: Grove Press.

—(1980) *The Documents of 20th Century Art: The Autobiography of Surrealism.* New York: Viking Press.

Johnson, Philip (1933) *Objects: 1900 and Today.* New York: Museum of Modern Art.

Jung, C. G. (1956) *Symbols of Transformation.* New York: Pantheon.

Keens, William (1986) "Serving Up Culture," *Museum News*, April.

Kimmelman, Michael (1989) "Nonprofit Gallery in TriBeCa Finds Itself at Storm's Center," *New York Times*, Section C, p. 33, November 10.

—(1990a) "The High Cost of Selling Art," *New York Times*, Section 2, p. 1, April 1.

—(1990b) "What on Earth is the Guggenheim Up To?," *New York Times*, Section 2, p. 1, October 14.

Kopper, Philip (1991) *America's National Gallery of Art.* New York: Abrams.

Kramer, Hilton (1985) *The Revenge of the Philistines: Art and Culture, 1972–1984.* New York: Free Press.

Krens, Thomas (1992) *Guggenheim Commemorative Magazine.* New York: Solomon R. Guggenheim Foundation.

Kuhn, Charles, L. *et al.* (1971) *Concepts of the Bauhaus: The Busch-Reisinger Museum Collection.* Cambridge, MA: Harvard University Press.

Laclotte, Michel (1989) *The Louvre.* Paris: Scala.

LaFarge, John (1979) Quoted in Richard Wilson, *The American Renaissance.* New York: Brooklyn Museum.

Lee, Sherman E. (1972) "The Art Museum as a Wilderness Area," *Museum News.*

—(ed.) (1975) *On Understanding Art Museums.* Englewood Cliffs: Prentice Hall.

—(1983) "A More Certain and Precise Perimeter," an interview by Pamela M. Banks and David W. Ewing, *Museum News*, June.

Lerman, Leo (1969) *The Museum: One Hundred Years and the Metropolitan Museum.* New York: Viking Press.

Leymarie, Jean (1962) *French Painting: The Nineteenth Century.* Geneva: Skira.

Life (1949) "Jackson Pollock," August.
Locke, John (1964) *Concerning Human Understanding*. New York: Dutton.
Lynes, Barbara Bahler (1989) *O'Keefe, Stieglitz and the Critics, 1916–1929*. Ann Arbor: UMI Research Press.
Lynes, Russell (1973) *The Good Old Modern*. New York: Atheneum.
—(1980) *The Tastemakers: The Shaping of American Popular Taste*. New York: Dover.
McClellan, Andrew (1994) *Inventing the Louvre; Art, Politics, and the Origins of the Modern Museum in Eighteenth Century Paris*. Cambridge: Cambridge University Press.
McMullen, Roy (1962) *Art, Affluence and Alienation: The Fine Arts Today*. New York: Praeger.
Marquis, Alice Goldfarb (1989) *Missionary for the Modern*. Chicago: Contemporary Books.
Mattingly, Garrett, *et al.* (1961) *Renaissance Profiles*. New York: Harper and Row.
Mayer, A. Hyatt (1957) "The Gifts that Made the Museum," *Museum of Modern Art Bulletin*, **16**(3), November.
Mendelowitz, Daniel (1970) *A History of American Art*. New York: Holt, Rinehart and Winston.
Messer, Thomas (1971) "Great Editorial," *New York Arts Magazine*, **45**(8), Summer.
Metropolitan Museum of Art *Annual Reports*: 1876, 1878, 1887, 1890, 1902, 1905, 1962–63. 1967–68, 1972–73, 1975–76.
—*Bulletin*, 1872.
—*Bulletin*, 1873.
—*Bulletin*, January, 1904.
—*Bulletin*, January, 1906, Vol. 1, No. 2.
—*Bulletin*, February, 1906, Vol. 1, No. 3.
—*Bulletin*, November, 1906, Vol. 1, No. 12.
—*Bulletin*, June, 1907, Vol. 2, No. 6.
—*Bulletin*, February, 1910, Vol. 5, No. 2.
—*Bulletin*, April, 1910, Vol. 5, No. 4.
—*Bulletin*, July, 1910, Vol. 5, No. 7.
—*Bulletin*, March, 1913, Vol. 8, No. 3.
—*Bulletin*, May, 1913, Vol. 8, No. 5.
—*Bulletin*, November, 1913, Vol. 8, No. 11.
—*Bulletin*, April, 1914, Vol. 9, No. 4.
—*Bulletin*, July, 1915, Vol. 10, No. 7.
—*Bulletin*, May, 1918, Vol. 13, No. 5.
—*Bulletin*, February, 1929, Vol. 24, No. 2.
—*Bulletin*, March, 1929, Vol. 25, No. 3.
—*Bulletin*, January, 1932, Vol. 27, No. 1.
—*Bulletin*, November, 1933, Vol. 28, No. 11.
—*Bulletin*, February, 1963, Vol. 21, No. 6.

—*Bulletin*, Summer, 1965, Vol. 24, No. 1.

Meyer, Karl E. (1979) *The Art Museum: Power, Money, Ethics*. New York: Morrow.

Mies van der Rohe, Ludwig (1984) Quoted in Hans M. Wingler, *The Bauhaus*. Cambridge, MA: M.I.T. Press

Mooney, Michael McDonald (1980) *The Ministry of Culture*. New York: Wyndam Books.

Morfogan, Zackary (1988) "The Business of Creating a Partnership," *Museum News*, January–February.

Moure, Gloria (1988) *Marcel Duchamp*. New York: Rizzoli.

Munro, Thomas (1940) *Educational Work at the Cleveland Museum of Art*. Cleveland: Cleveland Museum of Art.

—(1952) *Educational Work at the Cleveland Museum of Art*. Cleveland: Cleveland Museum of Art.

Murray, Peter and Murray, Linda (1979) *The Art of the Renaissance*. New York: Oxford University Press.

Museum of Modern Art. *Annual Reports*: 1938, 1939, 1940, 1941, 1943, 1945, 1948, 1955, 1959, 1961, 1965, 1988, 1994, 1995.

Museum of Modern Art Bulletin (April, 1934), Vol. 1, No.8.

—*Bulletin* (March–April, 1935), Vol. 2, Nos. 6–7.

—*Bulletin* (July, 1939), Vol. 6, No. 5.

—*Bulletin* (September, 1940), Vol. 7, No. 5.

—*Bulletin* (June, 1942) 5–6, Vol. 9, No. 5.

—*Bulletin* (October–November, 1942) Vol. 10, No. 1.

—*Bulletin* (February–March, 1944), Vol. 11, No. 4.

—*Bulletin* (November, 1944), Vol. 12, No. 2.

—*Bulletin* (January, 1945), Vol. 12, No. 3.

—*Bulletin* (February, 1946), Vol. 13, No. 3.

—*Bulletin* (Spring, 1948), Vol. 15, No. 3.

—*Bulletin* (Spring, 1950), Vol. 16, No. 3.

—*Bulletin* (June, 1951), Vol. 18, No. 4.

—*Bulletin* (Fall, 1951), Vol. 19, No. 1.

—*Bulletin* (Summer, 1954), Vol. 21, Nos. 3–4.

—*Bulletin* (Fall, 1958), Vol. 26, No. 1.

—"Expansion and Renovation Project Fact Sheet," 1984.

Naifeh, Steven and Smith, Gregory White (1989) *Jackson Pollock: An American Saga*. New York: HarperCollins.

National Gallery of Art *Annual Reports*: 1984, 1985, 1986, 1987, 1988, 1989, 1990, 1991, 1992, 1993, 1994.

Newsweek (1964) "Thinking of Today ... and Eternal Things," June 1.

New York Times (1984) Editorial, "Marvelous Museum of Modern Art," Section 4, p. 22, May 13.

O'Doherty, Brian (1986) *Inside the White Cube*. San Francisco, CA: The Lapis Press.

O'Hara, John (n.d.) *Cathedral of the Sacred Heart*. Newton, NJ: Harrison Conroy Co.

Ozouf, Mona (1988) *Festivals and the French Revolution.* Cambridge, MA: Harvard University Press.

Pelli, Cesar (1984) "Interview," New York: Museum of Modern Art.

Philadelphia Museum of Art *Annual Reports*: 1986, 1987, 1988, 1989, 1995.

Piles, Roger de (1979) *The Art of Painting and the Lives of the Painters.* London: J. Nutt near Stationers-Hall, 1706, reprinted by University Microfilms International, Ann Arbor, MI.

Pollock, Jackson (1944) "Jackson Pollock" (Answers to a questionnaire) *Arts and Architecture*, **61**(2), February.

—(1947–48) "My Painting," *Possibilities* **1**(1) Winter.

—and Wright, William (1951) *An Interview with Jackson Pollock.* Taped for presentation on Sag Harbor radio station 1951, printed in 1955.

Quoniam, Pierre (1977) *Le Louvre.* Paris: Editions des Musées Nationaux.

Read, Herbert (1960) *The Forms of Things Unknown, Essays toward an Aesthetic Philosophy.* Cleveland: World.

—(1968) *A Concise History of Modern Painting.* New York: Praeger Publishers.

Rockefeller, Abby Aldrich (1929) *Letters to Her Sister Lucy*, copyright 1957 by John D. Rockefeller, Jr., New York.

Rockefeller, Nelson (1941) CBS Radio Interview, Museum of Modern Art Library Archives.

Roosevelt, Franklin D. (1939) Broadcast at the dedication of the new building of the Museum of Modern Art.

—(1942) "Address," *Bulletin* Vol. 9, No. 4, New York: Museum of Modern Art, May, 1942.

Roth, Leland M. (1978) *The architecture of McKim, Mead and White 1870–1920.* New York: Garland.

Rubin, William (1984) "Interview," New York: Museum of Modern Art.

Ruch, Sandra (1988) "The Business of Creating a Partnership" (A Round Table), *Museum News*, January–February.

Ruskin, John (1964) *Stones of Venice.* London: Hill and Wang.

Russell, John (1984) "New Art and Tradition at the New Museum," *New York Times*, Section 2, p. 1, May 6.

Saarinen, Aline B (1958) *The Proud Possessors.* New York: Random House.

Sachs, Paul J (1939) "Tenth Anniversary Speech," *Museum of Modern Art Bulletin*, **6**(5).

—(1954) "The Early Years: Address delivered at the opening ceremonies of the 25th anniversary of the Museum of Modern Art, Oct. 19, 1954," *Museum of Modern Art Bulletin*, **22**(1–2).

Sandler, Irving (1970) *The Triumph of American Painting.* New York: Praeger.

Scheer, Robert (1975) "Nelson Rockefeller Takes Care of Everybody," *Playboy*, 22(10), October.

Schimmel, Paul (1986) *The Interpretive Link: Abstract Surrealism into Abstract Expressionism*. Newport, CA: Newport Harbor Art Museum.

Severinghaus, J. Walter; Miller, Dorothy C.; Rosenblum, Robert (1984) *Art at Work: The Chase Manhattan Collection*. New York: Dutton.

Shearer, Linda (1988) *Vito Acconci*. New York: Museum of Modern Art.

Slesinger, Larry H., and Richard L. Moyers (1995) *A Snapshot of America's Nonprofit Boards: Results of a National Survey*. Washington, D.C.: National Center for Nonprofit Boards.

Stella, Frank (1993) "A Museum News Interview" by Donald Garfield, *Museum News*, 72(5), September–October.

Time (1939) "Beautiful Doings," May 23.

Tomkins, Calvin (1989) *Merchants and Masterpieces: The Story of the Metropolitan Museum of Art*. New York: Henry Holt.

Ullberg, Alan D., with Patricia Ullberg (1981) *Museum Trusteeship*. Washington, D.C.: American Association of Museums.

Vasari, Giorgio (1987) *The Lives of the Artists* (1568), translated by George Bull 1965, New York: Viking Penguin.

Veysey, Laurence (1979) "Plural Organized Worlds of the Humanities," in *The Organization of Knowledge in Modern America, 1860–1920*, Alexandria Oleson and John Voss (eds), Baltimore: Johns Hopkins University Press.

Vogel, Carol (1996) "It's Art Squeezed, The Modern Buys Growing Room," *New York Times*, Section 1:1, February 5.

Wackernagel, Martin (1981) *The World of the Florentine Renaissance Artist*, Princeton. NJ: Princeton University Press.

Wakefield, David (1976) *Fragonard*. London: Oresko Books.

Walker, John (1984) *National Gallery of Art, Washington, D.C.* New York: Abrams.

—and Brown, J. Carter (1979) *National Gallery of Art*. New York: Abrams.

Wallis, Brian (1986) *Hans Haacke: Unfinished Business*. New York: Museum of Contemporary Art, Cambridge, MA: M.I.T. Press.

Warhol, Andy and Hackett, Pat (1983) *Popism; The Warhol 60s*. New York: Harper Colophon.

Warner, W. Lloyd (1965) *The Living and the Dead: A Study of the Symbolic Life of Americans*. New Haven: Yale University Press.

Weiss, Philip (1990) "Selling the Collection," *Art in America*, July.

Weisgall, Deborah (1989) "A Megamuseum in a Milltown," *New York Times*, Section 4, p. 32, March 5.

Welu, James A (1995) "From the Director," *Worcester Art Museum Calendar*, February 25–April 23.

Wheeler, Lawrence J (1989) "Preserving Integrity," *Museum News*, July–August.

Whitehill, Walter Muir (1970) *Museum of Fine Arts, Boston: A Centennial History*. Cambridge, MA: Belknap Press of Harvard University Press.

Whitford, Frank (1988) *Bauhaus*. London: Thames and Hudson.
Whitney Museum of American Art. *Bulletin*, 1988–89.
Wilson, Edmund (1946) *Memoirs of Hecate County*. New York: Doubleday.
Wilson, Richard Guy (1979) *The American Renaissance*. New York: Brooklyn Museum.
—(1983) *McKim, Mead and White*. New York: Rizzoli.
Wingler, Hans M. (1984) *The Bauhaus*. Cambridge, MA: MIT Press.
Wittlin, Alma S. (1970) *Museums: In Search of a Usable Future*. Cambridge, MA: M.I.T. Press.
Worcester Art Museum *Biennial Report, 1986–88*.
—*Calendar* May–August, 1994.
—*Calendar* January–April, 1995.
—*Calendar* May–August, 1995.
—*Calendar* September–December, 1995.
—*Calendar* January–April, 1996.

Index